Concise Introduction to EU Private

International Law

Prof. Dr. Michael Bogdan

Europa Law Publishing is a publishing company
specializing in European Union law, international trade
law, public international law, environmental law and
comparative national law.
For further information please contact Europa Law
Publishing via email: info@europalawpublishing.com
or visit our website at: www.europalawpublishing.com.

Typeset in Scala and Scala Sans, Graphic design by
G2K Designers, Groningen/Amsterdam

NUR 828
ISBN-10 90-76871-70-1
ISBN-13 978-90-76871-70-7

British Library Cataloguing-in-Publication Data
A catalogue record for this book is available from the
British Library

Foreword

This concise book is intended to be used mainly as an introduction to the
rules of private international law belonging to the legal system of the European
Union, more specifically to its core, the law of the European Community. It is
my hope that it can be useful as an introductory textbook in elective undergrad-
uate courses and master programs on EC law offered today by many law schools,
both to their own students and to exchange students from other countries.

Provisions of EC law dealing with private international law issues have
become so numerous and voluminous that they cover hundreds of pages in
the Official Journal, and a detailed analysis of them all probably would require
much more than a thousand pages. Substantial selections and simplifications
thus were made in order to keep the size of the book within reasonable limits.
Hopefully, the book will serve as a spring-board towards more profound studies
of statutory texts, case law and legal literature. The bibliography and the footnote
references to legal writing are highly selective, mainly because the amount of
literature has become too large; for example, the subject is treated to some extent
in practically all current textbooks on private international law published in
Europe.

I wish to express my sincere gratitude to The Institute for Research in Legal
Science (*Institutet för rättsvetenskaplig forskning*) for its support during my work
on this book. I also wish to thank Professor Trevor Hartley (London) and Professor Christian Kohler (Luxemburg) for their valuable comments on a preliminary
version of the manuscript and Assistant Professor Christoffer Wong (Lund)
for correcting the English of the final version thereof. The responsibility for all
remaining mistakes and errors is, however, exclusively mine.

Critical suggestions by readers are welcome and will be considered seriously
if and when this book appears in a new edition.

Lund, 1 August 2006
Michael Bogdan

Abbreviations

Clunet	Journal du droit international
C.M.L.R.	Common Market Law Review
Consumer L.J.	Consumer Law Journal
EC	European Community (Communities)
ECJ	Court of Justice of the European Communities
ECR	European Court Reports
EEA	European Economic Area
EU	European Union
I.C.L.Q.	International and Comparative Law Quarterly
Int.Insolv.Rev.	INSOL International Insolvency Review
JT	Juridisk Tidskrift
OJ	Official Journal of the European Union
	(formerly Official Journal of the European Communities)
PIL	Private International Law
RabelsZ	Rabels Zeitschrift für ausländisches
	und internationales Privatrecht
Rec.des cours	Recueil des cours de l'Académie
	de droit international de La Haye
Rev.crit.d.i.p.	Revue critique de droit international privé
Rev.trim.dr.eur.	Revue trimestrielle de droit européen
SvJT	Svensk Juristtidning
TfR	Tidsskrift for rettsvitenskap
Yearb.PIL	Yearbook of Private International Law
ZEuP	Zeitschrift für Europäisches Privatrecht
ZfRV	Zeitschrift für Rechtsvergleichung,
	Int. Privatrecht und Europarecht

CHAPTER I

Introduction

1.1 The Subject

The field of law called Private International Law (PIL) deals with private-law relationships and civil proceedings having international implications. Examples of these situations are a marriage or a contract entered into by parties who are citizens and/or habitual residents of different countries; a tort is committed or the resulting damage arises in a country other than those where the parties habitually reside; an object pledged while situated in one country may be moved to another country where the validity of the pledge is challenged, *etc.*

Whenever a private-law relationship having connections to more than one country (and thereby to more than one legal system) gives rise to a legal controversy, one may ask which law should govern the substance of the dispute: should the court apply its own law (*lex fori*) or foreign law? If foreign law is to be applied, which of the legal systems involved is to govern? The problem often is perceived as involving a conflict between the legal systems of the countries connected in some way with the legal relationship in question. The legal provisions determining the national legal system to be applied are therefore commonly called conflict rules (*règles de conflit, Kollisionsregeln, etc.*) and constitute the very core of PIL, which is the reason why the whole subject is sometimes called Conflict of Laws (*conflit des lois, Kollisionsrecht, etc.*). An example of a conflict rule is Article 8 of the EC Regulation No 1346/2000 on Insolvency Proceedings,[1] which provides that:

> [t]he effects of insolvency proceedings on a contract conferring the right to acquire or make use of immoveable property shall be governed solely by the law of the Member State within the territory of which the immoveable property is situated.

This example illustrates the fact that conflict rules are mainly of a "technical" nature, as they do not deal with the substance of the dispute but merely with the question about which national legal system is to be applied to that substance. Conflict rules are therefore "rules about applicable rules", rather than rules about "reality".

The conflict rule quoted above is taken from an EC Regulation, but many, probably most, conflict rules in force in the EU Member States continue to be of national origin. The word "international" in "Private International Law" thus may be somewhat misleading, as it does not refer to the nature of the sources of law, but rather to the character of the legal relationships the subject deals with. The sources of most conflict rules are the same as the sources of other fields of law in the country of the forum (Acts of Parliament and other statutes, judicial

---

[1]   See section 10.3 *infra.*

precedents, preparatory legislative materials, opinions of legal writers, *etc.*). Each country has thus its own PIL, which may, and in fact does, vary largely from country to country, even among the EU Member States. Those parts of PIL that have been subjected to unification or harmonization by international conventions or by EC law, of course, constitute an exception.

The principal theoretical idea behind most of the conflict rules is that each private-law relationship preferably should be governed by the legal system with which the relationship has the closest and most relevant connection, but different countries often hold different views on which connecting factor is the most appropriate one. For example, while the PIL of some countries gives in family and succession matters decisive weight to citizenship (nationality) of the person(s) concerned, other countries prefer to apply the law of the country of habitual residence or domicile to those matters. There are also conflict rules which do not specify the decisive connecting factor at all, and provide rather in general terms for the application of the law of the country that has the closest relationship to the legal relationship under scrutiny.[2] Such approach often may lead to the application of a suitable legal system, but, at the same time, has the serious drawback of often making the applicable law difficult to predict.

In a wider sense, PIL comprises not only conflict rules, but also procedural rules dealing with certain situations having international character. In procedural matters, there are normally no conflict rules prescribing the application of foreign law. The courts of each country usually follow their own procedural rules, but the procedural rules of *lex fori* may include special provisions on situations having international character. Similarly to conflict rules, some of these special procedural rules have been unified or harmonized through international conventions or EC law. The most important of the procedural rules regulate the international jurisdiction of courts (*i.e.*, they specify which connection – or which combination of connections – between a dispute and the country of the forum is sufficient to make the courts of that country competent to adjudicate), without necessarily designating the locally competent court of first instance. A typical jurisdictional provision is, for example, Article 8(1) of the EC Regulation No 2201/2003 concerning Jurisdiction and the Recognition and Enforcement of Judgments in Matrimonial Matters and the Matters of Parental Responsibility (the so-called Brussels II Regulation):[3]

> The courts of a Member State shall have jurisdiction in matters of parental responsibility over a child who is habitually resident in that Member State at the time the court is seised.

---

[2] See, for example, Article 4(1) of the 1980 Rome Convention on the Law Applicable to Contractual Obligations (section 7.3 *infra*).

[3] See section 5.3.1 *infra*.

Also of great importance are rules on the recognition and enforcement of foreign judgments, for example Article 33(1) of the EC Regulation No 44/2001 on Jurisdiction and the Recognition and Enforcement of Judgments in Civil and Commercial Matters (the so-called Brussels I Regulation):[4]

> A judgment given in a Member State shall be recognised in the other Member States without any special procedure being required.

Among other procedural issues within the scope of PIL are the service of documents or taking of evidence in one country upon a request from a court conducting civil proceedings in another country, and the treatment in civil proceedings of foreign nationals and persons habitually residing abroad. In some EU countries, the concept of PIL is much wider and includes, at least for teaching purposes, even some public-law issues (such as citizenship and immigration) and international criminal law (such as the jurisdiction of courts in penal proceedings), but this work limits itself to civil matters and civil proceedings, which constitute the core of PIL in all of the Member States.

The rules on applicable law, jurisdiction of courts and the recognition and enforcement of judgments are interconnected. Thus, a very restrictive approach to recognition and enforcement of foreign judgments makes it necessary to extend jurisdiction even to cases with only a relatively weak connection with the forum country, in order to avoid the risk of creating a legal vacuum wherein the forum has no jurisdiction at the same time as foreign judgments are not recognized and enforced. The extension of jurisdiction to such cases leads, in turn, to a more frequent application of foreign law, as the forum will more frequently face situations with a dominant connection with a foreign country (and consequently with a foreign legal system).

International cooperation is of particularly great importance to PIL, due to the international nature of the situations and legal problems involved. Such cooperation has a long tradition and there is even a special international body created for that purpose, The Hague Conference on Private International Law (*Conférence de La Haye de droit international privé*).[5] In spite of its name, this is not a mere conference or meeting place but a properly constituted intergovernmental organization, with a long history starting far back in the nineteenth century. There are today about 35 "Hague conventions" dealing with a variety of issues pertaining to PIL along with varying numbers of ratifications. The Conference counts at present 65 members, including all Member States of the EU, and the European Community as such intends to become a member, too.[6]

---

[4] See section 3.4 *infra*.

[5] See the Conference's home page on the Internet, <www.hcch.net>.

[6] See section 1.2 *infra*.

1.2   EC Involvement

The involvement of PIL in the European integration process is of a much more recent date.[7] When the European Economic Community (EEC) was founded in 1957, the original Rome Treaty focused on the creation of a common market based on the freedom of movement for goods, persons, services and capital, and the rules intended to achieve this result were almost exclusively rules of administrative and other public law, such as rules regarding customs duties, qualitative and quantitative import restrictions, residence and labour permits, prohibition of anti-competitive behaviour, *etc.*

The original Rome Treaty contained, consequently, practically no mention of PIL or PIL-related problems. A small exception was Article 215 (today Article 288), stipulating that the contractual liability of the Community shall be governed by the law applicable to the contract in question, but this was hardly anything new. Of greater interest was the undertaking in Article 220 (now Article 293) by the Member States to enter, "so far as is necessary", into negotiations with each other with a view to securing for the benefit of their nationals *i.a.* the mutual recognition of juridical persons and the simplification of formalities governing the reciprocal recognition and enforcement of judgments and arbitration awards. While there have been so far no fruitful negotiations about EC statutes regulating the recognition of juridical persons[8] and recognition and enforcement of arbitration awards (mainly because there appears to be no acute

---

7   On the development of PIL within the EC legal order during the last decades, see the regularly appearing surveys by Jayme & Kohler in *IPRax* 1985 pp. 65-71, 1988 pp. 133-140, 1989 pp. 337-346, 1990 pp. 353-361, 1991 pp. 361-369, 1992 pp. 346-356, 1993 pp. 357-371, 1994 pp. 405-415, 1995 pp. 343-354, 1996 pp. 377-389, 1997 pp. 385-401, 1998 pp. 417-429, 1999 pp. 401-413, 2000 pp. 454-456, 2001 pp. 501-514, 2002 pp. 461-471, 2003 pp. 485-495, 2004 pp. 481-493, 2005 pp. 481-493. Among the general works on the interrelation between the EC law and PIL, see Ballarino & Ubertazi, *Yearb.PIL* 2004 pp. 85-128; von Bar (ed.), *Europäisches Gemeinschaftsrecht*; Baur, *YearbPIL* 2003 pp. 177-190; Besse, *ZEuP* 1999 pp. 107-122; Boele-Woelki & van Ooik, *Yearb.PIL* 2002 pp. 1-36; Fletcher, *Conflict*; Fuchs *etc.* (eds.), *Les conflits*; Hatzidaki-Dahlström, *EU:s internationella privat- och processrätt*; Hess, *IPRax* 2001 pp. 389-396; von Hoffmann, *ZfRV* 1995 pp. 45-54 and in von Hoffmann (ed.), *European Private International Law*, pp. 13-37; Hommelhoff *et al.* (eds.), *Europäisches Binnenmarkt*; Jayme, *Ein Internationales Privatrecht*; C. Kessedjian, *Essays Nygh*, pp. 187-196; Kohler, *Rev.crit.d.i.p.* 1999 pp. 1-30 and in *IPRax* 2003 pp. 401-412; Kreutzer, *RabelsZ* 2006 pp. 1-88; Lagarde & von Hoffmann (eds.), *L'européisation*; Lasok & Stone, *Conflict*; Lefranc, *Rev.crit.d.i.p.* 2005 pp. 413-446; Lefranc, *Rev.crit.d.i.p.* 2005, pp. 413-446; Meeusen in Meeusen, Pertegás & Straetmans (eds.), *Enforcement*, pp. 43-76; Partsch, *Le droit*; Philip, *EU-IP*; Picone, *Diritto*; Reichelt (ed.), *Europäisches Kollisionsrecht*; Roth, *RabelsZ* 1991 pp. 623-673 and in *IPRax* 1994 pp. 165-174; Rozehnalová & Týč, *Evropský justiční prostor*; Vékás, *Liber Memorialis Petar Šarčević*, pp. 171-187; Wilderspin & Lewis, *Rev.crit.d.i.p.* 2002 pp. 1-37 and 289-313.

8   A convention on the reciprocal recognition of juridical persons was signed by the six original Member States on 29 February 1968, but due to the lack of ratifications it never entered into force. See E.C.Bull.Supp. 2/69 pp. 5-16.

practical need of such instruments[9]), negotiations regarding the recognition and enforcement of judgments resulted in the 1968 Brussels Convention on Jurisdiction and the Enforcement of Judgments in Civil and Commercial Matters.[10] In view of the subsequent developments, in particular, in the amendments brought about in 1999 by the Treaty of Amsterdam (see *infra*), it is doubtful whether Article 293 (former Article 220) of the EC Treaty retains any practical importance as far as PIL is concerned.

Although the Rome Treaty did not pay much attention to PIL issues in the beginning, it is undeniable that even differences in the field of private law may constitute obstacles hindering the creation of a truly common internal market. The EC has attempted, therefore, with some success to harmonize substantive rules of the Member States regarding some limited questions of private law, such as rules on certain aspects of consumer contracts or companies. However, most of the harmonizing directives merely impose certain minimum requirements and do not forbid the Member States from going further, for example in matters of consumer protection. At present, it is not realistic to expect a total unification or harmonization of the private law of the Member States; within the foreseeable future, a European Civil Code will hardly be anything other than a dream. This is due not only to the existing differences of substantive law, but even to the differences in legal techniques, as the very idea of a comprehensive civil code is in some Member States, for example in the United Kingdom, Ireland and the Nordic Member States, regarded as peculiar and odd. Furthermore, the principle of subsidiarity expressed in Article 5 of the EC Treaty, which is one of the fundamental principles of EC law, requires that the Community regulate only those matters where the objectives of the proposed action cannot be satisfactorily achieved by the Member States on the national level[11] and can be better achieved by the Community. The example of the USA shows that a well-functioning integration does not require a total unification of private law. The ongoing process of European integration, consequently, will not make conflict rules superfluous in relations between the legal systems of the Member States.

On the other hand, the existing harmonization of certain parts of private law, especially rules on the protection of the weaker party in consumer and other similar relations, has, in spite of its limited character, given rise to the need to ensure that the harmonized rules shall be complied with whenever the situation has a sufficiently close (even if not necessarily the closest) connection

---

9 The New York Convention on the Recognition and Enforcement of Foreign Arbitral Awards of 1958 is considered to be sufficient even for relations between EC Member States, and the duty of a Member State to recognize juridical persons incorporated in another Member State today normally is considered to follow directly from the EC Treaty's rules on the freedom of establishment, see section 2.2 *infra* and the ECJ judgment *Überseering BV* v. *NCC*, case C-208/00, [2002] ECR I-9919.

10 See section 3.1 *infra*.

11 Some commentators interpret the principle of subsidiarity to mean also that the Community should not intervene when the objective can be better achieved by an international agreement.

with the Community as a whole, irrespective of whether pursuant to the usual conflict rules the matter is governed by the law of a Member State or not. For example, Article 9 of the EC Directive No 94/47 on the Protection of Purchasers in respect of Certain Aspects of Contracts relating to the Purchase of the Right to Use Immovable Properties on a Timeshare Basis (the Timesharing Directive) stipulates that the Member States shall take the measures necessary to ensure that, "whatever the law applicable may be", the purchaser is not deprived of the protection afforded by the Directive, if the immovable property concerned is situated within the territory of a Member State.[12] A similar conflict rule sometimes even may be considered to be tacitly implied in the directives harmonizing provisions of substantive law.[13]

The realization of the difficulties of achieving a uniform European substantive private law has led to an increased understanding of the importance of unifying or at least harmonizing the PIL of the Member States. Despite the continued diversity of substantive law, the unification or harmonization of the rules of PIL improves the chances that the outcome of a legal dispute normally will be the same regardless of where in the Community the judicial proceedings take place.

By introducing Articles K1 and K3 into Title VI of the EU Treaty, the Treaty of Maastricht placed judicial cooperation in civil matters under the "third pillar" of the European integration, and created in this manner a legal base for the negotiation and adoption of more comprehensive EC conventions (but not regulations and directives) in the field of PIL. This was not a very radical change, as such conventions, formally separate from EC law itself, could be adopted even before the Maastricht amendments despite the lack of express support in the EC Treaty, as is witnessed by the Rome Convention on the Law Applicable to Contractual Obligations of 1980.[14] Some PIL conventions were actually formulated on the basis of Article K3,[15] but before they could be ratified by the Member States and enter into force, the EC Treaty was amended again through the Treaty of Amsterdam. The Amsterdam amendments moved "judicial cooperation in civil matters" from the European integration's "third pillar" to its "first pillar".[16] It appears, however, that this move took place without much contemplation, and

---

[12] See section 9.1 *infra*.

[13] See the ECJ in *Ingmar* v. *Eaton Leonard Technologies*, case C-381/98, [2000] ECR I-9305, section 9.1 *infra*.

[14] See section 7.1 *infra*. In contrast, the 1968 Brussels Convention on Jurisdiction and the Enforcement of Judgments in Civil and Commercial Matters had its legal base in Article 220 of the original wording of the EC Treaty (see *supra*).

[15] See, for example, the Convention on the Service in the Member States of the European Union of Judicial and Extrajudicial Documents in Civil or Commercial Matters, OJ 1997 C 261 p. 1, and the Convention on Jurisdiction and the Recognition and Enforcement of Judgments in Matrimonial Matters, OJ 1998 C 221 p. 1.

[16] See, for example, Kohler, *Rev.crit.d.i.p.* 1999 pp. 1-30 and in *IPRax* 2003 pp. 401-412.

was mostly a by-product of the move of the rules on immigration and asylum matters contained in the same Title. This explains why the consequences of the Amsterdam Treaty affecting PIL were not well thought-out and, in some respects, remain unclear.

Article 61(c) of the EC Treaty, as it now stands after the entry into force in 1999 of the Treaty of Amsterdam, provides that the Council, in order to establish progressively an area of freedom, security and justice, has to adopt measures in the field of judicial cooperation in civil matters as provided for in Article 65. Article 65 stipulates, in turn, the following:

> Measures in the field of judicial cooperation in civil matters having cross-border implications, to be taken in accordance with Article 67 and insofar as necessary for the proper functioning of the internal market, shall include
> (a) improving and simplifying:
> - the system for cross-border service of judicial and extrajudicial documents;
> - cooperation in the taking of evidence;
> - the recognition and enforcement of decisions in civil an commercial cases, including decisions in extrajudicial cases;
> (b) promoting the compatibility of the rules applicable in the Member States concerning the conflict of laws and of jurisdiction;
> (c) eliminating obstacles to the good functioning of civil proceedings, if necessary by promoting the compatibility of the rules on civil procedure applicable in the Member States.

It is not quite clear whether the enumeration under (a) – (c) above is intended to be exhaustive, but it certainly covers the central issues of PIL, namely jurisdiction, applicable law and recognition and enforcement of foreign judgments. It follows from the wording of Article 65 that it deals with civil matters only, thus not with matters of penal or administrative law. While "civil" undoubtedly should be understood as being equal to "civil and commercial", it does not include public-law issues such as citizenship, even though in some Member States they may be considered to belong to the field of PIL in a wider sense.

Notwithstanding that Article 65 is found in Title IV of the EC Treaty bearing the heading "Visas, Asylum, Immigration and Other Policies Related to Free Movement of Persons", it is clear that its ambitions in no way are strictly limited to matters related to the freedom of movement of persons. Another way of expressing the same thing is to say that the concept of "free movement of persons" has a special, extensive meaning of its own as far as Title IV is concerned, including not only problems concerning natural persons such as issues of international family law but even commercial matters typically affecting companies, for example jurisdiction in business disputes and determination of the applicable legal system in insolvency proceedings. The heading of Title IV, in any case, must be interpreted so that it does not preclude the conclusion that Title IV encompasses practically the whole PIL.

On the other hand, Article 65 deals merely with "civil matters having cross-border implications", which means that it cannot serve as the legal basis for measures concerning purely domestic substantive or procedural situations unless these situations have, at least to some extent, an international aspect. What this requirement actually means is disputed, but it is clear that the scope of Article 65 is not limited to measures of PIL nature.[17] All PIL provisions fulfill, by definition, the requirement of international implications and, therefore, are within the scope of Article 65, at least as far as that requirement is concerned.

As pointed out by the very wording of Article 65, measures based on that Article can be taken only "insofar as necessary for the proper functioning of the internal market", but this condition appears to be interpreted very – some may even say too – liberally. It seems to be fulfilled by EC legislation in all parts of PIL, including jurisdictional and conflict rules pertaining to those matters of family and succession law that are not directly connected with the internal market. This can be defended by pointing out that even such matters may give rise to legal problems whenever EU citizens make use of their right of free movement by migrating from one Member State to another. It can be added that pursuant to the Treaty Establishing a Constitution for Europe,[18] Article 65 of the EC Treaty is to be replaced by the Constitution's Article III-269, which substitutes "insofar as necessary" with the much softer requirement "particularly when necessary"; however, at present, it is highly uncertain whether the European Constitution will ever enter into force.

Another limitation on the Community's legislative powers pursuant to Article 65 follows from the above-mentioned general principle of subsidiarity. It appears, however, that the requirements imposed by this principle are generally considered fulfilled as far as PIL is concerned. For example, recital 32 in the Preamble of the EC Regulation on Insolvency Proceedings[19] refers dutifully to the principle of subsidiarity, but does not provide any explanation or justification why the objectives of the Regulation cannot be sufficiently achieved by the Member States and can only be fully achieved at Community level.

Practically the whole PIL belongs thus today to the "first pillar" of European integration, which means that it can be regulated by Community instruments such as regulations and directives. An ambitious action plan was adopted by the Justice and Home Affairs Council on 3 December 1998 on how best to implement the provisions of the Treaty of Amsterdam on an area of freedom, security

---

[17] In particular, some of the Commission's proposals based on Article 65(c) have focused on the compatibility of national civil proceedings in general rather than on PIL issues. See, for example, the proposal, presented on 25 May 2004 by the Commission, for a Regulation Creating a European Order for Payment Procedure, COM(2004)173 final, and the Commission's proposal of 22 October 2004 for a Directive on Certain Aspects of Mediation in Civil and Commercial Matters, COM(2004)718 final. The international implications of these proposals were merely incidental.

[18] OJ 2004 C 310.

[19] See section 10.1 *infra*.

and justice.[20] These ambitions received full political support on the highest
level in the Presidency Conclusions of the Tampere European Summit on 15
and 16 October 1999.[21] A number of legal instruments, most of them foreseen
in the Action Plan and/or in the Presidency Conclusions, already have been
adopted and will be presented later in this book.[22] On the basis of the European
Council's Hague Programme of 2004 on Strengthening Freedom, Security and
Justice in the European Union[23] and the Council's and Commission's Action
Plan implementing this Programme,[24] a number of additional PIL-related EC
instruments are being prepared,[25] for example rules on the establishment of a
European small claims procedure[26] and a European payment order procedure,[27]
on the law applicable to non-contractual obligations (the so-called "Regulation Rome II"),[28] on the law applicable to maintenance and suppression of the
exequatur requirement with regard to maintenance judgments,[29] on the applicable law regarding divorce and legal separation,[30] property rights of married

---

[20] See OJ 1999 C 19 p. 1, in particular on p. 10.

[21] See <http://presidency.finland.fi/netcomm/news/showarticle1457.html>.

[22] The most important of these instruments are, in chronological order, Regulation No 1346/2000 of 29
May 2000 on Insolvency Proceedings, OJ 2000 L 160 p. 1; Regulation No 1348/2000 of 29 May 2000
on the Service in the Member States of Judicial and Extrajudicial Documents in Civil or Commercial
Matters, OJ 2000 L 160 p. 37; Regulation No 44/2001 of 22 December 2000 on Jurisdiction and the
Recognition and Enforcement of Judgments in Civil and Commercial Matters, OJ 2001 L 12 p. 1 (the
so-called Brussels I Regulation); Regulation No 1206/2001 of 28 May 2001 on Cooperation between
the Courts of the Member States in the Taking of Evidence in Civil or Commercial Matters, OJ 2001 L
174 p. 1; Directive No 2003/8 of 27 January 2003 to Improve Access to Justice in Cross-border Disputes
by Establishing Minimum Common Rules relating to Legal Aid for such Disputes, OJ 2003 L 26 p.
41; Regulation No 2201/2003 of 27 November 2003 concerning Jurisdiction and the Recognition and
Enforcement of Judgments in Matrimonial Matters and the Matters of Parental Responsibility, repealing Regulation No 1347/2000, OJ 2003 L 338 p. 1 (the so-called Brussels II Regulation); and Regulation
No 805/2004 of 21 April 2004 creating a European Enforcement Order for Uncontested Claims, OJ
2004 L 143 p. 15.

[23] See OJ 2005 C 53 p. 1.

[24] See OJ 2005 C 198 p. 1; Wagner, *IPRax* 2005 pp. 494-496.

[25] See, for example, Baur, *Yearb.PIL* 2003 pp. 177-190 and cf. Lagarde, *RabelsZ* 2004 pp. 225-243.

[26] See the proposal, presented on 15 March 2005 by the Commission, for a Regulation establishing a European Small Claims Procedure, COM(2005)87 final.

[27] See the amended proposal, presented on 7 February 2006 by the Commission, for a Regulation creating
a European Order for Payment Procedure, COM(2006)57 final.

[28] See section 8.1 *infra*.

[29] See the Commission's proposal, presented on 15 December 2005, for a Regulation on Jurisdiction,
Applicable Law, Recognition and Enforcement of Decisions and Cooperation in Matters relating to
Maintenance Obligations, COM(2005)649 final.

[30] See the Commission's proposal, presented on 17 July 2006, for a Regulation Amending Regulation No
2201/2003 as regards Jurisdiction and Introducing Rules concerning Applicable Law in Matrimonial
Matters, COM(2006)399 final. Concerning the competence of the EC to regulate the question of applicable law in divorce matters, see Wagner, *RabelsZ* 2004 pp. 119-153.

couples,[31] successions and wills,[32] mediation,[33] *etc.* The Council has made use of its new competence also by enacting some instruments intended to improve, simplify and expedite effective judicial cooperation between the Member States in civil and commercial matters and to provide information to the public in order to facilitate their access to the national judicial systems of the Member States. An important step in this direction was the establishment of the European Judicial Network for the exchange of information and other cooperation,[34] as well as the creation of a global framework for the Community's financial and other support for activities intended to facilitate the implementation of judicial cooperation in civil matters[35].

Furthermore, although Article 65 speaks modestly of "promoting the compatibility" of the rules concerning the conflict of laws and of jurisdiction, the experiences so far indicate that the usual ambition is rather to achieve a total uniformity of such rules in the Member States. It must, however, be stressed that a full uniformity of results would require much more than a unification of the conflict rules as such of the Member States, namely a unified approach to a number of general questions of PIL, such as whether foreign law is applied at the court's own initiative or merely upon the request of a party, whether the application of foreign law includes the application of its conflict rules (*renvoi*), to what extent foreign law can be refused application due to the public policy of the forum, *etc.*

Whenever the Community makes use of its legislative competence and adopts common rules, it excludes thereby the competence of individual Member States to enter into international agreements with non-member states, which could affect those rules. In the field of PIL, this means, for example, that the Member States can no longer undertake new obligations under the above-mentioned Hague conventions.[36] This is considered to follow from the ECJ judgment of 31 March 1971 in the case of *Commission* v. *Council* regarding the European Agreement concerning the Work of Crews of Vehicles Engaged in

---

[31] See the Commission's Green Paper of 17 July 2006 on Conflict of Laws in Matters concerning Matrimonial Property Regimes, Including the Question of Jurisdiction and Mutual Recognition, COM(2006)400 final.

[32] See the Commission's Green Paper of 1 March 2005 on Succession and Wills, COM(2005)65 final.

[33] See the Commission's Proposal of 22 October 2004 for a Directive on Certain Aspects of Mediation in Civil and Commercial Matters, COM(2004)718 final.

[34] See the Network's homepage <europa.eu.int/comm/justice_home/ejn> and the Council Decision No 2001/470 of 28 May 2001 establishing a European Judicial Network in Civil and Commercial Matters, OJ 2001 L 174 p. 25.

[35] See Regulation No 743/2002 of 25 April 2002 establishing a General Community Framework of Activities to Facilitate the Implementation of Judicial Cooperation in Civil Matters, OJ 2002 L 115 p. 1.

[36] See, for example, A. Borrás in Meeusen, Pertegás & Straetmans (eds.), *Enforcement*, pp. 99-125; B. Hess in Fuchs *et al.* (eds.), *Les conflits*, pp. 81-100; Struycken, *ZEuP* 2004 pp. 276-295; Traest, *YearbPIL* 2003 pp. 223-259; Wilderspin & Rochaud-Joët, *Rev.crit.d.i.p.* 2004 pp. 1-48.

International Road Transport (ERTA)[37] and was recently confirmed by the ECJ
in its Opinion of 7 February 2006 regarding the competence of the Community
to conclude a new Lugano Convention on Jurisdiction and the Enforcement of
Judgments in Civil and Commercial Matters.[38] According to the ECJ, each time
the Community, with a view to implementing a common policy envisaged by
the EC Treaty, adopts provisions laying down common rules, whatever form they
may take, the Member States no longer have the right to make agreements with
third countries which affect those rules or alter their scope. At the same time,
the Community as such until recently has not been competent to sign, ratify
or accede to the Hague conventions, as this could be done merely by sovereign states. This was, for the first time, changed in connection with the 2005
Hague Convention on Choice of Court Agreements, which makes it possible
for "Regional Economic Integration Organizations" to sign, accept, approve or
accede to the Convention, provided they are constituted solely by sovereign states
and have competence over some or all of the matters governed by the Convention (Articles 29 and 30). With regard to those conventions that are open to
states only, the dilemma has to be solved in other ways, such as that used in
connection with the 1996 Hague Convention on Jurisdiction, Applicable Law,
Recognition, Enforcement and Cooperation in respect of Parental Responsibility
and Measures for the Protection of Children, which was considered to make a
valuable contribution while affecting some of the provisions in the EC Regulation Brussels II.[39] The Council noted that the Community had exclusive competence in the areas of the Convention affecting Community law, but adopted
a special decision authorizing the Member States to sign the Convention "in
the interest of the Community".[40] The accession, as soon as possible, of the
Community to the Hague Conference is among the stated aims of the European
Council's Hague Programme of 2005.[41] Even though all EU Member States are
already members of the Conference, a formal decision to admit the Community
as a full member requires an amendment of the Conference's Statute.

The United Kingdom and Ireland, pursuant to a special protocol, are not
obliged to participate in the EC cooperation in civil matters, but so far, they have
opted to take part in it on a voluntary basis. Denmark, on the other hand, has
a more far-reaching exception making Danish participation impossible.[42] This
means, *i.a.*, that the instruments made on the basis of Title IV of the EC Treaty

---

[37] Case 22/70, [1971] ECR 263.

[38] See Opinion 1/03 of the ECJ (Full Court), [2006] ECR I-1145, and section 3.1 *infra*.

[39] See Chapter 5 *infra*.

[40] See OJ 2003 L 48 p. 1.

[41] See OJ 2005 C 53 p. 14 and the proposal, presented on 9 December 2005 by the Commission, for a
Council Decision on the Accession of the European Community to the Hague Conference on Private
International Law, COM(2005)639 final.

[42] See Article 69 of the EC Treaty and Articles 1 and 2 of the Protocol on the Position of Denmark, annexed
to the Treaty on European Union and the Treaty establishing the European Community.

do not bind Denmark, which is not considered a Member State as far as they are concerned. Efforts are, however, being made to connect Denmark to these instruments by means of separate agreements.[43]

Articles 61 and 65 do not have the monopoly to serve as legal bases for Community rules on PIL issues. Some of the original provisions of the EC Treaty itself – in particular the provisions on the freedom of movement of persons, goods, services and capital and on the prohibition of discrimination on grounds of nationality – affect directly all parts of the legal system, including PIL, of the Member States. Some scattered secondary rules of PIL relevance, both before and after 1999, were inserted into various directives dealing mainly with the approximation of laws for the purpose of the establishment and functioning of the internal market, *i.e.*, the implementation of the "four freedoms". Such approximation has today its main legal basis in Articles 94 and 95 of the EC Treaty (formerly Articles 100 and 100a)[44] on the approximation of legislation directly affecting the functioning of the common market, although it could theoretically be argued that the new, special provisions on PIL in Articles 61 and 65 should make Articles 94 and 95 inapplicable as far as the approximation of PIL of the Member States is concerned.

It is noteworthy that Article 220 (see *supra*) of the original EEC Treaty has survived all reforms, although it is now re-numbered as Article 293. It is not clear what role it can play today for PIL, especially its relation to Articles 61 and 65. It seems that it is no longer possible to use Article 293 as the legal basis for PIL conventions, although the same PIL issues can be regulated by instruments of Community law on the basis of Title IV of the EC Treaty.

---

[43] See, for example, the Council Decision of 20 September 2005 on the Signing, on behalf of the Community, of the Agreement between the European Community and the Kingdom of Denmark on Jurisdiction and the Recognition and Enforcement of Judgments in Civil and Commercial Matters (with the text of the Agreement attached), OJ 2005 L 299 p. 61, and the Council Decision of 20 September 2005 on the Signing, on behalf of the Community, of the Agreement between the European Community and the Kingdom of Denmark on the Service of Judicial and Extrajudicial documents in Civil or Commercial Matters (with the text of the Agreement attached), OJ 2005 L 300 p. 53. Both agreements have been approved by the Council but have not yet entered into force.

[44] Some other provisions of the Treaty can also serve as legal bases for secondary EC legislation in the PIL field. See, for example, Directives No 2001/17 of 19 March 2001 on the Reorganization and Winding-up of Insurance Undertakings, OJ 2001 L 110 p. 28 and No 2001/24 of 4 April 2001 on the Reorganization and Winding-up of Credit Institutions, OJ 2001 L 125 p. 15, which have their legal basis in Article 47(2) on the freedom of establishment.

1.3   The Sources

The purpose of this section is to present summarily the types of sources of EC law that are encountered in the field of PIL. The principal and primary source in this field, just like in all other parts of EC law, is the Treaty establishing the European Community (the EC Treaty, corresponding to the amended EEC Treaty of 1957 in accordance with its wording currently in force). The provisions of the EC Treaty, also called the Rome Treaty (not to be confused with the above-mentioned Rome Convention of 1980 on the Law Applicable to Contractual Obligations), are directly applicable in all Member States without the need of any further enactment, and they have direct effect in the sense that they create rights and obligations that can be relied on by individuals before national courts and other authorities in the Member States.

Secondary EC legislation, which is valid only if it has a legal basis in and is compatible with the EC Treaty, consists in principle of regulations and directives.[45] Like the Treaty itself, regulations are directly applicable and have direct effect, whereas a directive is in principle binding on the Member States only, and merely as to the result to be achieved, allowing individual Member States a degree of discretion regarding the means of implementation. Nevertheless, the European Court of Justice (ECJ) has held that some directives, under certain conditions, can have certain direct effects as well,[46] and that a failed or delayed implementation of a directive can create an obligation for the Member State in question to pay compensation for the losses this failure or delay may have caused to private persons.[47]

The EC Treaty, as well as the regulations and directives based on it, are subject to the authoritative interpretation by the ECJ. The competence of the ECJ to deliver authoritative interpretations is very important in view of the fact that the wording in EC legislation is often far from crystal clear, and the existence of each Community instrument in some twenty official, authentic, linguistic versions of equal legal standing does not always make interpretation easier. Although ECJ judgments appear to be formally binding only for the actual case before the Court, in reality they practically always are respected and followed whenever the same question arises subsequently in the national courts of the Member States.[48] Most of the Court's judgments on the validity or interpretation of EC law are preliminary rulings made upon request from a national "court or

---

[45] In addition to regulations and directives, secondary acts of EC law include decisions, which are binding for those to whom they are addressed, and non-binding recommendations and opinions.

[46] See *Marshall v. Southhampton*, case 152/84, [1986] ECR 723; *Unilever v. Central Food*, case 443/98, [2000] ECR I-7535.

[47] See *Francovich v. Italy*, joined cases C-6/90 and C-9/90, [1991] ECR I-5357.

[48] An almost complete collection of ECJ case law pertaining to PIL is Bogdan, M. & Maunsbach, U. (eds.), *EU Private International Law: An EC Court Casebook*, Groningen 2006.

tribunal"[49] of a Member State in accordance with Article 234 (formerly Article 177) of the Treaty.

Article 68 imposes some restrictions on the type of national court authorized to make such a request when the provision under scrutiny is found in or is based on the Treaty's Title IV, including *i.a.* the above-mentioned Articles 61 and 65. In principle, the question must have arisen in a case pending before a court "against whose decisions there is no judicial remedy under national law", meaning normally the highest judicial instance or instances in the country of the forum. The reason for this restriction seems to be the apprehension that the ECJ otherwise might be flooded by references for preliminary rulings within the scope of application of Title IV (while this risk is probably negligible in the field of PIL, it cannot be excluded with regard to other matters such as asylum and immigration).[50] The restriction imposed by Article 68 on the right of lower national courts to ask for a preliminary ruling does not apply when the provision of EC law to be interpreted is found in, or was enacted on the basis of, other provisions of the Treaty than its Title IV, for example on the basis of Articles 94 and 95 on the approximation of the laws of the Member States affecting the establishment or functioning of the common market.

The highest national court of a Member State always has the right to request a preliminary ruling from the ECJ, whether this has been proposed by a party or not. In fact, the highest national court has not only the right, but also the duty, to turn to the ECJ if it is of the opinion that a decision on the interpretation of a provision of EC law is necessary to enable it to give judgment; however, such a request does not have to be made if there is no doubt about the correct interpretation, for example if there is a recent ECJ judgment on the same point or if the Community instrument in question is absolutely clear (*"acte clair"*), or if the different conceivable interpretations lead to the same result in the case before the national court.[51]

A ruling of the ECJ on the interpretation of Title IV, or of EC instruments based on it, may be requested also by the Council, the Commission or any Member State, irrespective of whether there is a case pending in a national court or not (see Article 68(3)), although the ruling given by the ECJ in response to such requests shall not apply retroactively to judgments of the Member States that have become *res judicata*.

---

[49] The referring court, in the actual case, must exercise a judicial function and not merely administrative authority, see *Standesamt Stadt Niebüll*, case C-96/04, [2006] ECR I-0000.

[50] At the same time, the restriction may cause substantial delays in obtaining a final decision, as the national proceedings up to the highest court take often several years and the proceedings at the ECJ can be time-consuming, too, even though there is now a possibility to use an "accelerated procedure" pursuant to Article 104a of the ECJ Rules of Procedure. The delays are particularly problematic in family law disputes under the Brussels II Regulation (see Chapter 5 *infra*); as it was put by a commentator, the minors subject to a custody dispute may have minor children of their own before the dispute is resolved.

[51] See, for example, *CILFIT* v. *Ministerio della Sanità*, case 283/81, [1982] ECR 3115.

It must be stressed that EC law in general, thus not merely the EC Treaty as such, takes precedence over national law of the Member States in order to ensure that EC law is applied uniformly throughout the Union. This means that in case of incompatibility between EC law and a Member State's PIL, it is the former that prevails. It also should be kept in mind that instruments of EC law are normally to be interpreted autonomously,[52] i.e., the concepts and terms used in those instruments must in principle be given their own meaning and do not depend on the terminology of any particular national legal system, although there are exceptions where EC law refers to, or can be interpreted as referring to, national law.[53]

International conventions in principle are not a source of EC law, with the exception of the EC Treaty itself (as amended) and conventions to which the Community itself is a party. However, it has already been pointed out that due to the lack of legal basis for proper Community legislation on PIL issues prior to the Amsterdam Treaty, the Member States sometimes resorted to regulating PIL issues by concluding "EC conventions", which were in several respects assimilated to EC legislation. They were, for example, published in the Official Journal of the European Communities, all new Member States were obliged to ratify them, and the ECJ was by special protocols authorized – or was supposed to be authorized – to make rulings on their interpretation. After the 1968 Brussels Convention has been converted into a regulation (the Brussels I Regulation), the only remaining multilateral EC convention pertaining to PIL is the 1980 Rome Convention on the Law Applicable to Contractual Obligations, but even this convention is expected to be converted into a Community instrument (almost certainly an EC regulation) in the near future.[54] Future conventions with non-member states pertaining to PIL, such as the Hague conventions and bilateral agreements with Denmark (which is in this context not considered to be a Member State), will be negotiated and ratified by the Community as such.[55]

Compared to international conventions, EC regulations are much more efficient, in particular, because their entry into force does not require a certain minimum number of ratifications, which is a requirement that sometimes causes a long delay in the entry into force of conventions. In addition, there is no need to keep track of the varying dates when a convention entered into force in the various Contracting States. However, the principal advantage of EC regulations as compared to conventions is that they are directly applicable as such in all Member States without transposition into national law, which makes it easier to preserve their uniform interpretation and application throughout the Community.

---

[52] See, for example, Audit, *Clunet* 2004 pp. 789-816; Scholz, *Das Problem*.

[53] See, for example, *Tessili v. Dunlop*, case 12/76, [1976] ECR 1473.

[54] See the proposal for a Regulation on the Law Applicable to Contractual Obligations (Rome I), presented by the Commission of the European Communities on 15 December 2005, COM(2005)650 final.

[55] See section 1.2 *supra*.

CHAPTER 2

The Direct Impact of the EC Treaty on the PIL of the Member States

2.1 The Use of Citizenship as a Connecting Factor and the Prohibition of Discrimination on Grounds of Nationality

Article 12(1) of the EC Treaty stipulates that "[w]ithin the scope of application of this Treaty, and without prejudice to any special provision contained therein, any discrimination on grounds of nationality shall be prohibited". This prohibition is reiterated in, for example, Article 39(2), abolishing any discrimination based on nationality between workers of the Member States as regards employment, remuneration and other conditions of work and employment. If read literally, these provisions could be understood to mean that unless the Treaty provides for an exception, the Members States are forbidden to treat a citizen of the European Union (Union citizen) worse than another such citizen, if the only or a substantial reason of the unequal treatment is that they are citizens of two different Member States.

On several occasions, the ECJ has referred to the prohibition of discrimination on grounds of nationality in the context of PIL. An interesting case is *Boukhalfa* v. *Bundesrepublik Deutschland*,[1] where a Belgian national, locally recruited and employed by the German embassy in Algeria, demanded to receive the same treatment as the locally recruited staff of German nationality. A special provision of German PIL stipulated at that time that the legal status of local staff having German nationality was determined by German law, while the employment contracts of other local employees were governed by local (*in casu* Algerian) law.[2] The ECJ held that the prohibition of discrimination between workers of the Member States as regards employment, remuneration and other conditions of work and employment applied in this case, so that a Belgian citizen could not be treated worse than a German national.[3]

Another judgment of interest is *Data Delecta AB* v. *MSL Dynamics Ltd.*,[4] concerning a Swedish provision which required that a foreign national not resident in Sweden or a foreign juridical person wishing to bring an action before a Swedish court against a Swedish national or a Swedish juridical person must, on application by the defendant, furnish security to guarantee the costs of the

---

[1] Case C-214/94, [1996] ECR I-2253.

[2] It deserves to be mentioned that Ms. Boukhalfa's employment contract dated from 1982, which made the Rome Convention on the Law Applicable to Contractual Obligations inapplicable, due to Article 17 of the Convention.

[3] The holding of the ECJ in this case is far from clear, as it limits the prohibition of discrimination to those aspects of the employment relationship "which are governed by the legislation of the employing Member State". The Court seems to have been reasoning in a circle, because the dispute was about whether Ms. Boukhalfa's employment was or was not governed by German law; the ECJ could be understood to mean merely that she was entitled to treatment pursuant to German law to the extent German law applied.

[4] Case C-43/95, [1996] ECR I-4661. See also *Hubbard* v. *Hamburger*, case C-20/92, [1993] ECR I-3777 and *Hayes* v. *Kronenberger*, case C-323/95, [1997] ECR I-1711.

judicial proceedings (*cautio judicatum solvi*). The ECJ held that the prohibition of discrimination on grounds of nationality made the Swedish provision inapplicable in relation to a plaintiff who was a national of or a legal person established in another Member State.

The prohibition of discrimination on grounds of nationality may apply even in some situations where the difference in treatment is based on a criterion other than citizenship, provided that the actual result or effect of that difference is that nationals of other Member States *de facto* are treated worse than the nationals of the Member State of the forum. An ECJ judgment that deserves to be mentioned in this context is *Mund & Fester* v. *Hatrex*,[5] concerning a German procedural rule which permitted the provisional seizure of assets in civil proceedings on the condition that it was probable that enforcement of the ensuing judgment otherwise would be impossible or substantially more difficult, while imposing no such condition on provisional seizures when enforcement was expected to take place abroad (in the actual case in the Netherlands). Although the German rule did not refer in any way to the nationality of the parties, the ECJ found that its application *in casu* amounted to a forbidden discrimination on grounds of nationality, because the prohibition of such discrimination forbids not only overt forms of discrimination but also all covert forms which, by the application of other criteria of differentiation, lead in fact to the same result. The ECJ pointed out that the great majority of enforcements abroad are against persons who are not of German nationality or against legal persons not established in Germany, so that the German provision in question led in fact to the same result as discrimination based on nationality. Such difference in treatment could be justified by objective circumstances, if it were reasonable to fear, in the light of the circumstances of the case, that enforcement of the subsequent judgment would be substantially more difficult abroad than in Germany, but this was not the case where the enforcement was to take place in the territory of a Member State bound by the Brussels rules on recognition and enforcement of judgments.[6] This decision must not be understood as to mean that all connecting factors are forbidden if they usually in one way or another *de facto* result in nationals of different Member States being treated differently; such conclusion would mean, for example, that even differentiation based on habitual residence would be illegal, as most persons are habitually resident in the country of which they are citizens. It is submitted that such indirect difference of treatment is lawful if it is based on objective considerations independent of the nationality of the persons concerned, but not if the true aim of the use of a certain connecting factor other than citizenship is to achieve a covert discriminatory treatment on grounds of nationality or if such use results in a *de facto* difference between the nationals of different Member States without there being any objective reasons behind the choice of the connecting factor used.

---

[5]   Case C-398/92, [1994] ECR I-467.

[6]   See section 3.4 *infra*.

In the PIL of most of the Member States, conflict rules regarding matters of family and succession law use, at least to some extent, citizenship (nationality) as a connecting factor, *i.e.*, such matters are wholly or at least in part governed by the *lex patriae* (the law of the country of citizenship) of the person(s) concerned. Citizenship also is used frequently as a basis for jurisdiction in family and succession matters. By definition, this means that nationals of different Member States are not treated in the same manner. Before the entry into force of the Amsterdam Treaty, this difference in treatment could be explained and defended by saying that the prohibition of discrimination on grounds of nationality applied merely within the scope of application of the EC Treaty[7] and that the issues of family and succession law did not, at that time, fall within that scope.[8] This way of reasoning was explicitly accepted by the ECJ in the case of *Jutta Johannes* v. *Hartmut Johannes*[9], which was decided on 10 June 1999 (*i.e.*, a few weeks after the entry into force of the Amsterdam Treaty) but dealt with an earlier matrimonial dispute to which the amendments introduced by the Amsterdam Treaty were not applicable. The Court pointed out that neither the national provisions of PIL determining the substantive national law applicable to the effects of a divorce nor the national provisions of civil law substantively regulating those effects fell within the scope of the EC Treaty. From this followed, according to the Court, that the prohibition of discrimination on grounds of nationality did not preclude a Member State from considering the spouses' nationality as a connecting factor for the purposes of determining the substantive national law applicable to the effects of a divorce.

As pointed out above, it is today clear that Articles 61 and 65 of the EC Treaty, as amended by the Treaty of Amsterdam, are intended to comprise even conflicts of laws and jurisdictions in the field of family and succession law. Therefore, these matters must be considered now to belong within the EC Treaty's scope of application.[10] Nevertheless, it is far from clear whether this means that Article 12 makes it today unlawful under Community law to use citizenship to determine jurisdiction and applicable law with regard to such issues. Outlawing the use of citizenship as a connecting factor in PIL appears to have been neither intended nor contemplated when the Amsterdam Treaty was negotiated and adopted. It is also noteworthy that Article 3 of the Brussels II Regulation,[11] enacted by the Council of the European Union after the entry into force of the Amsterdam amendments and based on competences granted to the Council by the very

---

[7]   See, for example, *Collins* v. *Imtrat*, joined cases C-92/92 and C-326/92, [1993] ECR I-5145.

[8]   See, for example, Drobnig, *RabelsZ* 1970 pp. 636-662; G. Fischer in von Bar (ed.), *Europäisches Gemein-schaftsrecht*, pp. 157-182; Roth, *RabelsZ* 1991 p. 643; Struycken, *Rec. des cours* 1992, vol. 232, pp. 351-358.

[9]   Case C-430/97, [1999] ECR I-3475.

[10] About the consideration whether a national provision falls within the ambit of the EC Treaty, see, for example, points 10-12 of the ECJ's judgment in *Mund & Fester* v. *Hatrex*, case C-398/92, [1994] ECR I-467.

[11] See section 5.2.1 *infra*.

same amendments, in fact, does use citizenship in a particular Member State as one of the connecting factors which, alone or in combination with other factors, can serve as grounds for that Member State's divorce jurisdiction. This shows that the Council does not consider the use of this connecting factor as forbidden by Article 12 of the EC Treaty. The Council enacted the Brussels II Regulation having regard to the proposal from the Commission and the opinions of the European Parliament and the Economic and Social Committee, which had not objected to the use of nationality as a connecting factor for jurisdiction. Of course, theoretically, they can all be wrong and the final interpretation of the extent of the non-discrimination principle lies in the hands of the ECJ.

The case of *Avello* v. *Etat belge*, decided in 2003,[12] indicates that even the ECJ is probably of the view that it is not a forbidden discrimination on grounds of nationality to subject citizens of different Member States to different treatment in family matters, at least not as far as their surnames are concerned. The case concerned children having dual Belgian-Spanish citizenship and habitually residing in Belgium. Both Spanish and Belgian PIL subjected surnames to the law of the country of citizenship and, in cases of double nationality, gave priority to their own citizenship, so that the children had different surnames in the two countries. They asked the competent Belgian authorities to change their surnames so that they would comply with Spanish law, but the Belgian authorities refused. The matter ultimately was submitted to the ECJ, which referred in its judgment to the settled case law that the principle of non-discrimination requires that comparable situations must not be treated differently and that different situations must not be treated in the same way. According to the Court, an exception may be justified "only if it is based on objective considerations independent of the nationality of the person concerned".[13] With regard to the actual case, the Court noted that the Belgian authorities treated persons who had both Belgian and Spanish nationality in the same way as persons having only Belgian nationality. According to the Court, the situation of these two categories of persons is not the same, because Belgian nationals who also hold Spanish nationality may suffer serious inconvenience due to having different surnames under the two legal systems involved. Consequently, the Court concluded that Article 12 of the EC Treaty obliged the Belgian authorities to grant the children's request, although the only relevant link to Spain was that in addition to being Belgian citizens, the children were (also) Spanish citizens.[14]

The reasoning of the ECJ does not appear to be wholly consistent. According to the Court, dual Spanish-Belgian nationals do not have to be treated in

---

[12] Case C-148/02; [2003] ECR I-11613.

[13] See point 31 of the judgment.

[14] It is submitted that the outcome of the case would have been the same even if the children had not been dual citizens but merely Spanish nationals. If the ECJ holds that persons with dual Spanish-Belgian nationality are entitled to have their surname follow Spanish law, then persons possessing only Spanish nationality must reasonably have the same right.

the same way as persons holding only Belgian nationality, because these two categories of persons are not in the same situation. Nevertheless, as the Court itself made clear in point 31 of the judgment, such differentiated treatment may be justified only if it is based on objective considerations independent of the nationality of the persons concerned. If, due to the differences in their citizenships, citizens of different Member States are deemed to be in different situations and, therefore, can be legitimately subjected to different treatment, then most of the value of Article 12 as a shield against discrimination on grounds of nationality is lost.

However, it is important to note that the parents in the *Avello* Case did not demand that their children be treated by Belgian authorities in the same way as (other) Belgian nationals. Quite the opposite, they requested special treatment on grounds of their second, Spanish nationality. When such different treatment is requested by the affected persons themselves (or on their behalf), it can be assumed that it is to their advantage. Such *positive* discrimination of citizens of other Member States is tolerated by Community law, subject to certain conditions. Thus, it must be stressed that the *Avello* judgment cannot be interpreted as permitting or requiring the application of the law of the country of citizenship against the will of the person(s) concerned. In fact, it can be argued that Article 12 grants to Union citizens the right to demand the application of the law of the Member State where they habitually reside, in order to avoid being discriminated there in comparison with local nationals. Had the children in the *Avello* case been Spanish nationals only, and had their parents requested that their surnames be registered by Belgian authorities in accordance with Belgian rules on surnames in order to facilitate their assimilation in the Belgian society, it is both possible and plausible that a refusal by the Belgian authorities, on the grounds of the children's Spanish nationality, to grant that request would amount to a negative discrimination, incompatible with Article 12 of the EC Treaty.[15]

It can be added that in the *Avello* Case the ECJ referred also to Article 17 of the EC Treaty, which gives all nationals of the Member States a citizenship of the Union, intended to complement national citizenship. Even though that Article does not seem to give Union citizens any additional protection against discrimination on grounds of nationality, it can be understood as confirming that such protection exists today, even when there is no economic link to the internal market.

---

[15] See, for example, Kohler in *Internationales Familienrecht für das 21. Jahrhundert*, p. 18. It is, however, an open question whether Community law, as it is today, would oblige, in such a case, the Spanish authorities to recognize the surname acquired by the Spanish children in Belgium pursuant to Belgian law. This question has arisen in the case of *Standesamt Stadt Niebüll*, case C-96/04, [2006] ECR I-0000, but was not decided because the ECJ found itself to lack jurisdiction due to the administrative, rather than judicial, nature of the case pending before the referring national court.

2.2 The Freedom of Movement and the Principle of Control by the Country of Origin

Among the most central and almost sacred principles of EC law, the rules of the EC Treaty on the free movement of goods, persons, services and capital play a primordial role. All restrictions, capable of hindering, directly or indirectly, actually or potentially, this freedom of movement are normally forbidden,[16] unless the effects of the restriction are insignificant. As developed in the case law of the ECJ, this system requires, for example, that the free movement of a product or service produced and lawfully marketed in one Member State is not hindered in other Member States by the application of requirements and restrictions imposed by their local law.[17] Even when those requirements and restrictions are reasonable and not discriminatory *per se*, products or services crossing national borders would be exposed to a competitive disadvantage obstructing intra-Community trade if they had to comply simultaneously with the laws of two or more Member States. At the same time, the system seems to assume that the product or service really complies with the law of the Member State of origin, *i.e.* it must not be exempted from the requirements of that law because it is intended for export to the other Member States.

This so-called "country-of-origin principle", based on the effective control by the law of the country of origin and the recognition throughout the Community of what that law accepts as lawful and permissible (it is therefore sometimes also called "the principle of mutual recognition"),[18] is defined in various ways and implemented in more detail in some existing or proposed secondary Community legislation,[19] but it is embodied to some extent even in the EC Treaty itself, although the Treaty does not explicitly refer to it.

---

[16] See, for example, *Procureur du Roi* v. *Dassonville*, case 8/74, [1974] ECR 837.

[17] See the well-known judgment of the ECJ in the case of *Rewe-Zentral* v. *Bundesmonopolverwaltung*, case 120/78, [1979] ECR 649 (the case is better known under the name of *Cassis de Dijon*).

[18] The principle has given rise to much debate and is far from uncontroversial among PIL writers. See, for example, S. Bariatti in Meeusen, Pertegás & Straetmans (eds.), *Enforcement*, pp. 77-98; Basedow, *RabelsZ* 1995 pp. 1-55 and in *Liber Memorialis Petar Šarčević*, pp. 13-24; Drasch, *Das Herkunftslandprinzip*; M. Fallon in Fuchs *et al.* (eds.), *Les conflits*, pp. 31-80; Fallon & Meeusen, *YearbPIL* 2002 pp. 37-66; Fezer & Koos, *IPRax* 2000 pp. 350-354; Grundmann, *RabelsZ* 2000 pp. 457-477 and in Fuchs *et al.* (eds.), *Les conflits*, pp. 5-29; Halfmeier, *ZEuP* 2001 pp. 837-868; Hommelhoff *et al.* (eds.), *Europäisches Binnenmarkt*; Höpping, *Auswirkungen*; Mankowski, *IPRax* 2004 pp. 385-395; Paefgen, *ZEuP* 2003 pp. 266-294; Radicati di Brozolo, *Rev.crit.d.i.p.* 1993 pp. 401-424; Spindler, *RabelsZ* 2002 pp. 633-709; von Wilmowski, *RabelsZ* 1998 pp. 1-37.

[19] See, *e.g.*, Article 3 of the Directive on Electronic Commerce (section 9.2 *infra*). Article 22 of the proposed Rome I Regulation on the Law Applicable to Contractual Obligations (see section 7.7 *infra*) and Article 3 of the proposed Rome II Regulation on the Law Applicable to Non-contractual Obligations (see section 8.1 *infra*) stipulate that the Regulation will not prejudice the application or adoption by the EC institutions of acts which lay down rules to promote the smooth operation of the internal market.

The country-of-origin principle is, however, subject to exceptions. Some exceptions are stipulated in the EC Treaty itself (see, for example, Article 30 permitting restrictions on the free movement of goods[20] on grounds of public morality, public policy, public security, protection of health and life, national treasures or industrial and commercial property), but even other restrictions based on legitimate objective considerations may under certain additional conditions be acceptable in non-harmonized areas of law, if they are necessary to satisfy the mandatory requirements of public good in the Member State of the forum (for example fairness in commerce or protection of consumers, workers or the environment). In the words of the ECJ, such national measures liable to hinder or make less attractive the exercise of fundamental freedoms guaranteed by the Treaty must fulfil four conditions: they must be applied in a non-discriminatory manner; they must be justified by imperative requirements in the general interest; they must be suitable for securing the attainment of the objective which they pursue; and they must not go beyond what is necessary in order to attain it.[21] The force and intensity of the country-of-origin principle is thus subject to a "rule of reason" and varies from case to case. It is often quite difficult to ascertain whether and to what extent it applies in a particular situation.

As seen from the viewpoint of the receiving Member State, the country-of-origin principle does not necessarily require a general application of the law of the country of origin, but merely that the law of the receiving country is not applied in a way hindering the free movement. This means that the principle does not restrict the receiving country's right to apply its own law on all those points where that law is more permissive than the law of the country of origin. In fact, insisting on the application of a more demanding law of the country of origin would place enterprises established in another Member State in a situation worse than that of domestic enterprises and, therefore, could be perceived sometimes as discriminatory and contrary to EC law. The country-of-origin principle is thus more a corrective "escape clause" to be used in a particular case than a general conflict rule of its own.

All this is mainly of interest for restrictions imposed by public law, for example various safety requirements for products, but, in some cases, it can be relevant for the applicability of private-law rules as well.[22] If applied strictly

---

[20] Concerning restrictions pertaining to the right of establishment, the freedom to provide services and the movement of capital, see Articles 46, 55 and 58 of the EC Treaty.

[21] See *Gebhard* v. *Consiglio degli Avvocati*, case 55/94, [1995] ECR I-4165.

[22] See, for example, Fallon, *Rec.des cours* 1995, vol. 253, pp. 59-91. In the case law of the ECJ, see, for example, *Alsthom Atlantique SA* v. *Sulzer*, case C-339/89, [1991] ECR I-107, where the ECJ held that the application of a provision of French law on strict liability of sellers for hidden defects did not violate EC law, but only after the Court had established that the French rule did not favor French products. The ECJ pointed out, furthermore, that the French rule could be contracted out by a choice of another legal system. Cf. also the older case of *Société Générale* v. *Walter Koestler*, case 15/78, [1978] ECR 1971,

even in the private-law area, the country-of-origin principle would mean that even regarding civil and commercial matters (contracts, torts, *etc.*), the supplier normally would be allowed to rely on the law of the Member State in which he is established in order to avoid the more exacting rules of the Member States to which he directs his activities.

The functioning of the country-of-origin principle can be illustrated by the case law concerning freedom of establishment of juridical persons registered in another Member State.[23] An ECJ judgment of great interest in this context is *Centros v. Erhvervs- og Selskabsstyrelsen*,[24] where two persons residing habitually in Denmark and dissatisfied with the minimum capital requirements of Danish company law registered a private limited company in England for the sole purpose of pursuing business activities in Denmark through a Danish branch of the English company. The Danish administrative authorities refused to register the branch, arguing that the scheme constituted a circumvention of Danish law and exposed creditors to the risk of fraud. The ECJ did not accept this reasoning. It held that the refusal to register the branch prevented the English company from exercising its freedom of establishment, and was thus contrary to the EC Treaty (today Articles 43 and 48). This case concerned merely the refusal to perform an administrative measure (registration of a branch), but in the subsequent decision in the case of *Überseering BV v. NCC* the ECJ held that it is equally forbidden for a Member State to attempt to achieve a similar result by means of PIL, for example by refusing to recognize the legal capacity of companies created in accordance with the laws of another Member State.[25] According to the ECJ, where a company formed in accordance with the law of and having its registered office in a Member State exercises its freedom of establishment in another Member State, the latter must recognize its legal capacity under the law of the former. In a third case, *Kamer van Koophandel v. Inspire Art*, the ECJ stated that a Member State must not impose additional requirements and conditions provided for in its domestic company law on the exercise of freedom of establishment by companies from other Member States, save where the existence of an abuse is established on a case-by-case basis.[26]

The country-of-origin principle plays an important role also for the freedom of movement and the right of establishment of natural persons. It is, for

---

where it was held that the freedom to provide services did not hinder the application by German courts of German provisions barring recovery of wagering debts with regard to a contract made in France between a French bank and its customer, provided that the treatment of such debts was not discriminatory compared with the treatment of similar debts contracted in Germany.

[23] See, for example, Ballarino, *Rev.crit.d.i.p.* 2003 pp. 373-402; Behrens, *IPRax* 2003 pp. 193-207; Bogdan, *Ny Juridik* 2004, no. 1, pp. 7-20; Østergaard, *Nordisk Tidsskrift for Selskabsret* 2005 pp. 110-122; Roth, *IPRax* 2003 pp. 117-127; Zimmer, *RabelsZ* 2003 pp. 298-317.

[24] Case C-212/97, [1999] ECR I-1459.

[25] Case C-208/00, [2002] ECR I-9919.

[26] Case C-167/01, [2003] ECR I-10155.

example, doubtful to what extent the Member State to which an EU citizen immigrates has the right to impose on him its own law on personal and family matters on the ground of the immigrant's new domicile or habitual residence. It can be argued that the application of the new *lex domicilii*, in any case against the immigrant's will, is incompatible with the freedom of movement stipulated in Article 18 of the EC Treaty if it precludes or deters a national of a Member State from leaving his country of origin to exercise that freedom. The risk of such incompatibility is illustrated by the case of *Christos Konstantinidis*, decided by the ECJ in 1993,[27] where the ECJ held that it was contrary to the freedom of establishment stipulated in Article 52 (now 43) of the EC Treaty to oblige a Greek national to use, in the pursuit of his occupation in Germany,[28] a Latin-alphabet spelling of his Greek name whereby its pronunciation was distorted in a way causing him serious inconvenience. This judgment can be interpreted as to mean that the ECJ recognizes that most people consider their name to be very important and that a grave risk of interference by another Member State regarding names may consequently be sufficient to deter, or at least discourage, many EU citizens from exercising their right to move to such a Member State. There is no doubt that a change in the marital property regime that affects a spouse adversely or the loss of the freedom to dispose of one's estate by a will is by many people perceived as a hindrance, which is at least as serious as an involuntary change of name.[29]

---

[27] Case C-168/91; [1993] ECR I-1191.

[28] At the time of the decision, the reference to Mr. Konstantinidis' economic activities was important in order to demonstrate that the situation fell within the scope of Community law. Today, the combined effect of Articles 17 and 18(1) of the EC makes it unnecessary to establish any economic link in order to demonstrate an infringement of the right to freedom of movement. See points 48 and 54 in the Opinion of Advocate General Jacobs in the case of *Standesamt Stadt Niebüll*, case C-96/04, [2006] ECR I-0000.

[29] Cf. also *Dafeki v. Landesversicherungsanstalt*, case C-336/94, [1997] ECR I-6761, where the ECJ held that as the exercise of the rights arising from the freedom of movement for workers is not possible without production of documents relative to personal status issued by the Member State of the worker's origin, the administrative and judicial authorities of the Member State to which the worker moves must accept such certificates and analogous documents relative to personal status, unless their accuracy is seriously undermined by concrete evidence relating to the individual case in question. The judgment concerned a matter of fact (the date of birth in a birth certificate), but there are no reasons to believe that the same principle does not apply to other matters of personal status, such as marriages and adoptions. On such matters, however, the presumption of correctness of the document issued by the Member State of the person's origin may, it seems, in principle be refuted even by the application of the rules of PIL of the Member State where the document is relied on. A different question is whether each Member State can rely on its own PIL when granting or refusing admission to a person claiming to be a family member within the meaning of Article 2(2) of Directive 2004/38 of 29 April 2004 on the Right of Citizens of the Union and their Family Members to Move and Reside freely within the Territory of the Member States, OJ 2004 L 158 p. 77. See, for example, Kohler in *Internationales Familienrecht für das 21. Jahrhundert*, p. 25.

The combined result of the non-discrimination rule in Article 12[30] and the freedom of movement pursuant to Article 18 seems to be that an EU citizen moving from his own country to another Member State is entitled to demand the application of the family and succession law of the country of his new habitual residence, but, *if he so desires,* he may choose to have his personal matters governed by the law of his country of origin instead, at least as long as he retains his original nationality.[31] This freedom of choice will probably function well with regard to surnames and some other issues, but it must be admitted that it will not solve corresponding problems concerning certain other family-law situations, for example a dispute regarding the division of matrimonial property, where different parties may have mutually incompatible preferences as to the legal system to be applied.

---

[30] See section 2.1 *supra.*

[31] See, for example, Kohler in *Internationales Familienrecht für das 21. Jahrhundert,* p. 18.

CHAPTER 3

Regulation Brussels I

3.1 History of the Regulation and its Relationship to the Brussels and Lugano Conventions

The EC Treaty itself contains no rule directly obliging the Member States to recognize and enforce each other's judgments. The original Article 220 of the EEC Treaty of 1957 stipulated, however, that Member States should enter, so far as necessary, into negotiations with each other with a view to securing for the benefit of their nationals the simplification of formalities governing the reciprocal recognition and enforcement of judgments. This provision demonstrates the awareness of the founding Member States of the fact that a community based on the freedom of movement for persons, goods, services and capital also requires a free movement of court decisions on matters related to the functioning of the common market (some speak in this context of a "common market for judgments" or "the fifth freedom").

In compliance with the above-mentioned Article 220 (today Article 293) of the Treaty, the six original Member States concluded in 1968 the Brussels Convention on Jurisdiction and the Enforcement of Judgments in Civil and Commercial Matters.[1] The Convention became effective in 1973 and subsequently was amended repeatedly, mainly to accommodate new Member States (in the context of the Convention called "Contracting States"). In order to secure a uniform interpretation, the ECJ was authorized, by a special protocol (the Luxembourg Protocol of 1971[2]), to interpret the Convention, although the right to request a preliminary ruling was not given to all courts in the Contracting States, but only to the highest courts and courts sitting in an appellate capacity. There is now an impressive amount of relevant ECJ case law.[3] Also of particular value for the interpretation of the Convention and its amendments are the semi-official explanatory reports published in the Official Journal.[4]

The Brussels Convention went far beyond the ambitions of Article 220 of the Treaty, which were limited to simplifying recognition and enforcement of judgments. The Convention was designed as a "double instrument", which means that it regulated not only the recognition and enforcement of judgments but even the jurisdiction of courts. In fact, the jurisdictional provisions in the Brussels Convention seem to have played a much more important role in practice

---

[1]   OJ 1990 C 189 p. 2.

[2]   OJ 1990 C 189 p. 25.

[3]   Almost all ECJ judgments concerning the Brussels Convention until 1995 can be found in M. Bogdan (ed.), *The Brussels Jurisdiction and Enforcement Convention – an EC Court Casebook*, Kluwer 1996. More recent cases are found in the official European Court Reports (ECR) and are freely available on the Internet as well, for example through the ECJ website <www.curia.eu.int>.

[4]   The report on the original text of the Convention was written by P. Jenard, who served as reporter of the committee which prepared the Convention, see OJ 1979 C 59 p. 1. Subsequent amendments are commented on by P. Schlosser in OJ 1979 C 59 p. 71, D.I. Evrigenis and K.D. Karameus in OJ 1986 C 298 p. 1 and by M. de Almeida Cruz, M. Desantes Real and P. Jenard in OJ 1990 C 189 p. 35.

and have given rise to much more case law and legal writing than its rules on recognition and enforcement.

A double instrument makes recognition and enforcement simpler. As it can be assumed that the Contracting States abide by the jurisdictional rules of the instrument, there normally is no need to allow a Contracting State to subject judgments made in the other Contracting States to examination and conditions regarding the adjudicating court's jurisdiction. At the same time, the rules on recognition and enforcement make it possible to eliminate certain exorbitant jurisdictional grounds favouring directly or indirectly domestic plaintiffs at the expense of foreign defendants. The best example of such exorbitant juris-dictional grounds is the mere presence in the forum country of some assets belonging to the defendant. The countries using this ground of jurisdiction, for example Germany and Sweden, usually defend it by pointing out the plaintiff's need for a domestic judgment due to non-recognition and non-enforcement of foreign decisions. More generous recognition and enforcement rules make it possible to do away with this jurisdictional ground without the risk of creating a legal vacuum, *i.e.*, a situation where the assets are beyond the reach of the credi-tors because foreign judgments are not accepted while domestic courts have no jurisdiction.

The Brussels Convention went further than Article 220 of the Treaty also in another respect. Article 220 obliged the Member States to enter into negotia-tions "for the benefit of their nationals", whereas the resulting Convention did not, with some very minor exceptions, give any relevance to the nationality of the parties.

The Brussels Convention was generally considered to be a success, and even those Western European countries that were not members of the EC, in particular members of the European Free Trade Association (EFTA), wished to join the system created by the "Brussels rules". As direct accession to the Brus-sels Convention was not open to these countries, a solution was found in the form of the parallel Lugano Convention on Jurisdiction and the Enforcement of Judgments in Civil and Commercial Matters of 1988.[5] The rules of the Lugano Convention are in almost all respects identical to those of the Brussels Conven-tion, and even the numbering of the articles is practically the same. Some minor differences exist however between the contents of the two instruments[6] and it must also be kept in mind that questions on the interpretation of the Lugano Convention cannot be submitted to the ECJ. The Lugano Convention applies

---

[5]   OJ 1988 L 319 p. 9. A commentary on the Lugano Convention is found in a semi-official explanatory report by P. Jenard and G. Möller, OJ 1990 C 189 p. 57. See also Bogdan, 9 *Saint Louis University Public Law Review* 113-129 (1990); Briggs & Rees, *Civil Jurisdiction*, pp. 179-186 and 332-333; Byrne, *The Euro-pean Union*; Donzallaz, *La Convention*; Fisknes, *Luganokonvensjonen*; Gaudemet-Tallon, *Compétence*, pp. 393-417; Gillard (ed.), *L'espace*; Pålsson, *Brysselkonventionen*, pp. 22-25; Rognlien, *Luganokonvensjonen*; Wahl, *The Lugano Convention*.

[6]   See, in particular, Articles 5(1), 16(1), 17, 28, 55 and 57 of both conventions.

today in relations between Iceland, Norway and Switzerland and between any of them and the majority of the EC Member States (some of the ten most recent EC members are not yet bound by the Lugano rules, but this is expected to change relatively soon). A special protocol (Protocol No 2) and two declarations attached to the Lugano Convention make it clear that this Convention is to be interpreted paying due account to the ECJ case law concerning the Brussels rules and there is a practically unanimous consensus that the ECJ precedents on those rules are more-or-less automatically to be followed even for the interpretation of the Lugano Convention, except in those rare cases where the wording of the Lugano Convention differs from that of the Brussels rules.[7]

The Brussels Convention, which applied between the EC Member States themselves, was replaced on 1 March 2002 by Regulation No 44/2001 on Jurisdiction and the Recognition and Enforcement of Judgments in Civil and Commercial Matters (the so-called Brussels I Regulation).[8] The Regulation applies in principle to legal proceedings initiated after its entry into force, but, for most Member States, this date (1 March 2002[9]) did not bring about any revolutionary changes, because the main principles of the Regulation stem from the Brussels Convention. Nevertheless, the numerous differences regarding various details made it impossible to retain the Convention's numbering of articles (except for the first six of them). This means that although most of the explanatory reports, legal writing and ECJ case law regarding the Brussels Convention continue to be relevant for the interpretation of the Regulation, it requires a little more effort to localize precedents and other statements pertaining to a particular provision.

The Brussels Convention continues to apply in relation to Denmark (see Article 1(3) of the Regulation), as well as in relation to certain of the territories belonging to the Member States, but situated outside of Europe (see Article 68(1) of the Regulation and Article 299 of the EC Treaty). A special agreement has been reached between the EC and Denmark to replace the Brussels Convention with a new instrument resulting in the application of rules, which are almost identical to those in the Brussels I Regulation.[10] The Lugano Convention is expected to be adapted to the Regulation within the foreseeable future, too.[11] The following text therefore deals with the Regulation only. The amount of literature on the Regulation is so far limited,[12] but there are many works dealing

---

[7]   See, for example, Duintjer Tebbens, *YearbPIL* 2001 pp. 1-25; Schmidt-Parzefall, *Die Auslegung*.

[8]   OJ 2001 L 12 p. 1. The Regulation has subsequently undergone some minor changes, mainly in order to accommodate the new Member States, see *e.g.* OJ 2003 L 236 p. 711.

[9]   For those Member States, which jointed the EU in 2004, the Regulation entered into force on the day when they became Member States, *i.e.* 1 May 2004.

[10] See OJ 2005 L 299 p. 61 and section 1.2 *supra*. The agreement has not yet entered into force.

[11] According to Opinion 1/03 of the ECJ, dated 7 February 2006, the EC – and not the Member States – has exclusive competence to conclude the new Lugano Convention.

[12] Among the more general works on the Regulation see, for example, Ancel, *YearbPIL* 2001 pp. 101-114; Beraudo, *Clunet* 2001 pp. 1033-1106; Droz & Gaudemet-Tallon, *Rev.crit.d.i.p.* 2001 pp. 601-652;

with the Brussels and Lugano Conventions. As mentioned above, most of them, to some extent, remain relevant for the interpretation of the Regulation as well[13].

3.2 The Scope and Other General Features of the Regulation

In its very first preliminary ruling on the interpretation of the Brussels Convention,[14] the ECJ pointed out that the Brussels rules frequently use words and legal concepts drawn from civil, commercial and procedural law and capable of a different meaning from one Member State to another. This gives rise to the question of whether these words and concepts must be regarded as having their own independent meaning, and thus as being common to all the Member States, or as referring to substantive rules of one or another national law, for example the *lex fori* or the law applicable to the substance of the dispute. According to the ECJ, neither of these two options (autonomous interpretation or interpretation according to some national law) rules out the other since the appropriate choice between them can only be made individually in respect of each of the Brussels rules. In its above-mentioned first decision on the Brussels rules, concerning the interpretation of the reference made in Article 5(1) to the "place of performance" of contractual obligations, the ECJ opted for national law, as due to the differences prevailing between national legal systems, at that time it did not appear possible to give more substantive guidance to the interpretation of that concept. Nevertheless, it is clear that most of the Brussels rules, in the same way as most other rules of EC law, are to be interpreted autonomously

---

Gaudemet-Tallon, *Compétence*; Geimer, *IPRax* 2002 pp. 69-74; Geimer & Schütze, *Europäisches Zivilverfahrensrecht*; Kropholler, *Europäisches Zivilprozessrecht*; Layton & Mercer (eds.), *European Civil Practice*; Pålsson, *Brysselkonventionen*, Rauscher (ed.), *Europäisches Zivilprozessrecht*; Rozehnalová & Týč, *Evropský justiční prostor*, pp. 171-336; Strömholm, *Upphovsrätt*, pp. 111-135.

[13] Among the more general works on the Brussels and Lugano Conventions see, for example, Briggs & Rees, *Civil Jurisdiction*; Byrne, *The European Union*; Calvo Caravaca (ed.), *Comentario*; Carpenter *et al.*, *The Lugano and San Sebastian Conventions*; Czernich & Tiefenthaler, *Die Übereinkommen*; Dashwood, Hacon & White, *A Guide*; Donzalaz, *La Convention*; Droz, *Compétence*; Droz, *Pratique*; Droz, *Rev.crit.d.i.p.* 1987 pp. 251-303 and 1989 pp. 1-51; Duintjer Tebbens, *YearbPIL* 2001 pp. 1-25; Fentiman *et al.* (eds.), *L'espace*; Fisknes, *Luganokonvensjonen*; Fletcher, *Conflict*, pp. 103-146; Gillard (ed.), *L'espace judiciaire européen*; Gothot & Holleaux, *La Convention*; Hartley, *Civil Jurisdiction*; Jayme (ed.), *Ein internationales Zivilverfahrensrecht*; Jenard, *La Convention*; Kaye, *Civil Jurisdiction*; Kaye (ed.), *European Case Law*; Kaye, *Law*; Klinke, *Brüsseler Übereinkommen*; Mari, *Il diritto*; Mercier & Dutoit, *L'Europe*; Newton, *The Uniform Interpretation*; Nielsen, *International privat- og procesret*, pp. 132-219; Pålsson, *Brysselkonventionen*; Philip, *EU-IP*, pp. 27-123; Pocar, *La Convenzione*; Rognlien, *Luganokonvensjonen*; Schack, *ZEuP* 1999 pp. 783-796; F. Salerno in von Hoffmann (ed.), *European Private International Law*, pp. 115-158; Schlosser, *EuGVÜ*; Schmidt-Parzefall, *Die Auslegung*; Scholz, *Das Problem*; Trunk, *Die Erweiterung*; Wahl, *The Lugano Convention*; Weiss, *Die Konkretisierung*; Werlauff, *Common European Procedural Law*; Weser, *Convention*.

as much as possible, *i.e.*, they are not based on the legal terminology of any individual Member State but rather have their own meaning, binding on all the Member States. Such autonomous interpretation of the Brussels rules' terms and concepts is, in the words of the ECJ, necessary to ensure that these rules are fully effective,[15] and must be based in the first place on their objectives and scheme and, secondly, on the general principles which stem from the corpus of the national legal systems.[16]

This is true also with regard to the delimitation of the scope of application of the Regulation, as defined in Article 1.[17] The concept of "civil and commercial matters", referred to in Article 1(1), is autonomous and independent of the corresponding national legal concepts.[18] The second sentence in Article 1(1), excluding revenue, customs and administrative matters, was added simply to clarify, by means of examples, the types of matters that do not fall within the scope of "civil and commercial matters", and it neither limits nor modifies that concept.[19] The interpretation of "civil and commercial matters" has given rise to several ECJ judgments. As the main rule, the Court has held that a dispute, or a judgment given in a dispute, between a public authority and a person governed by private law, in which the public authority acts in the exercise of its powers, is excluded from the area of application of the Brussels rules.[20] It makes no difference whether the proceedings are brought by or on behalf of a public authority (for example, for the purpose of collecting a tax debt), or against a public authority (for example, by a private person claiming a tax refund).[21]

The delimitation between, on the one hand, civil and commercial matters and, on the other hand, matters of public law, is not always manifest and clear.[22]

---

[14] *Tessili v. Dunlop*, case 12/76, [1976] ECR 1473.

[15] See, for example, the case of *Suhadiwarno Panjan*, case C-440/97, [1999] ECR I-6307, point 11.

[16] See, for example, Audit, *YearbPIL* 2001 pp. 101-114; Layton & Mercer (eds.), *European Civil Practice*, vol. I, pp. 293-299; Pålsson, *Brysselkonventionen*, pp. 35-42; Scholz, *Das Problem*.

[17] See, for example, *LTU v. Eurocontrol*, case 29/76, [1976] ECR 1541; *Bavaria v. Eurocontrol*, joined cases 9 and 10/77, [1977] ECR 1517; *Gourdain v. Nadler*, case 133/78, [1979] ECR 733; *Netherlands v. Rüffer*, case 814/79, [1980] ECR 3807.

[18] See, for example, Soltész, *Der Begriff*.

[19] *TIARD v. The Netherlands*, case C-266/01, [2003] ECR I-4867.

[20] See, for example, *LTU v. Eurocontrol*, case 29/76, [1976] ECR 1541, concerning a judgment obliging a private company to pay charges unilaterally fixed and imposed by a public authority for its obligatory and exclusive services. See also *Netherlands v. Rüffer*, case 814/79, [1980] ECR 3807.

[21] It must be added that judicial proceedings against a *foreign* public authority will normally be barred by the foreign state's sovereign immunity.

[22] See, for example, Briggs & Rees, *Civil Jurisdiction*, pp. 30-31; Byrne, *The European Union*, pp. 14-20; Czernich & Tiefenthaler, *Die Übereinkommen*, pp. 41-42; Dashwood, Hacon & White, *A Guide*, pp. 9-11 and 69-72; Donzallaz, *La Convention*, vol. I, pp. 327-344; Gaudemet-Tallon, *Compétence*, pp. 25-28; Geimer & Schütze, *Europäisches Zivilverfahrensrecht*, pp. 65-74; Hartley, *Civil Jurisdiction*, pp. 11-16; Kaye, *Civil Jurisdiction*, pp. 62-84; Lasok & Stone, *Conflict*, pp. 166-170; Layton & Mercer (eds.), *European Civil*

For example, the ECJ has held that an action for damages against a teacher in a state school, who by negligent lack of supervision caused injury to a pupil, is a civil matter even where cover for the damages is provided by an insurance scheme governed by public law.[23] The ECJ also has held that the concept of civil law encompasses an action under a right of recourse whereby a public body seeks from a private person recovery of sums it has paid to that person's child and former spouse by way of social assistance, provided that the right of recourse is governed by the rules of the ordinary law regarding maintenance obligations and not by provisions giving the public body a prerogative of its own.[24] Similarly, an action by a state against a private person, who had voluntarily agreed by contract to guarantee a customs debt of another person, was deemed a civil and commercial matter insofar as the legal relationship between the state and the guarantor was governed by the rules applicable to relations between private individuals.[25]

There are also several types of issues that, although having a civil or commercial nature, are excluded from the scope of the Regulation by its Article 1(2), such as almost the whole of family law, insolvency, social security and arbitration. In some of these areas, there are other instruments of EC law[26] or such instruments are being prepared, while the exclusion of arbitration is made possible by the existence of the relatively well-functioning, worldwide New York Convention of 1958 on the Recognition and Enforcement of Foreign Arbitral Awards. The enumeration of exceptions in Article 1(2) is intended to be exhaustive, so that civil and commercial matters not listed there come within the scope of the Regulation.[27]

The family-law exception in Article 1(2)(a) states that the Regulation does not apply to the status or legal capacity of natural persons, rights in property arising out of a matrimonial relationship, wills and succession.[28] Questions of the status

---

Practice, vol. I, pp. 336-349; Pålsson, Brysselkonventionen, pp. 51-54; Philip, EU-IP, pp. 30-31; Rauscher (ed.), Europäisches Zivilprozessrecht, pp. 47-50; Rognlien, Luganokonvensjonen, pp. 122-123; Rozehnalová & Týč, Evropský justiční prostor, pp. 184-186; Schlosser, EuGVÜ, pp. 18-23; Soltész, Der Begriff.

[23] Sonntag v. Waidmann, case C-172/91, [1993] ECR I-1963.

[24] Gemeente Steenbergen v. Baten, case C-271/00, [2002] ECR I-10489 . See also Freistaat Bayern v. Blijdenstein, case C-433/01, [2004] ECR I-981.

[25] See TIARD v. The Netherlands, case C-266/01, [2003] ECR I-4867. Concerning the action for recourse by such guarantor against the original debtor, see Frahuil v. Assitalia, case C-265/02, [2004] ECR I-1543.

[26] See, e.g., the Brussels II Regulation (Chapter 5 infra) and the Insolvency Regulation (Chapter 10 infra).

[27] See de Cavel v. de Cavel, case 120/79, [1980] ECR 731 (see in particular point 5 of the judgment).

[28] See, for example, M. Bogdan in Meeusen, Pertegás & Straetmans (eds.), Enforcement, pp. 211-223; Briggs & Rees, Civil Jurisdiction, p. 32; Byrne, The European Union, pp. 21-25; Czernich & Tiefenthaler, Die Übereinkommen, p. 43; Dashwood, Hacon & White, A Guide, pp. 11-13 and 74-76; Donzallaz, La Convention, vol. I, pp. 355-372; Gaudemet-Tallon, Compétence, pp. 28-31; Geimer & Schütze, Europäisches Zivilverfahrensrecht, pp. 80-85; Hartley, Civil Jurisdiction, pp. 16-20; Kaye, Civil Jurisdiction, pp. 85-129; Lasok & Stone, Conflict, pp. 172-180; Layton & Mercer (eds.), European Civil Practice, vol. I, pp. 350-356;

of natural persons comprise, for example, the validity of a marriage, divorce, adoption, paternity, guardianship, custody, name and declaration of death. The validity and dissolution of a registered partnership and other similar new family formations is also a matter of status of natural persons and is, as such, probably excluded from the scope of the Regulation. The exception regarding rights in property arising out of a matrimonial relationship comprises not only the property rights themselves but also closely connected matters such as the husband's management of his wife's property resulting from the marriage bond.[29] It is questionable whether disputes concerning rights in property arising out of a registered partnership or of a *de-facto* cohabitation are excluded as well, since although being family relationships, they are not "matrimonial". One part of family law that is not excluded is maintenance.[30] Distinguishing between maintenance disputes and disputes regarding marital property rights sometimes may be difficult, especially because the courts in some countries can award a lump sum intended both to enable a spouse to provide for himself and to divide property between the spouses.[31] Disputes between family members are excluded only to the extent they arise out of the family relationship but not if they are based on general rules, for example if one spouse sold his car to the other spouse and a dispute arises about the payment of the price.

The exclusion in Article 1(2)(b) of "bankruptcy, proceedings relating to the winding-up of insolvent companies or other legal persons, judicial arrangements, compositions and analogous proceedings" excludes from the scope of the Regulation insolvency proceedings in the strict sense, but also other matters deriving directly from the bankruptcy or winding-up and closely connected with such proceedings, for example proceedings regarding the liability of the manager of a bankrupt enterprise to make good a deficiency in the assets, provided that liability is based on the provisions of insolvency law.[32] The gap

---

Pålsson, *Brysselkonventionen*, pp. 56-58; Philip, *EU-IP*, pp. 31-32; Rauscher (ed.), *Europäisches Zivilprozessrecht*, pp. 51-54; Rognlien, *Luganokonvensjonen*, pp. 124-125; Rozehnalová & Týč, *Evropský justiční prostor*, pp. 186-187; Schlosser, *EuGVÜ*, pp. 24-26.

[29] See *CHW v. GJH*, case 25/81, [1982] ECR 1189. Cf. also *de Cavel v. de Cavel*, case 143/78, [1979] ECR 1055.

[30] In matters relating to maintenance obligations, the Regulation's rules, however, will probably be replaced by the proposed Regulation on Jurisdiction, Applicable Law, Recognition and Enforcement of Decisions and Cooperation in Matters relating to Maintenance Obligations, see Article 48(1) of the proposal presented by the Commission on 15 December 2005, COM(2005)649 final.

[31] See *de Cavel v. de Cavel*, case 120/79, [1980] ECR 731; *van den Boogaard v. Laumen*, case C-220/95, [1997] ECR I-1147.

[32] *Gourdain v. Nadler*, case 133/78, [1979] ECR 733. See also Briggs & Rees, *Civil Jurisdiction*, pp. 32-33; Byrne, *The European Union*, pp. 25-27; Czernich & Tiefenthaler, *Die Übereinkommen*, pp. 43-44; Dashwood, Hacon & White, *A Guide*, pp. 76-77; Donzallaz, *La Convention*, vol. I, pp. 372-376; Gaudemet-Tallon, *Compétence*, pp. 31-32; Geimer & Schütze, *Europäisches Zivilverfahrensrecht*, pp. 85-88; Hartley, *Civil Jurisdiction*, pp. 20-21; Kaye, *Civil Jurisdiction*, pp. 129-144; Layton & Mercer (eds.), *European Civil*

created by this exclusion is in some respects filled by Article 25 of the EC Insolvency Regulation,[33] which provides for recognition and enforcement, not merely of judgments concerning the opening, the course and the closure of insolvency proceedings but also of other judgments deriving directly from the insolvency proceedings and closely linked with them, even if they were handed down by another court.

The exclusion in Article 1(2)(c) of matters regarding social security[34] appears to be unnecessary to the extent social security is perceived as a public-law matter (see *supra*). Article 1(2)(c) thus is relevant only in relation to social security matters governed by civil and commercial law. In any case, it excludes both an individual's claim for a social security benefit and claims of the body administering the social security system for fees to be paid by the individual or his employer. On the other hand, it does not exclude actions under a right of recourse, by which a public body seeks to recover, in accordance with the rules of ordinary civil law, the sums it has paid to the defendant's family by way of social insurance.[35] This means that such actions for recourse are within the scope of the Regulation.

Arbitration is excluded by Article 1(2)(d),[36] which does not mean that the jurisdictional rules of the Regulation cannot be set aside by an arbitration agreement between the parties or that an arbitration award cannot be recognized, but merely that jurisdiction in disputes and recognition of judgments regarding arbitration as such are not governed by the Regulation. This exclusion applies only if the arbitral matter is raised as a main issue in the proceedings, for

---

Practice, vol. I, pp. 356-360; Lasok & Stone, *Conflict,* pp. 180-183; Pålsson, *Brysselkonventionen,* pp. 58-59; Philip, *EU-IP,* p. 32; Rauscher (ed.), *Europäisches Zivilprozessrecht,* pp. 54-56; Rognlien, *Luganokonvensjonen,* pp. 125-126; Schlosser, *EuGVÜ,* pp. 27-28.

[33] See OJ 2000 L 160 p. 1 and Chapter 10 *infra.*

[34] See, for example, Briggs & Rees, *Civil Jurisdiction,* p. 33; Dashwood, Hacon & White, *A Guide,* pp. 14 and 79; Donzallaz, *La Convention,* vol. I, pp. 379-380; Gaudemet-Tallon, *Compétence,* pp. 32-33; Geimer & Schütze, *Europäisches Zivilverfahrensrecht,* pp. 88-90; Hartley, *Civil Jurisdiction,* pp. 21-22; Kaye, *Civil Jurisdiction,* pp. 144-146; Lasok & Stone, *Conflict,* pp. 183-185; Layton & Mercer (eds.), *European Civil Practice,* vol. I, pp. 360-362; Pålsson, *Brysselkonventionen,* pp. 59-60; Philip, *EU-IP,* p. 32; Rauscher (ed.), *Europäisches Zivilprozessrecht,* pp. 56-58; Rognlien, *Luganokonvensjonen,* pp. 126-127; Schlosser, *EuGVÜ,* pp. 28-29.

[35] *Gemeente Steenbergen v. Baten,* case C-271/00, [2002] ECR I-10489.

[36] See, for example, Briggs & Rees, *Civil Jurisdiction,* pp. 33-34; Byrne, *The European Union,* pp. 28-35; Czernich & Tiefenthaler, *Die Übereinkommen,* p. 45; Dashwood, Hacon & White, *A Guide,* pp. 14-15 and 78-79; Donzallaz, *La Convention,* vol. I, pp. 382-390; Gaudemet-Tallon, *Compétence,* pp. 33-36; Geimer & Schütze, *Europäisches Zivilverfahrensrecht,* pp. 90-92; Hartley, *Civil Jurisdiction,* p. 22; Kaye, *Civil Jurisdiction,* pp. 146-150; Lasok & Stone, *Conflict,* pp. 185-187; Layton & Mercer (eds.), *European Civil Practice,* vol. I, pp. 362-370; Pålsson, *Brysselkonventionen,* pp. 60-61; Philip, *EU-IP,* p. 33; Rauscher (ed.), *Europäisches Zivilprozessrecht,* pp. 58-61; Ronglien, *Luganokonvensjonen,* pp. 127-128; Rozehnalová & Týč, *Evropský justiční prostor,* pp. 188-189; Schlosser, *EuGVÜ,* pp. 29-31.

example, when the court is requested to appoint an arbitrator[37] or to set aside an arbitral award. The court having jurisdiction pursuant to the Regulation to deal with a contractual dispute, on the other hand, is competent to deal also with the defendant's procedural objection that the court's jurisdiction is excluded due to the existence of a valid arbitration agreement.

What has just been said about arbitration applies also to the other above-mentioned exclusions in Article 1(2): they refer only to cases where the excluded matter is the main issue in dispute, and not to situations where such matter arises merely as a preliminary or incidental question, even though the answer to the preliminary question may be decisive for the main issue, for example, when the validity of a marriage or of an adoption is contested by the defendant in a dispute on maintenance. The court having jurisdiction pursuant to the Regulation to adjudicate the maintenance dispute thus is competent to examine even objections regarding the validity of a marriage or adoption, but its decision about those objections has no legal force beyond the maintenance dispute pending before the court.

A restriction, not explicitly stated in the Regulation, of the scope of its jurisdictional provisions is that they intend to regulate jurisdiction only with regard to disputes having some kind of international character.[38] Purely internal disputes are considered to be excluded, which is of importance in particular for the right of the parties to such internal disputes to take advantage of Article 23 concerning prorogation of jurisdiction.[39] This does not mean that the dispute must necessarily involve parties from different countries, since a case may have international character due to some other circumstance(s), such as that it concerns a contract to be performed abroad or compensation for a tort committed in another country. According to the ECJ, it is not necessary for the applicability of the Regulation that at least two of the countries involved are Member States.[40] There is no requirement of any international background of the dispute when it comes to the Regulation's provisions on *lis pendens*, recognition and enforcement. These provisions apply whenever proceedings ongoing in a Member State or judgments made in a Member State are relied on in another Member State, provided of course that they fall within the scope of the Regulation as defined in Article 1.

---

[37] *Rich* v. *Impianti*, case C-190/89, [1991] ECR I-3855.

[38] See *Owusu* v. *Jackson*, case C-281/02, [2005] ECR I-1383; Jenard's Report on the Brussels Convention, OJ 1979 C 59, p. 8; Donzallaz, *La Convention*, vol. I, pp. 418-431; Geimer & Schütze, *Europäisches Zivilverfahrensrecht*, pp. 114-118; Kaye, *Civil Jurisdiction*, pp. 216-226; Pålsson, *Brysselkonventionen*, pp. 61-63; Rauscher (ed.), *Europäisches Zivilprozessrecht*, pp. 65-67; Rognlien, *Luganokonvensjonen*, p. 105.

[39] See section 3.3.5 *infra*.

[40] *Owusu* v. *Jackson*, case C-281/02, [2005] ECR I-1383. Cf. also *Group Josi* v. *UGIC*, case C-412/98, [2000] ECR I-5925.

Pursuant to Article 1(1), the Regulation applies in civil and commercial matters "whatever the nature of the court or tribunal". It is thus irrelevant whether the court in question is a court of general jurisdiction or a special court, such as a labor court for employment disputes. It may even be a criminal court, to the extent it is competent, under national law, to deal also with matters of civil liability. However, it must be a court or tribunal, and not an administrative organ. This is the reason why a special provision in Article 62 had to declare the Swedish enforcement authorities, which handle summary proceedings such as payment orders, to be courts, because Swedish summary proceedings and the decisions made therein would otherwise fall outside the field of application of the Regulation.[41]

Some limitations of the scope of the Regulation follow from its relationship to other international instruments, both international conventions and provisions of EC law. Article 67 gives precedence to rules about jurisdiction and recognition and enforcement of judgments in other instruments of EC law, including those national laws of the Member States that have been harmonized in implementation of EC directives.[42] Article 71 of the Regulation gives precedence to earlier conventions to which Member States are parties and which govern jurisdiction and/or the recognition and enforcement of judgments in relation to particular matters. Such particular rules are found, for example, in some conventions on nuclear damage, maintenance, intellectual property and international transports.[43] The Regulation supersedes, on the other hand, the earlier general recognition and enforcement conventions between the Member States, although they continue to apply in relation to those matters to which the Regulation does not apply,[44] for example, most matters of family law. These superseded earlier general conventions are enumerated in Article 69. After the entry into force of the Regulation, it appears that the Member States are not allowed to conclude any new conventions concerning jurisdiction and the enforcement of judgments in disputes within the Regulation's scope, not even in relation to particular matters.

---

[41] Articles 63-65 contain a few other special rules relating to certain Member States, but these exceptions cannot be dealt with in this concise presentation.

[42] See Chapter 6 *infra*.

[43] See, for example, *Tatry*, case C-406/92, [1994] ECR I-5439; *Nürnberger* v. *Portbridge*, case C-148/03, [2004] ECR I-10327.

[44] See *Bavaria* v. *Eurocontrol*, joined cases 9 and 10/77, [1977] ECR 1517.

3.3   The Jurisdictional Rules of the Regulation

3.3.1   The Main Rule of the Defendant's *Forum Domicilii*

The main jurisdictional principle of the Regulation is that persons domiciled in a Member State must ("shall") be sued in the courts of that Member State, regardless of their nationality (Articles 2 and 3).[45] The domicile of the plaintiff, as well as the nationality or nationalities of the parties, in principle are irrelevant.[46] This means, on the one hand, that the courts of the country of the defendant's domicile must not refuse to try the case (according to the ECJ, the doctrine of *forum non conveniens*[47] cannot be used in order to deviate from Article 2[48]) and, on the other hand, that the courts in the other Member States in principle are obligated to dismiss the case because of lack of jurisdiction.

A person domiciled in a Member State may be sued in another Member State only in situations mentioned among the exceptions explicitly permitted by the Regulation.[49] The use of national jurisdictional rules of the forum Member State against defendants domiciled in other Member States in principle is forbidden. The "black list" of forbidden jurisdictional rules in Annex I is not exhaustive but rather a mere catalogue of the most notorious examples of national jurisdictional grounds not permitted by the Regulation when the defendant is domiciled in another Member State. Even jurisdictional grounds that are not mentioned in Annex I are forbidden unless belonging to the explicitly permitted exceptions. It could be argued, however, that jurisdictional grounds not accepted by the Regulation, including the explicitly forbidden grounds on the black list in Annex I, in some very rare situations, could be used in order to avoid a legal vacuum, for example, in a Member State where the defendant debtor has sequestrable assets that otherwise would be beyond the reach of his creditors because the judgment made in the Member State, where the defendant is domiciled, has

---

[45]   See, for example, Byrne, *The European Union*, pp. 38-39; Czernich & Tiefenthaler, *Die Übereinkommen*, p. 46; Dashwood, Hacon & White, *A Guide*, pp. 83-88; Gaudemet-Tallon, *Compétence*, pp. 59-61; Geimer & Schütze, *Europäisches Zivilverfahrensrecht*, pp. 124-127; Kaye, *Civil Jurisdiction*, pp. 339-345; Lasok & Stone, *Conflict*, pp. 202-205; Layton & Mercer (eds.), *European Civil Practice*, vol. I, pp. 393-399; Pålsson, *Brysselkonventionen*, pp. 92-93; Philip, *EU-IP*, pp. 41-42; Rauscher (ed.), *Europäisches Zivilprozessrecht*, pp. 73-77; Rognlien, *Luganokonvensjonen*, pp. 129-133; Schlosser, *EuGVÜ*, pp. 27-28.

[46]   Cf. *Group Josi* v. *UGIC*, case C-412/98, [2000] ECR I-5925.

[47]   The doctrine of *forum non conveniens* allows a court having jurisdiction to decline to exercise it when another court is better placed to hear the case. Cf. Article 15 of the Brussels II Regulation (section 5.3.1 *infra*).

[48]   *Owusu* v. *Jackson*, case C-281/02, [2005] ECR I-1383. The reasoning of the ECJ indicates that the doctrine of *forum non conveniens* must not be used in order to deviate from other of the Regulation's jurisdictional rules either. See Cuniberti, 54 *I.C.L.Q.* 973-981 (2005); Harris, 54 *I.C.L.Q.* 933-950 (2005); Hartley, 54 *I.C.L.Q.* 824-828 (2005).

[49]   See sections 3.3.2-3.3.5 *infra*.

been refused recognition and enforcement, for instance, on the ground of public policy (Article 34(1)).

If the defendant is not domiciled in any of the Member States, the jurisdiction of each of them, in accordance with Article 4, may be determined by the forum's own national jurisdictional rules, including the rules on the black list in Annex I. Many of these national rules are rather excessive, as some Member States consider their courts to have jurisdiction on the basis of such factors as the citizenship of the plaintiff (France, Luxembourg), the presence of the defendant's assets (Germany, Sweden), or the service of documents on the defendant during his temporary presence within the country (United Kingdom). Article 4(2) extends in fact the use of some of these national jurisdictional rules beyond their original scope, because it provides that a foreigner domiciled in a Member State having such rules there can avail himself of them in the same way as local nationals. This is of particular importance where the national jurisdictional rule is based on the plaintiff's citizenship in the forum country. The foreigner in question does not even have to be a national of any of the Member States. Thus, an American citizen domiciled in France, when acting as plaintiff, can rely on the French jurisdictional rules as if he were a French national, provided of course that the defendant is not domiciled in any of the Member States.

The fact that only defendants domiciled in a Member State are protected against the – often exorbitant – national jurisdictional rules, while other defendants are not, for example, those domiciled in the USA, has been criticized as being discriminatory.[50] It certainly can be a disadvantage from the point of view of a US defendant to be subjected to the jurisdiction of a French court on the sole ground that the plaintiff carries a French passport, especially as the resulting judgment will be recognized and enforced in almost all European countries.[51] With regard to contractual disputes, both European and non-European parties have, subject to certain restrictions, normally the possibility to avoid the effects of Article 4 by insisting on an arbitration or a choice-of-court agreement.

It follows from the aforesaid that the defendant's domicile is of central importance for the Regulation. The domicile of the plaintiff is relevant in exceptional cases only, for example, according to Articles 5(2), 9(1), 16(1) and 23(1). The concept of domicile has different meaning in different Member States and, therefore, it is useful that the Regulation defines it in Articles 59 and 60. Regarding companies and other legal persons and associations, the domicile is defined in Article 60 as the place of the statutory seat, the place of the central administration or the principal place of business.[52] This means that a legal

---

[50] See, for example, Juenger, *Rev.crit.d.i.p.* 1983 pp. 37-51.

[51] Of course, the judgment will be so recognized even if the French plaintiff loses the case on its merits, in which case the recognition of the French judgment all over Europe will be to the advantage of the defendant.

[52] There are special rules regarding the domicile of legal persons in Ireland or the United Kingdom and the domicile of trusts, see Article 60(2-3).

person at the same time can have its domicile and, at the option of the plaintiff, be sued in several Member States, although the first action precludes subsequent actions in other Member States due to the *lis pendens* rule in Article 27. To enjoy protection against national jurisdictional rules (see *supra*), it suffices that the legal person is domiciled in a Member State according to one of the criteria listed in Article 60.

As far as domicile of natural persons is concerned, Article 59 contains no substantive definition but merely two conflict rules.[53] The first conflict rule concerns the situation where the defendant's domicile in the Member State of the forum is decisive for the forum's jurisdiction, usually pursuant to Article 2. Article 59(1) stipulates that the question of whether the defendant is domiciled in the country of the forum must be decided by the law of that country. It may happen that two or more Member States consider the same person to be domiciled within their respective territories; the solution is the same as for legal persons domiciled in more than one Member State (see *supra*), *i.e.*, in principle, the court first seized will have sole jurisdiction pursuant to Article 27. The second conflict rule in Article 59(2) deals mainly with the situation where the defendant is not domiciled in the forum state, but it is necessary to determine whether he is domiciled in any of the other Member States in order to decide whether he is entitled to protection against the application of the national jurisdictional rules of the forum according to Article 4. The determination of the defendant's domicile in such cases is made in accordance with the law of the Member State in which the defendant is allegedly domiciled. If, for example, the defendant sued in a Swedish court claims protection against national Swedish jurisdictional rules on the ground that he is domiciled in Germany (*i.e.*, in another Member State), the Swedish court must determine whether he really is domiciled there by applying the German concept of domicile.

It can be added that in most Member States the domicile of natural persons corresponds more to the concept of habitual residence than to the English and Irish concept of "domicile", which in some respects is closer to nationality. Several provisions in the Regulation (Articles 5(2), 13(3) and 17(3)) use the expression "domiciled or habitually resident", but the two concepts are practically synonymous in the majority of the Member States.

---

[53] See, for example, Briggs & Rees, *Civil Jurisdiction*, pp. 80-81 and 87-88; Byrne, *The European Union*, pp. 231-239; Czernich & Tiefenthaler, *Die Übereinkommen*, pp. 259-260; Dashwood, Hacon & White, *A Guide*, pp. 183-184; Donzallaz, *La Convention*, vol. I, pp. 391-409; Geimer & Schütze, *Europäisches Zivilverfahrensrecht*, pp. 713-717; Hartley, *Civil Jurisdiction*, pp. 23-30; Kaye, *Civil Jurisdiction*, pp. 278-319; Lasok & Stone, *Conflict*, pp. 205-207; Layton & Mercer (eds.), *European Civil Practice*, vol. I, pp. 1052-1059; Nielsen, *International privat- og procesret*, pp. 154-155; Pålsson, *Brysselkonventionen*, pp. 86-91; Philip, *EU-IP*, pp. 37-39; Rauscher (ed.), *Europäisches Zivilprozessrecht*, pp. 470-475; Schlosser, *EuGVÜ*, pp. 232-233.

3.3.2   Special Jurisdictional Rules

The main jurisdictional principle in Articles 2 and 3 of the Regulation, protecting the defendant by forcing the plaintiff to sue in the defendant's *forum domicilii*, is subject to some important exceptions, in the first place those in Articles 5 and 6. These exceptions give the plaintiff the option, in some situations, to sue the defendant, even though he is domiciled in a Member State, in the courts of another Member State. The inconvenience and other disadvantages this may cause to the defendant in these cases are considered to carry less weight than the close connection between the dispute and that other Member State. This close connection is considered to make a particular court in that country especially suitable for adjudicating the dispute, for example, because of the easy access to relevant evidence or other similar advantages.

It must be noted that when referring to the courts for a particular place, the special jurisdictional rules in Articles 5 and 6 do not point out merely the alternative Member State where the action can be brought but normally even the competent local court in that Member State. This is an important difference in comparison with most of the other jurisdictional rules in the Regulation, including the main rule in Article 2, which refer generally to the courts of a certain Member State and leave it to the law of that state to specify the competent local court. Another thing to keep in mind is that Articles 5 and 6 do not deprive the plaintiff of his right to sue in the Member State of the defendant's domicile, but give him rather an additional, alternative choice.

The special jurisdictional rules, being derogations from the main rule, are supposed to be interpreted and applied with restraint.[54] In practice, however, the ECJ has chosen sometimes to give Article 5 a rather extensive scope.

Pursuant to Article 5(1), which is one of the more problematic provisions in the Regulation, in matters relating to a contract a defendant domiciled in a Member State can be sued, in another Member State, in the courts for the place of performance of the contractual obligation in question (the so-called *forum solutionis*).[55] The concept of contract is interpreted autonomously and does not depend on whether the relationship is classified as contractual in the national

---

[54]   See, *e.g.*, *Kalfelis* v. *Bankhaus Schröder,* case 189/87, [1988] ECR 5565.

[55]   See, for example, Briggs & Rees, *Civil Jurisdiction*, pp. 91-100; Byrne, *The European Union*, pp. 43-70; Czernich & Tiefenthaler, *Die Übereinkommen*, pp. 54-62; Dashwood, Hacon & White, *A Guide*, pp. 88-95; Donzallaz, *La Convention*, vol. III, pp. 98-258; Gaudemet-Tallon, *Compétence*, pp. 127-164; Geimer & Schütze, *Europäisches Zivilverfahrensrecht*, pp. 160-186; Gsell, *IPRax* 2002 pp. 484-491; Hager & Bentele, *IPRax* 2004 pp. 73-77; Hartley, *Civil Jurisdiction*, pp. 43-48; Hertz, *Jurisdiction*, pp. 85-171; Lasok & Stone, *Conflict*, pp. 212-221; Layton & Mercer (eds.), *European Civil Practice*, vol. I, pp. 409-456; Newton, *The Uniform Interpretation*, pp. 43-161; Nielsen, *International privat- og procesret*, pp. 157-162; Pålsson, *Brysselkonventionen*, pp. 95-107; Philip, *EU-IP*, pp. 46-49; Rauscher, *Verpflichtung*; Rauscher (ed.), *Europäisches Zivilprozessrecht*, pp. 88-115; Rognlien, *Luganokonvensjonen*, pp. 138-143; Rozehnalová & Týč, *Evropský justiční prostor*, pp. 204-206; Schlosser, *EuGVÜ*, pp. 44-50; Valloni, *Der Gerichtsstand*.

law of the Member State of the forum or the national law governing the relation-ship in question.[56] For example, the ECJ has held that the concept of contractual dispute ("matters relating to a contract") includes a dispute between an associa-tion and its member, regardless of whether the disputed obligation arose simply from the membership or from membership in conjunction with decisions made by the association.[57] Article 5(1) does not require an actual conclusion of a bilateral contract and applies even to disputes relating to one-sided obligations of contractual nature, such as the assumption of suretyship (guarantee) or the promise of a prize.[58] In fact, a dispute is considered to relate to a contract even when the very existence of that contract is contested by the defendant, since Article 5(1) otherwise could be deprived of its effect by a simple assertion by the defendant that the contract did not exist.[59] It appears that Article 5(1) can be used even if it is the plaintiff himself who denies the very existence of a valid contract, for example, when he institutes an action for a judicial declaration that the contract is null and void.

On the other hand, Article 5(1), according to the ECJ, does not apply to an action between a manufacturer and a sub-buyer of goods, because belonging to such a chain of contracts (between the manufacturer and the buyer and between the buyer and the sub-buyer) does not create an obligation freely assumed between the manufacturer and the sub-buyer.[60] The pre-contractual liability for unjustifiedly breaking off contractual negotiations falls also outside Article 5(1).[61]

If the action is caused by the non-performance or a defective performance of a contractual obligation, it is not the place of the claimed remedy (*e.g.*, the replacement of defective goods or payment of compensation) but the place of performance of the original obligation that is decisive.[62] Most contracts involve two reciprocal performances, normally one performance in kind (specific performance) and another in money, and the ECJ has held that in principle it is the place of the disputed performance that is decisive.[63] If the dispute is about a faulty or late performance in kind, then *forum solutionis* is the court for the place where the specific performance has or should have been carried out, while for disputes concerning payment, it is the court for the place where the payment

---

[56] See, for example, *Arcado* v. *Haviland*, case 9/87, [1988] ECR 1539; M. Pertegás in Meeusen, Pertegás & Straetmans (eds.), *Enforcement*, pp. 175-190.

[57] *Peters* v. *ZNAV*, case 34/82, [1983] ECR 987. Cf. also *Powell Duffryn* v. *Petereit*, case 214/89, [1992] ECR I-1745.

[58] *Engler* v. *Janus*, case C-27/02, [2005] ECR I-481.

[59] *Effer* v. *Kantner*, case 38/81, [1982] ECR 825. Cf. also *Sanders* v. *van der Putte*, case 73/77, [1977] ECR 2383.

[60] *Handte* v. *Traitements*, case C-26/91, [1992] ECR I-3967.

[61] *Tacconi* v. *HWS*, case C-334/00, [2002] ECR I-7357.

[62] See *de Bloos* v. *Bouyer*, case 14/76, [1976] ECR 1497.

[63] *De Bloos* v. *Bouyer*, case 14/76, [1976] ECR 1497; *Shenavai* v. *Kreischer*, case 266/85, [1987] ECR 239.

has or should have been made. This is today, however, more an exception than the main rule, because in contrast to Article 5(1) of the Brussels and Lugano Conventions, Article 5(1)(b) of the Regulation contains a special, partly autonomous definition of the place of performance in respect of the two most common and most important types of contract, namely, contracts for the sale of goods and contracts regarding the provision of services.[64] The place of all performances under such contracts, including the obligation to pay the price, is for the purposes of Article 5(1) deemed to be the place in a Member State where, under the contract, the goods were or should have been delivered or the services were or should have been provided. The place of payment is thus irrelevant as far as these two types of contracts are concerned. Regarding those contractual relations that are neither for the sale of goods nor for the provision of services, for example, a barter transaction, a loan of money, a trademark licence or a rental of equipment, it is the original main rule, referring to the court for the place of the disputed performance, that continues to apply.

The place of performance of the relevant obligation, for example, the place of delivery of the goods sold, is in most cases explicitly or implicitly agreed upon by the parties. The Regulation leaves it to the applicable national law to regulate the formal and material validity of such agreements.[65] However, if the agreement on the place of performance is not designed to determine the actual place of performance, but is made solely for the purpose of indirectly establishing jurisdiction, it will not have effect pursuant to Article 5(1), although if it complies with the formal requirements imposed by Article 23, it conceivably can have the effects of a valid choice-of-court agreement.[66]

If there is no agreement between the parties on the place of performance, that place in principle must be determined by the law governing the contract in question pursuant to the PIL of the forum,[67] which is nowadays normally the law determined by the conflict rules in the 1980 Rome Convention on the Law Applicable to Contractual Obligations.[68] This means that the law governing the contract may have to be ascertained even before the court decides whether it has jurisdiction to deal with the dispute. It appears that the PIL of the forum can and should be used in this way irrespective of whether the place of performance is relevant under Article 5(1)(a) or Article 5(1)(b), although it has been argued that the words "under the contract" in Article 5(1)(b) indicate that that provision

---

[64] See, for example, Beraudo, *Clunet* 2001, pp. 1040-1048; Gaudemet-Tallon, *Compétence*, pp. 158-164; Geimer & Schütze, *Europäisches Zivilverfahrensrecht*, pp. 175-179; Gsell, *IPRax* 2002 pp. 484-491; Hager & Bentele, *IPRax* 2004 pp. 73-77; Layton & Mercer (eds.), *European Civil Practice*, vol. I, pp. 448-452; Pålsson, *Brysselkonventionen*, pp. 101-103; Rauscher (ed.), *Europäisches Zivilprozessrecht*, pp. 108-115.

[65] *Zelger* v. *Salinitri*, case 56/79, [1980] ECR 89.

[66] See section 3.3.5 *infra* and *MSG* v. *Gravières Rhénanes*, case C-106/95, [1997] ECR I-911.

[67] *Tessili* v. *Dunlop*, case 12/76, [1976] ECR 1473; *Custom* v. *Stawa*, case C-288/92, [1994] ECR I-2913; *Suhadiwarno Panjan*, case C-440/97, [1999] ECR I-6307.

[68] See Chapter 7 *infra*.

can be used only if the place of performance has been determined by the parties themselves.

If the dispute concerns several parallel obligations under the same contract, and one of these obligations is the principal obligation while the other are merely accessory, then pursuant to the principle of *accessorium sequitur principale*, the determination of jurisdiction for the whole dispute may be based on the place of performance of the main obligation.[69] For example, if the essence of the contract is the sale and delivery of a piece of machinery, the court for the place of delivery is competent also with regard to a dispute concerning the accessory obligation of the seller to train an employee of the buyer to operate the machine, regardless of in which country that training has taken or is to take place. However, if the two (or more) obligations arising from the same contract are of equal rank, then jurisdiction concerning each of them must be determined separately.[70]

Article 5(1) does not apply when the relevant place of performance is situated outside the territory of the Member States.[71] The ECJ has also held that Article 5(1) cannot be used, and the plaintiff consequently is compelled to sue in the Member State of the defendant's domicile pursuant to Article 2, when the contractual obligation is to be performed without any geographical limitation, for example, in the case of a negative contractual undertaking to refrain, in the whole world, from certain behavior.[72]

Article 5(2) provides for a special forum for disputes in matters relating to maintenance obligations[73] (towards children, a spouse or a former spouse, a parent, *etc.*).[74] In such matters, a defendant domiciled in a Member State can be sued in another Member State in the courts for the place where the maintenance creditor is domiciled. If the issue of maintenance is ancillary to proceedings concerning the status of a person, for example, divorce proceedings or a lawsuit concerning the determination of paternity or custody, the national court enter-

---

[69] *Shenavai* v. *Kreischer*, case 266/85, [1987] ECR 239.

[70] *Leathertex* v. *Bodetex*, case C-420/97, [1999] ECR I-6747.

[71] Cf. *Six Constructions* v. *Humbert*, case 32/88, [1989] ECR 341.

[72] *Besix* v. *WABAG*, case C-256/00, [2002] ECR I-1699.

[73] With regard to maintenance disputes, the Regulation, however, may soon be replaced with the proposed Regulation on Jurisdiction, Applicable Law, Recognition and Enforcement of Decisions and Cooperation in Matters relating to Maintenance Obligations, see the proposal presented by the Commission on 15 December 2005, COM(2005)649 final and Chapter 6 *infra*.

[74] See, for example, Byrne, *The European Union*, pp. 70-71; Czernich & Tiefenthaler, *Die Übereinkommen*, p. 66; Dashwood, Hacon & White, *A Guide*, pp. 95-96; Donzallaz, *La Convention*, vol. III, pp. 310-336; Gaudemet-Tallon, *Compétence*, pp. 164-167; Geimer & Schütze, *Europäisches Zivilverfahrensrecht*, pp. 187-194; Hartley, *Civil Jurisdiction*, pp. 48-50; Lasok & Stone, *Conflict*, pp. 233-235; Layton & Mercer (eds.), *European Civil Practice*, vol. I, pp. 456-469; Pålsson, *Brysselkonventionen*, pp. 107-111; Philip, *EU-IP*, pp. 51-52; Rauscher (ed.), *Europäisches Zivilprozessrecht*, pp. 116-121; Rognlien, *Luganokonvensjonen*, pp. 145-147; Schlosser, *EuGVÜ*, pp. 50-52.

taining those proceedings has jurisdiction as to maintenance as well, but only if its jurisdiction regarding status (which is as such not governed by the Regulation but by the court's own jurisdictional rules including other international instruments, such as the Brussels II Regulation[75]) is not based solely on the nationality of one of the parties. Another precondition, albeit not clearly stated in the wording of Article 5(2), is that the procedural law of the country of the forum permits such cumulation of proceedings.

The plaintiff is for jurisdictional purposes considered to be a maintenance creditor even when bringing a maintenance action for the first time, *i.e.*, before it has been established that, on the whole, he is entitled to maintenance.[76] For the application of Article 5(2), it makes, furthermore, no difference whether maintenance is provided in the form of periodical payments or a lump sum or other transfer of property, as long as the transfer is designed to enable the person claiming maintenance to provide for himself.[77] Maintenance awarded as part of the distribution of a deceased person's estate is probably also included if it has this purpose, although there are diverging opinions. On the other hand, Article 5(2) is intended to give an advantage to maintenance creditors because they are the weaker party in the proceedings, and, therefore, it cannot be relied on by a public body seeking to obtain the reimbursement of sums it paid to a maintenance creditor, to whose rights it is subrogated against the maintenance debtor.[78] The same probably applies if maintenance is claimed by a professional debt-collecting agency to which the claim has been assigned by the original maintenance creditor. It is disputed whether Article 5(2) is intended to apply when the proceedings are initiated by the maintenance debtor, for example, when he sues in order to have the amount of alimonies reduced due to changed circumstances, but this question is of limited importance, as the courts of the maintenance creditor's domicile in such a case normally will have jurisdiction on the basis of Article 2.

Article 5(3) deals with disputes in matters relating to "tort, *delict* or *quasi-delict*", where a defendant domiciled in a Member State can be sued in another Member State in the courts for the place where the harmful event occurred or may occur (the so-called *forum delicti*).[79] This rule is interpreted by the ECJ

---

[75] See Chapter 5 *infra*.

[76] *Farrell* v. *Long*, case C-295/95, [1997] ECR I-1683.

[77] *Van den Boogaard* v. *Laumen*, case C-220/95, [1997] ECR I-1147. Cf. also *de Cavel* v. *de Cavel*, case 120/79, [1980] ECR 731.

[78] *Freistaat Bayern* v. *Blijdenstein*, case C-433/01, [2004] ECR I-981.

[79] See, for example, Briggs & Rees, *Civil Jurisdiction*, pp. 111-126; Byrne, *The European Union*, pp. 71-79; Czernich & Tiefenthaler, *Die Übereinkommen*, pp. 67-70; Dashwood, Hacon & White, *A Guide*, pp. 96-97; Donzallaz, *La Convention*, vol. III, pp. 337-396; Gaudemet-Tallon, *Compétence*, pp. 167-182; Geimer & Schütze, *Europäisches Zivilverfahrensrecht*, pp. 194-207; Hartley, *Civil Jurisdiction*, pp. 50-52; Hertz, *Jurisdiction*, pp. 237-283; Lasok & Stone, *Conflict*, pp. 229-233; Layton & Mercer (eds.), *European Civil Practice*, vol. I, pp. 469-490; Nielsen, *International privat- og procesret*, pp. 164-168; Pålsson, *Brysselkon-*

to mean that when the place of the harmful act and the place of the resulting damage are not identical, the plaintiff can choose between the courts for these two places[80] (in addition, of course, to the option of suing in the *forum domicilii* of the defendant pursuant to the main jurisdictional rule in Article 2). The court for the place of the resulting damage has, however, jurisdiction only in respect of the direct[81] and immediate[82] damage arising in the country of the forum[83]. The requirement that the damage must have arisen or may arise in the Member State of the forum is of particularly great importance when the same harmful act causes or risks to cause damage in several Member States, for example, a defamatory statement spread on the Internet. In such a case, the plaintiff can choose between instituting parallel proceedings in each Member State with regard to the damage that arose there and suing, regarding the total damage, in the Member State of the harmful act or where the defendant is domiciled.[84] Damage arising on board a ship under certain circumstances may be regarded as having occurred (also) in the Member State where the ship is registered.[85]

The terms "tort, *delict* or *quasi-delict*" do not mean the same thing in all Member States, but according to the ECJ the Regulation has its own, autonomous concept meaning that Article 5(3) encompasses all liability, which does not relate to a contract and falls consequently outside the field of application of Article 5(1).[86] This means that there can be neither gaps nor overlapping between Article 5(1) and Article 5(3). It would probably be more appropriate to replace "tort, *delict* or *quasi-delict*" in the wording of Article 5(3) with "non-contractual liability"; an action by a sub-buyer of goods against the manufacturer (see *supra*)

---

ventionen, pp. 111-118; Philip, *EU-IP*, pp. 53-54; Rauscher (ed.), *Europäisches Zivilprozessrecht*, pp. 121-129; Rognlien, *Luganokonvensjonen*, pp. 147-151; Rozehnalová & Týč, *Evropský justiční prostor*, pp. 207-209; Schlosser, *EuGVÜ*, pp. 52-56.

[80] *Bier* v. *Mines de potasse d'Alsace*, case 21/76, [1976] ECR 1735.

[81] In *Dumez* v. *Helaba*, case C-220/88, [1990] ECR I-49, the ECJ held that Article 5(3) refers to the place where the direct victim suffered the harmful effects, not the place where other persons (for example, the parent company or a family member) were indirectly harmed as a result of the direct victim's damage.

[82] The ECJ has held that Article 5(3) does not refer to the place where the direct victim claims to have suffered financial loss (for example, loss of income) consequential upon the initial damage (for example bodily harm) suffered by him elsewhere, see *Marinari* v. *Lloyd's Bank*, case C-364/93, [1995] ECR I-2719; *Kronhofer* v. *Maier*, case C-168/02, [2004] ECR I-6009.

[83] *Shevill* v. *Presse Alliance*, case C-68/93, [1995] ECR I-415.

[84] The plaintiff may even choose to combine the two alternatives, for example, by suing in some selected Member States regarding the damage caused there and in the Member State of the harmful act or of the defendant's domicile for the rest. The *lis pendens* provision in Article 27 does not prevent such combinations, because the parallel proceedings do not concern the same damage and, consequently, do not involve the same cause of action.

[85] *Danmarks Rederiforening* v. *LO*, case C-18/02, [2004] ECR I-1417.

[86] *Kalfelis* v. *Bankhaus Schröder*, case 189/87, [1988] ECR 5565; *Réunion* v. *Spliethoff*, case C-51/97, [1998] ECR I-6511; *Tacconi* v. *HWS*, case C-334/00, [2002] ECR I-7357.

or an action based on *negotiorum gestio* do not, for example, really deal with any tort or delict, even though they fall within the field of application of Article 5(3), because they are not based on any contractual obligation freely assumed between the parties.[87]

Article 5(3) applies not only to actions for compensation but even to preventive (anticipatory) actions, where the plaintiff petitions the court for an injunction or restraining order forbidding the defendant to commit harmful acts, for example, an action brought by a consumer protection organization for the purpose of preventing a businessman from using certain unfair terms in his contracts with consumers.[88] On the other hand, Article 5(3) cannot be relied on by a creditor challenging the validity – in respect of him – of fraudulent transactions made by his debtor.[89] Article 5(3) can be invoked even by plaintiffs other than the direct victim of the tort, for example, by an insurer who has compensated the victim and sues the wrongdoer for recourse; and it can also be used against other defendants than the wrongdoer himself, for example, against his vicariously liable employer. Furthermore, it can probably be relied on even by the alleged wrongdoer, for example, when he sues for a declaratory judgment holding that he is not liable for certain damage or that he is not obliged to refrain from certain allegedly harmful behavior.

A claim for damages based on an act giving rise to criminal proceedings may be raised in the court for those proceedings if such cumulation is permitted by the law of the forum (Article 5(4)); this means that national rules on criminal jurisdiction, which at present are not harmonized by EC law at all, may in these cases indirectly serve as bases for civil jurisdiction as well.[90]

As regards disputes arising out of the operations of a branch, agency or other establishment, a defendant domiciled in a Member State can be sued in another Member State in the courts for the place where the establishment is situated (Article 5(5)).[91] Although it does not say so explicitly, this provision seems to

---

[87] Cf. also *Tacconi* v. *HWS*, case C-334/00, [2002] ECR I-7357; *Frahuil* v. *Assitalia*, case C-265/02, [2004] ECR I-1543.

[88] *Verein für Konsumenteninformation* v. *Henkel*, case C-167/00, [2002] ECR I-8111. See also Bogdan, *JT* 2002-03 pp. 410-416.

[89] *Reichert* v. *Dresdner Bank*, case C-261/90, [1992] ECR I-2149.

[90] See, for example, Donzallaz, *La Convention*, vol. III, pp. 397-416; Gaudemet-Tallon, *Compétence*, pp. 182-184; Geimer & Schütze, *Europäisches Zivilverfahrensrecht*, pp. 207-210; Layton & Mercer (eds.), *European Civil Practice*, vol. I, pp. 490-491; Pålsson, *Brysselkonventionen*, pp. 118-119; Rauscher (ed.), *Europäisches Zivilprozessrecht*, pp. 129-131.

[91] See, for example, Bogdan, *SvJT* 1998 pp. 832-835; Briggs & Rees, *Civil Jurisdiction*, pp. 126-128; Byrne, *The European Union*, pp. 79-83; Czernich & Tiefenthaler, *Die Übereinkommen*, pp. 70-71; Dashwood, Hacon & White, *A Guide*, pp. 97-100; Donzallaz, *La Convention*, vol. III, pp. 417-452; Gaudemet-Tallon, *Compétence*, pp. 184-192; Geimer & Schütze, *Europäisches Zivilverfahrensrecht*, pp. 210-214; Hartley, *Civil Jurisdiction*, pp. 53-54; Layton & Mercer (eds.), *European Civil Practice*, pp. 491-500; Nielsen, *International privat- og procesret*, pp. 168-170; Pålsson, *Brysselkonventionen*, pp.119-122; Philip, *EU-IP*, pp. 55-56;

have in mind only an establishment of the defendant, not of the plaintiff. The concept of "branch, agency or other establishment" (in short, establishment) was discussed by the ECJ in several judgments. The leading case is *Somafer* v. *Saar-Ferngas*, decided in 1978,[92] where the Court declared that the concept would require an independent interpretation, common to all the Contracting States, and defined establishment as:

> a place of business which has the appearance of permanency, such as the exten-
> sion of a parent body, has a management and is materially equipped to negotiate
> business with third parties so that the latter, although knowing that there will if
> necessary be a legal link with the parent body, the head office of which is abroad,
> do not have to deal directly with such parent body but may transact business at
> the place of business constituting the extension.

This definition indicates that the establishment must have the capacity to represent the parent body (the defendant) at the conclusion of contracts, so that the mere collecting of orders does not seem to be sufficient. At the same time, the establishment must not be too independent. A distributor (re-seller) buying and selling products on his own behalf thus would not qualify, since he is subject neither to the control nor to the direction of the parent body,[93] and the same seems to be true of an independent commercial agent who acts in the name of the defendant but is free to arrange his own work and at the same time represent several competing firms[94]. The establishment, from the legal view-point, can be a mere physical extension and part of the parent body, but it also can be a separate legal or even a natural person, such as an agent. In fact, even a parent company acting in the name and on behalf of its daughter company can be deemed to be an establishment of its own daughter.[95] The establishment must have a management, but this can be identical to the management of the defendant himself.[96] Much depends on the appearance, as third parties must normally be able to rely on the impression created by the establishment behav-ing as an extension of the foreign defendant.[97] In order to make Article 5(5) applicable, the dispute must arise out of the operations of the establishment in question, such as from the contractual undertakings made by the establish-ment in the name of the defendant (the parent body), but it is not necessary that

---

Rauscher (ed.), *Europäisches Zivilprozessrecht*, pp. 131-135; Rognlien, *Luganokonvensjonen*, pp. 152-155; Rozehnalová & Týč, *Evropský justiční prostor*, pp. 209-210; Schlosser, *EuGVÜ*, pp. 58-60.

[92] Case 33/78, [1978] ECR 2183.

[93] See *de Bloos* v. *Bouyer*, case 14/76, [1976] ECR 1497.

[94] See *Blanckaert* v. *Trost*, case 139/80, [1981] ECR 819.

[95] *SAR Schotte* v. *Parfums Rothschild*, case 218/86, [1987] ECR 4905.

[96] *SAR Schotte* v. *Parfums Rothschild*, case 218/86, [1987] ECR 4905.

[97] *SAR Schotte* v. *Parfums Rothschild*, case 218/86, [1987] ECR 4905 (see, in particular, point 15 of the judg-ment).

these undertakings be performed in the Member State of the establishment.[98] Article 5(5) also applies to disputes arising out of the management proper of the establishment (such as renting of premises or employment of local staff) and non-contractual obligations arising for the parent body out of the actions of the establishment.[99]

Article 5(6) deals with actions against defendants in their capacity of settlers, trustees or beneficiaries of trusts, provided that the trust was created by the operation of a statute or by a written instrument or orally and evidenced in writing.[100] Article 5(6) permits that such defendants, even if domiciled in a Member State, can be sued in another Member State where the trust is domiciled. In order to determine whether a trust is domiciled in the forum country, the court shall apply its own rules of PIL (see Article 60(3)).

Finally, Article 5(7) contains a provision regarding disputes concerning the payment of freight or remuneration for the salvage of a cargo. This provision, as well as another maritime-related rule in Article 7 concerning jurisdiction over claims for limitation of liability from the use or operation of a ship, cannot be described here in more detail.[101]

A number of special jurisdictional rules of a different type, created for the purpose of procedural economy, efficiency and convenience, are found in Article 6 (the so-called *fora connexitatis*).[102] Their common feature is that they extend, under certain circumstances, the jurisdiction of a court, which is competent under the Regulation to deal with a certain defendant or a certain issue, to some other related parties or issues. Thus, a defendant domiciled in a Member State,

---

[98] *Lloyd's Register* v. *Campenon Bernard*, case C-439/93, [1995] ECR I-961.

[99] *Somafer* v. *Saar-Ferngas*, case 33/78, [1978] ECR 2183.

[100] See, for example, Briggs & Rees, *Civil Jurisdiction*, p. 129; Byrne, *The European Union*, p. 84; Donzallaz, *La Convention*, vol. III, pp. 453-463; Gaudemet-Tallon, *Compétence*, pp. 192-194; Geimer & Schütze, *Europäisches Zivilverfahrensrecht*, pp. 214-217; Lasok & Stone, *Conflict*, pp. 341-243; Layton & Mercer (eds.), *European Civil Practice*, vol. I, pp. 500-502; Rauscher (ed.), *Europäisches Zivilprozessrecht*, pp. 135-137.

[101] See, for example, Byrne, *The European Union*, pp. 85-86 and 89; Donzallaz, *La Convention*, vol. III, pp. 464-678; Gaudemet-Tallon, *Compétence*, pp. 194-198; Geimer & Schütze, *Europäisches Zivilverfahrensrecht*, pp. 217-219 and 241-243; Layton & Mercer (eds.), *European Civil Practice*, vol. I, pp. 503-504 and 527-528; Pålsson, *Brysselkonventionen*, pp. 123-129; Rauscher (ed.), *Europäisches Zivilprozessrecht*, pp. 137-138 and 155-156; Rognlien, *Luganokonvensjonen*, pp. 180-189.

[102] See, for example, Briggs & Rees, *Civil Jurisdiction*, pp. 130-137; Byrne, *The European Union*, pp. 86-89; Czernich & Tiefenthaler, *Die Übereinkommen*, pp. 72-79; Dashwood, Hacon & White, *A Guide*, pp. 101-102; Donzallaz, *La Convention*, vol. III, pp. 479-556; Gaudemet-Tallon, *Compétence*, pp. 199-211; Geimer & Schütze, *Europäisches Zivilverfahrensrecht*, pp. 219-241; Layton & Mercer (eds.), *European Civil Practice*, vol. I, pp. 504-527; Nielsen, *International privat- og procesret*, pp. 170-176; Pålsson, *Brysselkonventionen*, pp. 129-137; Philip, *EU-IP*, pp. 57-60; Rauscher (ed.), *Europäisches Zivilprozessrecht*, pp. 138-155; Rognlien, *Luganokonvensjonen*, pp. 156-162; Rozehnalová & Týč, *Evropský justiční prostor*, pp. 212-215; Schlosser, *EuGVÜ*, pp. 62-67.

who is one of several defendants regarding closely connected claims, normally can be sued in another Member State in the court for the place where any one of the other defendants is domiciled. This follows from Article 6(1), which requires that the claims are so closely connected that it is expedient to hear and determine them together in order to avoid the risk of irreconcilable judgments resulting from separate proceedings. It must be noted that according to Article 6(1), it is not sufficient for establishing the jurisdiction of the court in a Member State over a particular defendant that one of the other defendants can be sued there pursuant to Article 5. Article 6(1) requires rather that one of the other defendants actually is domiciled in the forum country. On the other hand, Article 6(1) can be relied on even when the action against the defendant domiciled in the forum country is inadmissible pursuant to national law, for example, because of ongoing bankruptcy proceedings.[103] It is disputed whether Article 6(1) presupposes that both (all) defendants are sued at the same time. The purpose of Article 6(1) is similar to that of Article 28,[104] *i.e.* to avoid irreconcilable judgments resulting from separate proceedings, but it seems that Article 6(1), being an exception from the main rule in Article 2, is to be interpreted and used with more restraint.[105]

In third-party proceedings, for example, actions against a guarantor or a person that the defendant in the main (original) proceedings can sue for recourse if he loses, such third party domiciled in another Member State can be sued in the court seized of the original proceedings, unless the sole purpose of the original proceedings was to create jurisdiction against him (Article 6(2)). The bringing of the third-party proceedings in the court of the original proceedings, consequently, must not amount to an abuse,[106] and a similar restriction is considered implied in the above-mentioned Article 6(1),[107] for example, when the only purpose of an action brought by a creditor against a destitute co-debtor is to make it possible for the creditor to sue in the same court the other co-debtors domiciled in other Member States. Article 6(2) does not require that the defendant in the original proceedings is domiciled in the forum country, which means that it is sufficient that the court has jurisdiction over him pursuant to any of the other jurisdictional rules in the Regulation, for example, Article 5.[108] In fact, it is probably sufficient that the court has jurisdiction over the defendant in the original proceedings according to national jurisdictional rules, provided that he is not domiciled in a Member State (see Article 4[109]). At the same time,

---

[103] See *Reisch* v. *Kiesel*, case C-103/05, [2006] ECR I-0000.

[104] See section 3.3.6 *infra*.

[105] Cf. *Roche* v. *Primus*, case C-539/03, [2006] ECR I-0000, where the ECJ found it unnecessary to decide the issue.

[106] See *Réunion* v. *Zurich*, case C-77/04, [2005] ECR I-4509.

[107] See *Reisch* v. *Kiesel*, case C-103/05, [2006] ECR I-0000, in particular point 32 of the judgment.

[108] See *Kongress Agentur Hagen* v. *Zeehaghe*, case C-365/88, [1990] ECR I-1845; *Réunion* v. *Spliethoff*, case C-51/97, [1998] ECR I-6511.

[109] See section 3.3.1 *supra*.

Article 6(2) does not apply unless the third party is domiciled in a Member State. If the third party is domiciled in a non-member state, jurisdiction over him is regulated by the national jurisdictional rules of the forum.

A counter-claim[110] against a plaintiff/defendant domiciled in another Member State, arising from the same contract or facts as the original claim, can be adjudicated by the court where that original claim is pending (Article 6(3)). Finally, a contractual action against a defendant domiciled in another Member State can be combined with an action against the same defendant in matters relating to rights *in rem* in immovable property in the court of the Member State in which that immovable property is situated, provided that the law of that Member State permits such combining of the two actions (Article 6(4)). The purpose of this rule is to make it possible, for example, to bring an action in Sweden against a debtor domiciled in England for the repayment of a debt secured by a mortgage on the debtor's Swedish immovable property.

3.3.3 Weak-party Disputes

Certain disputes, where one of the parties is assumed to be in a substantially weaker position and therefore in need of enhanced procedural protection, are subject to separate jurisdictional provisions in the Regulation, namely, some insurance disputes (Articles 8-14), consumer disputes (Articles 15-17) and disputes on individual[111] employment contracts (Articles 18-21).[112] The main idea behind these provisions is to protect the weaker party (the person claiming insurance benefits, the consumer, the employee) against being sued in a Member State other than his own, while at the same time giving the same weaker party the option to sue in his own country even when the defendant is domiciled in another Member State. Of course, the Regulation can fully guarantee this enhanced protection only if the weaker party is domiciled in a Member State. The rules on weak-party disputes are largely self-contained, and the previously described jurisdictional provisions in the Regulation are not applicable to them, with the exception of Article 5(5) on disputes arising out of the operation of a branch, agency or other establishment. The right to bring a counterclaim also in principle remains unaffected by the special rules on weak-party disputes, see Articles 12(2), 16(3) and 20(2). The references in Articles 8, 15(1) and 18(1) to Article 4 mean that national jurisdictional rules of the Member State of the

---

[110] A counter-claim, seeking the pronouncement of a separate judgment, must be distinguished from a mere set-off, which is a defence rather than a counter-attack and does not amount to an action under procedural law, see *Danvaern* v. *Otterbeck*, case C-341/93, [1995] ECR I-2053. The question of jurisdiction does not normally arise in connection with a mere set-off, but cf. *AS-Autoteile* v. *Malhé*, case 220/84, [1985] ECR 2267.

[111] As opposed to collective agreements between employers and trade unions.

[112] Cf. also Article 5(2) on maintenance disputes (see section 3.3.2 *supra*).

[113] Cf. *Brenner* v. *Reynolds*, case C-318/93, [1994] ECR I-4275.

forum apply when the defendant is not domiciled in any of the Member States, but Articles 9(2), 15(2) and 18(2) protect to some extent defendant enterprises that are not domiciled in a Member State by stipulating that in insurance, consumer and employment disputes arising out of the operation of their establishment in a Member State, such enterprises must be treated as if they were domiciled in that Member State.[113] This fictitious domicile means namely that they, being considered domiciled in a Member State, are protected against the use of national jurisdictional rules on the basis of Article 4.

The Regulation's rules on weak-party disputes, which are to a large extent one-sidedly mandatory to the benefit of the weaker party, are relatively voluminous and cannot be presented here in detail. This applies especially to jurisdiction in matters relating to insurance, which can be dealt with in a summary fashion only.[114] The Regulation differentiates between insurance covering large risks of a mainly commercial nature and other insurance. In disputes regarding large risks, as enumerated in Article 14, the jurisdictional rules of Articles 8-12 can be departed from through agreement between the parties, while in other insurance disputes the same provisions in principle are mandatory to the benefit of the weaker party (the policyholder, the insured or the beneficiary), except in some special situations, such as where the agreement is entered into after the dispute has arisen (Article 13). The jurisdictional rules in Articles 8-12 stipulate in principle that an insurer domiciled in a Member State may be sued not only in the courts of the Member State of his domicile but also in the Member State of his establishment whose operations gave rise to the dispute or where the plaintiff is domiciled (Articles 8 and 9). An insurer may bring proceedings against the policyholder, the insured or a beneficiary only in the Member State where the defendant is domiciled (Article 12). Some special rules apply to co-insurance, liability insurance, insurance of immovable property, *etc.*

The privileged treatment given to consumers,[115] defined in Article 15(1) as persons having concluded contracts for a purpose which can be regarded as

---

[114] On the special jurisdictional rules on insurance disputes, see for example *Group Josi* v. *UGIC*, case C-412/98, [2000] ECR I-5925 and *Réunion* v. *Zurich*, case C-77/04, [2005] ECR I-4509; Briggs & Rees, *Civil Jurisdiction*, pp. 55-59; Byrne, *The European Union*, pp. 90-98; Czernich & Tiefenthaler, *Die Übereinkommen*, pp. 79-98; Dashwood, Hacon & White, *A Guide*, pp. 103-110; Donzallaz, *La Convention*, vol. III, pp. 578-659; Gaudemet-Tallon, *Compétence*, pp. 216-224; Geimer & Schütze, *Europäisches Zivilverfahrensrecht*, pp. 243-268; Hertz, *Jurisdiction*, pp. 187-189; Kaye, *Civil Jurisdiction*, pp. 806-823; Lasok & Stone, *Conflict*, pp. 221-226; Layton & Mercer (eds.), *European Civil Practice*, vol. I, pp. 529-570; Nielsen, *International privat- og procesret*, pp. 178-185; Pålsson, *Brysselkonventionen*, pp. 140-147; Philip, *EU-IP*, pp. 87-92; Rauscher (ed.), *Europäisches Zivilprozessrecht*, pp. 157-183; Rognlien, *Luganokonvensjonen*, pp. 163-173; Rozehnalová & Týč, *Evropský justiční prostor*, pp. 216-221; Schlosser, *EuGVÜ*, pp. 68-76.

[115] See, for example, de Bra, *Verbraucherschutz*; Briggs & Rees, *Civil Jurisdiction*, pp. 59-63; Byrne, *The European Union*, pp. 99-107; Czernich & Tiefenthaler, *Die Übereinkommen*, pp. 98-109; Dashwood, Hacon & White, *A Guide*, pp. 110-114; Donzallaz, *La Convention*, vol. III, pp. 660-758; Gaudemet-Tallon, *Compétence*, pp. 225-234; Geimer & Schütze, *Europäisches Zivilverfahrensrecht*, pp. 268-292; Hertz, *Juris-*

being outside their trade or profession, is described in Article 16: a consumer may bring proceedings against the other party to the contract either in the courts of the Member State in which that other party is domiciled or in the courts where the consumer himself is domiciled, while proceedings against a consumer may be brought by the other party to the contract only in the courts of the Member State in which the consumer is domiciled.

The procedural advantages given to consumers in Article 16 apply, however, only under certain circumstances. To begin with, the wording of Article 15 presupposes that an actual contract has been concluded by the consumer, so that a unilateral offer of a prize made by a businessman to a consumer, even if of contractual nature, is not sufficient.[116] Furthermore, it would be clearly inappropriate if, for example, a consumer domiciled in Sweden and dissatisfied with a purchase he made in a shop when visiting Spain could bring proceedings in Swedish courts against the Spanish shopkeeper, who did not direct his activities to the Swedish consumer market and probably did not even know that his customer was a Swedish tourist. Therefore, Article 15(1) states that Article 16 applies only to disputes concerning installment sales of goods,[117] installment loans or other credits made to finance a sale of goods, and – and this is certainly the most important category of cases – any other contract concluded by the consumer with a person who pursues commercial or professional activities[118] in the Member State of the consumer's domicile or directs by any means such activities to that Member State (or several countries including that Member State), an additional condition being that the contract falls within the scope of such activities. The interpretation and application of this delimitation may cause difficulties, for example, when it must be determined whether marketing activities on the Internet, which can be accessed from anywhere in the world, are directed to the consumer's country or not. Circumstances such as the language or currency used on the Internet in some cases may be relevant, but if

---

diction, pp. 191-210; Kaye, *Civil Jurisdiction*, pp. 823-870; Lasok & Stone, *Conflict*, pp. 226-229; Layton & Mercer (eds.), *European Civil Practice*, vol. I, pp. 571-605; Nielsen, *International privat- og procesret*, pp. 185-190; Pålsson, *Brysselkonventionen*, pp. 147-154; Philip, *EU-IP*, pp. 92-95; Rauscher (ed.), *Europäisches Zivilprozessrecht*, pp. 183-201; Rognlien, *Luganokonvensjonen*, pp. 174-179; Rozehnalová & Týč, *Evropský justiční prostor*, pp. 222-232; Schlosser, *EuGVÜ*, pp. 76-83; G. Straetmans in Meeusen, Pertegás & Straetmans (eds.), *Enforcement*, pp. 315-322.

[116] *Engler* v. *Janus*, case C-27/02, [2005] ECR I-481. Cf. *Gabriel*, case C-96/00, [2002] ECR I-6367, and *Kapferer* v. *Schlank & Schick*, case C-234/04, [2006] ECR I-2585.

[117] However, the fact that the purchaser has been allowed to pay the price in several installments does not entitle him to the special protection referred to in Article 15(1) when the full price must be paid before the transfer of possession. See *Mietz* v. *Intership*, case C-99/96, [1999] ECR I-2277.

[118] The wording of Article 15(1) may create the impression that it does not presuppose that the consumer's counterpart acts in a commercial or professional capacity when the dispute concerns an installment sale of goods or a credit made to finance the sale of goods. However, it seems that Article 15 in its totality is not intended to apply to disputes between two parties who both act outside their trade or profession.

the contract in dispute actually and knowingly has been concluded over the web-site with a consumer in a particular country, the language or currency which the web-site uses do not necessarily constitute relevant factors.[119] The business enterprise also may make it clear to which country or countries it directs itself, for example, by stating on its commercial website that it does not wish to do business with consumers domiciled in particular countries or domiciled else-where than in particular countries. In situations not meeting the requirements of Article 15(1), the disputes relating to a consumer contract may be treated as falling within the scope of Article 5(1).[120]

The Regulation gives consumers, who must be individual natural persons, special procedural protection mainly because they act outside their trade or profession. The privileged position given by the Regulation to consumers therefore is not enjoyed by a plaintiff acting in pursuance of his business, not even if the disputed claim has been assigned to him by a consumer,[121] and the same applies when the dispute concerns a contract concluded by a person before he started to pursue a trade or profession but with a view to pursuing it in the future.[122] If the consumer enters into a contract which is partly for a profes-sional purpose, for example, if a professional farmer buys construction material intended for repairs of a building which houses both his family and his farm-ing equipment, Articles 15 and 16 apply only if the professional use is marginal and negligible (it is thus not sufficient that the private use prevails).[123] A further restriction is that disputes concerning rights *in rem* in immovable property or tenancies of immovable property, as well as insurance disputes, fall outside the scope of Articles 15 and 16 even if concerning consumer transactions, as they are governed by other special jurisdictional rules in Articles 8-14 and 22(1). Contracts of transportation, with the exception of package tours (*i.e.* with the exception of contracts, which for an inclusive price provide for a combination of travel and accommodation), are also excluded (see Article 15(3)), which means that they are governed by the Regulation's general rules to the extent they are not subject to special provisions in international transport conventions.

The provisions in Articles 15 and 16 in principle are mandatory and can be deviated from only by an agreement, which is entered into after the dispute has arisen, or which allows the consumer to bring proceedings in additional courts, or which is entered into by parties from the same Member State and confers jurisdiction on the courts of that Member State (Article 17). The last-mentioned exception presupposes that the agreement is valid according to the law of the Member State in question. On the other hand, the ECJ has held that a consumer

---

[119] See http://europa.eu.int/comm/justice_home/unit/civil/justciv_conseil/justciv_en.pdf (the Joint Decla-ration by the Council and the Commission on Articles 15 and 73 of Regulation No 44/2001).

[120] See section 3.3.2 *supra* and *Engler* v. *Janus*, case C-27/02, [2005] ECR I-481.

[121] *Shearson Lehman Hutton* v. *TVB*, case C-89/91, [1993] ECR I-139.

[122] *Benincasa* v. *Dentalkit*, case C-269/95, [1997] ECR I-3767.

[123] *Gruber* v. *Bay Wa AG*, case C-464/01, [2005] ECR I-439.

who by his own behavior creates the impression that he enters into the contract within the framework of his trade or profession (for example, by using a business letterhead or by claiming the right to restitution of value-added tax), must be considered to have validly abstained from the protection offered by Articles 15 and 16, provided that his counterpart has acted in good faith.[124]

Jurisdiction over individual contracts of employment is regulated in Articles 18-21,[125] which remind one in most respects of the rules about consumer disputes described above. There are, however, even some important differences. For example, the employee is not offered the option of suing the employer in the Member State where the employee is domiciled, but Article 19(2)(a) instead offers to the employee the alternative of bringing proceedings in the Member State where the employee habitually carries (or where he last habitually carried) out his work. This complements well Article 6(2) in the 1980 Rome Convention on the Law Applicable to Contractual Obligations, which presumes that in the absence of a valid choice of law by the parties, an individual employment contract is governed by the law of the country in which the employee habitually carries out his work.[126]

The localization of the habitual place of work sometimes may be problematic, but it is clear that a purely temporary posting in another country does not affect jurisdiction according to Article 19(2)(a).[127] It is not unusual that employees of a parent company, temporarily posted to a daughter company in another country, conclude a new employment contract with the daughter company while preserving or merely temporarily suspending their employment with the parent company. According to the ECJ, the place where the employee works for the daughter company under such circumstances can be regarded as the place where he habitually carries out his work for the parent company as well, provided that the parent company has an interest in his work for the daughter company.[128] The ECJ has also held that the work carried out by an employee on a fixed or floating installation on or above the continental shelf adjacent to a Member State in the context of the prospecting or exploitation of its natural resources is to be regarded, for the purposes of Brussels jurisdictional rules, as work carried out in the territory of that Member State.[129]

---

[124] *Gruber* v. *Bay Wa AG*, case C-464/01, [2005] ECR I-439.

[125] See, for example, Gaudemet-Tallon, *Compétence*, pp. 234-243; Geimer & Schütze, *Europäisches Zivilverfahrensrecht*, pp. 292-306; Layton & Mercer (eds.), *European Civil Practice*, vol. I, pp. 606-621; Pålsson, *Brysselkonventionen*, pp. 154-160; Rauscher (ed.), *Europäisches Zivilprozessrecht*, pp. 201-220; Rozehnalová & Týč, *Evropský justiční prostor*, pp. 233-239.

[126] See section 7.4 *infra*.

[127] See, however, Article 6 in Directive No 96/71 of 16 December 1996 concerning the Posting of Workers in the Framework of the Provision of Services (see sections 6 and 9.1 *infra*), which allows posted workers to sue their employer in the Member State where they are or were posted, in order to enforce their rights under the Directive.

[128] *Pugliese* v. *Finmeccanica*, case C-437/00, [2003] ECR I-3573.

[129] *Weber* v. *Universal Ogden*, case C-37/00, [2002] ECR I-2013.

It may also happen that the employee habitually divides his working time between several countries, for example, spending one week each month working in another Member State. Under such circumstances, for the application of Article 19, he is considered to habitually carry out his work in the Member State where he has established the effective centre of his working activities, taking into consideration such factors as where he spends most of his working time and where he has an office from which he organizes his activities for his employer and to which he returns after each business trip abroad.[130] In other words, he is considered to habitually carry out his work in the Member State where, taking account of all the circumstances of the case, he in fact performs the essential part of his duties towards his employer[131]. In the rare cases where the employee has no such base in any of the Member States, he can sue the employer in the Member State where the business, which engaged him, is or was situated (Article 19(2)(b)).

The employer, as well as the employee, can be sued also in the Member State where he is domiciled (Articles 19(1) and 20(1)). The jurisdictional rules in Articles 18-21 of the Regulation in principle are mandatory to the employee's benefit and can be departed from only by a choice-of-court agreement entered into after the dispute has arisen or by allowing the employee to bring proceedings in additional courts (Article 21).

3.3.4   Exclusive Jurisdiction

There are some disputes for which the Regulation in Article 22 assigns exclusive jurisdiction to one Member State only, irrespective of the domicile of the defendant and of the plaintiff. In these cases, it is even irrelevant whether any of the parties is or is not domiciled in any of the Member States, although the rules require other types of connection with the territory of the Member States, such as that the immovable property involved is situated in a Member State or that the dispute concerns the validity of an entry in a public register in a Member State (see *infra*). The main jurisdictional rule in Article 2, the special jurisdictional rules in Articles 5 and 6, and the jurisdictional rules on weak-party disputes in Articles 8-21 do not apply when Article 22 is applicable. On the other hand, the rules on exclusive jurisdiction constitute exceptions from the main principles of the Regulation and, therefore, should be interpreted and applied restrictively, *i.e.*, they must not be given a wider interpretation than is required by their objective, in particular, because they sometimes result in forcing the parties to litigate before a court in a Member State where none of them is domiciled.[132]

---

[130] *Rutten* v. *Cross Medical*, case C-383/95, [1997] ECR I-57.

[131] *Weber* v. *Ogden*, case C-37/00, [2002] ECR I-2013. Cf. also *Mulox* v. *Geels*, case C-125/92, [1993] ECR I-4075.

[132] See, for example, *Sanders* v. *van der Putte*, case 73/77, [1977] ECR 2383; *Gaillard* v. *Chekili*, case C-518/99, [2001] ECR I-2771.

The most important exclusive jurisdictional rule, Article 22(1), concerns proceedings having as their object rights *in rem* in immovable property or tenancies of immovable property.[133] Such proceedings must take place exclusively in the courts of the Member State where the immovable property is situated. An exception is made merely for disputes pertaining to temporary tenancies for private use for a maximum period of six consecutive months if the tenant is a natural person domiciled in the same Member State as the landlord (such disputes also can be tried in the courts of the Member State where both the landlord and the tenant are domiciled).[134]

It is not entirely clear whether the characterization of property as movable or immovable should be made according to some autonomous common standards or on the basis of national law (probably the law of the Member State where the property is situated). Article 22(1) does not apply when the immovable property in dispute is not situated in any of the Member States, and opinions are divided on whether jurisdiction in such a case should be governed by Article 2 and the other rules in the Regulation or by the national jurisdictional rules of the Member State of the forum. If the immovable property consists of components situated in two Member States, each Member State has exclusive jurisdiction over the part situated within its borders, unless the components are adjacent to each other and the property is situated almost entirely in one of the Member States involved, in which case that state has exclusive jurisdiction over the whole property.[135]

The ECJ has defined rights *in rem* as those rights that have effect not merely *vis-à-vis* a particular debtor but can be claimed against everybody (*erga omnes*),[136] such as ownership. In addition, in order to fall within the scope of Article 22(1) as pertaining to a right *in rem*, the proceedings, in the rather obscure language of the ECJ, must "seek to determine the extent, content, ownership or possession of immovable property or the existence of other rights *in rem* therein and to provide the holder of those rights with the protection of the powers which attach

---

[133] See, for example, Briggs & Rees, *Civil Jurisdiction*, pp. 42-48; Byrne, *The European Union*, pp. 108-121; Czernich & Tiefenthaler, *Die Übereinkommen*, pp. 109-121; Dashwood, Hacon & White, *A Guide*, pp. 114-118; Donzallaz, *La Convention*, vol. III, pp. 778-823; Gaudemet-Tallon, *Compétence*, pp. 73-79; Geimer & Schütze, *Europäisches Zivilverfahrensrecht*, pp. 319-338; Hartley, *Civil Jurisdiction*, pp. 64-66; Hertz, *Jurisdiction*, pp. 211-229; Kaye, *Civil Jurisdiction*, pp. 892-933; Layton & Mercer (eds.), *European Civil Practice*, vol. I, pp. 630-648; Nielsen, *International privat- og procesret*, pp. 192-196; Pålsson, *Brysselkonventionen*, pp. 160-172; Philip, *EU-IP*, pp. 67-70; Rauscher (ed.), *Europäisches Zivilprozessrecht*, pp. 224-233; Rognlien, *Luganokonvensjonen*, pp. 192-197; Rozehnalová & Týč, *Evropský justiční prostor*, pp. 244-247; Schlosser, *EuGVÜ*, pp. 85-92.

[134] Cf. *Dansommer* v. *Götz*, case C-8/98, [2000] ECR I-393.

[135] *Scherrens* v. *Maenhout*, case 158/87, [1988] ECR 3791.

[136] *Gaillard* v. *Chekili*, case C-518/99, [2001] ECR I-2771. See also *Reichert* v. *Dresdner Bank*, case C-115/88, [1990] ECR I-27; *Webb* v. *Webb*, case C-294/92, [1994] ECR I-1717; *Lieber* v. *Göbel*, case C-292/93, [1994] ECR I-2535.

to their interest".[137] A dispute concerning the rescission of a contract for the sale of land and compensation for the breach of such a contract,[138] the payment of a purchase price for immovable property, the cost of repairing such property or the compensation for using[139] or damaging it, thus is not included.[140] The same is true about a preventive action for cessation of a nuisance caused to immovable property.[141]

In addition to proceedings having as their object rights *in rem* in immovable property, Article 22(1) also encompasses disputes regarding tenancies. The ECJ rather surprisingly has held that this includes all disputes concerning the mutual obligations of the landlord and the tenant, thus not merely matters concerning the existence, validity, termination or prolongation of the tenancy as such. Even disputes concerning damage to the premises caused by the tenant[142] and disputes about mere payment of rent[143] are subject to the exclusive jurisdiction under Article 22(1). On the other hand, disputes concerning a lease of a whole retail business,[144] the procurement of holiday accommodation by a package travel organizer[145] or the membership in a time-sharing club[146] are not included, as these are complex contractual relationships where the principal aim of the agreement is not the tenancy of immovable property. The same approach is used by the ECJ in respect of disputes concerning the obligations of a trustee with regard to immovable property held by him in trust, because the immovable nature of the asset in question is of no importance for the trust as such and for the issues in dispute.[147]

Another exclusive forum is stipulated in Article 22(2) for proceedings, which have as their object the validity of constitution or dissolution of companies or other legal persons or the validity of the decisions of their organs.[148] Such

---

[137] *Reichert* v. *Dresdner Bank*, case C-115/88, [1990] ECR I-27, in particular point 11 of the judgment.

[138] *Gaillard* v. *Chekili*, case C-518/99, [2001] ECR I-2771.

[139] *Lieber* v. *Göbel*, case C-292/93, [1994] ECR I-2535. Article 22(1) applies, nevertheless, if the disputed use relates to a tenancy.

[140] Cf,, however, Article 6(4) on the *possibility* to combine a contractual action with an action against the same defendant in matters relating to rights *in rem* in immovable property (section 3.3.2 *supra*).

[141] *Land Oberösterreich* v. *ČEZ*, case C-343/04, [2006] ECR I-0000.

[142] *Dansommer* v. *Götz*, case C-8/98, [2000] ECR I-393.

[143] *Rösler* v. *Rottwinkel*, case 241/83, [1985] ECR 99.

[144] *Sanders* v. *van der Putte*, case 73/77, [1977] ECR 2383.

[145] *Hacker* v. *Euro-Relais*, case C-280/90, [1992] ECR I-1111.

[146] *Klein* v. *Rhodos Management*, case C-73/04, [2005] ECR I-8667.

[147] *Webb* v. *Webb*, case C-294/92, [1994] ECR I-1717.

[148] See, for example, Briggs & Rees, *Civil Jurisdiction*, pp. 48-50; Czernich & Tiefenthaler, *Die Übereinkommen*, pp. 121-122; Donzallaz, *La Convention*, vol. III, pp. 824-835; Gaudemet-Tallon, *Compétence*, pp. 80-81; Geimer & Schütze, *Europäisches Zivilverfahrensrecht*, pp. 338-350; Hartley, *Civil Jurisdiction*, pp. 66-67; Kaye, *Civil Jurisdiction*, pp. 933-949; Layton & Mercer (eds.), *European Civil Practice*, vol. I, pp. 648-651; Nielsen, *International privat- og procesret*, p. 196; Pålsson, *Brysselkonventionen*, pp. 172-174; Philip, *EU-IP*, p. 70; Rauscher (ed.), *Europäisches Zivilprozessrecht*, pp. 233-236; Schlosser, *EuGVÜ*, pp. 92-93.

proceedings are within the exclusive jurisdiction of the Member State where the legal person in question has its seat, as determined by the PIL of the forum. It is noteworthy that this seat is not necessarily identical to the domicile of the legal person as defined in Article 60(1). If more than one Member State consider the seat to be in their respective territories, the court first seized will have exclusive jurisdiction pursuant to Article 29. For other types of disputes regarding company law than those mentioned in Article 22(2), the general rules of the Regulation apply.

Proceedings concerning the validity of entries in public registers, such as land, ship or aircraft register, must take place in the Member State where the register is kept (Article 22(3)), and a similar exclusive jurisdictional rule applies in principle also to proceedings concerning the registration or validity of patents, trade marks, designs and other similar industrial or intellectual property rights required to be registered or deposited[149] (Article 22(4)).[150] Disputes about the legal effects of registration or deposition, however, are not subject to the exclusive jurisdiction under Article 22(3-4). A contractual dispute about the ownership of or a license to use a registered industrial right falls also outside the exclusive jurisdiction of the country of registration,[151] and the same is true about non-contractual disputes concerning infringements of such rights irrespective of whether the plaintiff demands compensation, requests an injunction against the infringer, or petitions for a declaratory judgment affirming that he is not guilty of an infringement. However, the ECJ has held that this applies only if the validity of the registered right is not called into question in the proceedings. According to the Court, Article 22(4) provides for exclusive jurisdiction in all disputes relating to the registration or validity of a patent, irrespective of whether the issue is raised by way of an action or as an objection.[152] This constitutes a departure from the previously widely held view that the courts, which were competent pursuant to the other provisions of the Regulation to deal with an infringement, could handle, as a preliminary issue, even the defendant's objections regarding the registration or validity of the industrial right

---

[149] See, for example, Briggs & Rees, *Civil Jurisdiction*, pp. 50-51; Czernich & Tiefenthaler, *Die Übereinkommen*, pp. 123-124; Donzallaz, *La Convention*, vol. III, pp. 836-848; Gaudemet-Tallon, *Compétence*, pp. 82-86; Geimer & Schütze, *Europäisches Zivilverfahrensrecht*, pp. 350-359; Kaye, *Civil Jurisdiction*, pp. 949-955; Layton & Mercer (eds.), *European Civil Practice*, vol. I, pp. 652-660; Mäder, *Die Anwendung*; Nielsen, *International privat- og procesret*, pp. 196-197; Pålsson, *Brysselkonventionen*, pp. 174-178; Philip, *EU-IP*, pp. 70-71; Rauscher (ed.), *Europäisches Zivilprozessrecht*, pp. 236-242; Schlosser, *EuGVÜ*, pp. 93-95.

[150] See also the special rule in Article 22(4) para. 2 on proceedings concerned with the registration or validity of European patents. Special provisions apply, furthermore, to disputes concerning industrial property rights created by Community law, such as Community trade marks (OJ 1994 L 11 p. 1), Community plant variety rights (OJ 1994 L 227 p. 1) and Community designs (OJ 2002 L 3 p. 1).

[151] *Duijnstee* v. *Goderbauer*, case 288/82, [1983] ECR 3663.

[152] *GAT* v. *LuK*, case C-4/03, [2006] ECR I-0000.

concerned, although their decision regarding such objections would not be binding outside the framework of the dispute at hand. It is an open question how the ECJ would solve the corresponding problem with regard to the other exclusive jurisdictional rules in Article 22, for example an objection, in a dispute about compensation for the burning down of a building, that the plaintiff was not the rightful owner of the house.

Finally, Article 22(5) provides for exclusive jurisdiction of the Member State where a judgment has been or is to be enforced to carry out proceedings concerned with the enforcement, for example, disputes about whether certain of the judgment debtor's assets are sequestrable or not.

3.3.5   Prorogation of Jurisdiction (Choice-of-court Agreements)

The Regulation recognizes, in Article 23, choice-of-court agreements between the parties regarding the court in a Member State that shall have jurisdiction to settle their dispute(s).[153] Such agreements refer usually to a particular court, but it happens that the agreement limits itself to pointing out the Member State where the adjudication shall take place, while leaving the determination of the particular court to that Member State's national law. Article 23 probably also can be relied on by parties wishing to conclude a pure derogation agreement, *i.e.* to exclude the jurisdiction of the courts of one or several of the Member States without indicating the court that is to have jurisdiction. The parties can point out the chosen court by naming it directly or choose it indirectly by specifying the objective factors on the basis of which the competent court can be ascertained, for example, by referring to the courts of the country "where the seller has his principal place of business".[154] They even can agree on several alternative courts, leaving the final choice to the (future) plaintiff or to a future circumstance, for example, by agreeing that all disputes shall be settled by the court of the domicile of the (future) defendant.[155]

---

[153] See, for example, Briggs & Rees, *Civil Jurisdiction*, pp. 63-79; Byrne, *The European Union*, pp. 125-144; Czernich & Tiefenthaler, *Die Übereinkommen*, pp. 125-155; Dashwood, Hacon & White, *A Guide*, pp. 121-130; Donzellaz, *La Convention*, vol. III, pp. 869-1149; Gaudemet-Tallon, *Compétence*, pp. 89-118; Geimer & Schütze, *Europäisches Zivilverfahrensrecht*, pp. 361-418; Hartley, *Civil Jurisdiction*, pp. 68-74; Kaye, *Civil Jurisdiction*, pp. 1031-1115; Killias, *Die Gerichtsstandsvereinbarungen*; Lasok & Stone, *Conflict*, pp. 255-268; Layton & Mercer (eds.), *European Civil Practice*, vol. I, pp. 668-743; Merrett, 55 *I.C.L.Q.* 315-336 (2006); Newton, *The Uniform Interpretation*, pp. 163-279; Nielsen, *International privat- og procesret*, pp. 198-209; Pålsson, *Brysselkonventionen*, pp. 180-205; Philip, *EU-IP*, pp. 73-84; Rauscher (ed.), *Europäisches Zivilprozessrecht*, pp. 246-280; Rognlien, *Luganokonvensjonen*, pp. 200-211; Rozehnalová & Týč, *Evropský justiční prostor*, pp. 252-276; E.R. Sachpekidou in Fentiman *et al.* (eds.), *L'espace*, pp. 69-83; Schlosser, *EuGVÜ*, pp. 98-119; C. Soulard in Fentiman *et al.* (eds.), *L'espace*, pp. 57-67.

[154] *Coreck v. Handelsveem*, case C-387/98, [2000] ECR I-9337.

[155] *Meeth v. Glacetal*, case 23/78, [1978] ECR 2133. Cf. also *Coreck v. Handelsveem*, case C-387/98, [2000] ECR I-9337.

Article 23(1) also stipulates that the agreed court or courts will have exclusive jurisdiction unless the parties have agreed otherwise. In other words, choice-of-court clauses are presumed to be exclusive, so that they deprive all courts other than the one(s) agreed upon of jurisdiction. The agreed upon court has exclusive jurisdiction even with regard to disputes about the validity of the choice-of-court clause itself.[156]

Article 23(1) imposes some restrictions though. To begin with, the choice-of-court agreement must not deviate from the Regulation's rules on exclusive jurisdiction or the Regulation's mandatory jurisdictional rules regarding weak-party disputes.[157] Another condition is that the choice of court must pertain to disputes which have already arisen or may arise in connection with a particular legal relationship, such as a particular contract. A general prorogation, concerning all future disputes between the parties, thus is not recognized. Furthermore, Article 23(1) requires that at least one of the parties be domiciled in a Member State; it is probably sufficient that this condition is fulfilled either at the time of the conclusion of the agreement or at the time of the initiation of the proceedings. If none of the parties is domiciled in a Member State, their freedom to conclude a valid choice-of-court agreement is not governed by the Regulation but depends on national law, although Article 23(3) provides that the courts of the Member States other than the agreed one, even in such a case, are obliged to refrain from exercising jurisdiction unless the agreed court declines to adjudicate.

Article 23(1) does not require any connection between, on the one hand, the agreed upon court or country and, on the other hand, the parties or the dispute.[158] However, it appears that the dispute must not be a purely internal matter connected with only one single country.[159] Furthermore, as mentioned above, Article 23(1) deals in principle merely with those agreements that choose the courts of a Member State. This does not mean that other choice-of-court agreements are null and void, but merely that their validity and effect depend, in principle, on the attitude of each particular Member State. It is thus in principle the national law of each Member State that decides whether its courts are deprived of their jurisdiction by the choice of a court in a non-member state. The Regulation's exclusive and mandatory jurisdictional rules, nevertheless, must be complied with even in such cases, for example, Article 22(1) if the dispute concerns a right *in rem* in immovable property situated in a Member State.[160]

---

[156] *Benincasa* v. *Dentalkit*, case C-269/95, [1997] ECR I-3767.

[157] See sections 3.3.3 and 3.3.4 *supra*. Some additional restrictions may be found in international instruments enjoying precedence in relation to the Regulation, such as the Warsaw Convention for the Unification of Certain Rules relating to International Carriage by Air.

[158] See *Zelger* v. *Salinitri*, case 56/79, [1980] ECR 89; *MSG* v. *Gravières Rhénanes*, case C-106/95, [1997] ECR I-911; *Benincasa* v. *Dentalkit*, case C-269/95, [1997] ECR I-3767; *Trasporti Castelletti* v. *Trumpy*, case C-159/97, [1999] ECR I-1597.

[159] See section 3.2 *supra*.

[160] See section 3.3.4 *supra*.

In Article 23(4-5), there are some rules on choice-of-court agreements in trust instruments, but they are too special to be dealt with here.

Choice-of-court agreements are usually mere clauses in larger contracts. In accordance with the so-called doctrine of separability, the validity of the choice-of-court clause does not depend on the validity of the contract as a whole, so that such a clause can be valid even if the contract as a whole is not. The Regulation does not say anything about the rules governing the validity of the choice-of-court agreement in such respects as incapacity, coercion or fraud. Such issues seem to be subjected to the law determined by the PIL of the court before which they have arisen. On the other hand, Article 23(1) contains relatively detailed substantive rules about the required form of choice-of-court agreements,[161] offering three alternatives. The first alternative is that the agreement is in writing or evidenced in writing (Article 23(1)(a)). The second alternative recognizes a form in accord with practices established between the parties (Article 23(1)(b)). The third and last alternative, stipulated in Article 23(1)(c), is available only in international trade or commerce and accepts a form in accordance with a widely known and regularly observed usage in the particular trade concerned, provided that the parties were or ought to have been aware of the usage in question; the fact that the existence of a usage is challenged in court, of course, does not mean necessarily that the usage does not exist[162]. A special rule in Article 23(2) makes electronic communications equivalent to writing, if they provide a durable record of the agreement. These formal requirements in Article 23(1) are exhaustive, so that Member States are not allowed to impose additional formal conditions, such as the presence of witnesses, affirmation by a Notary Public or the use of the official language of the forum.[163]

"Tacit prorogation", where the defendant enters an appearance without contesting jurisdiction of the court, is recognized by Article 24.[164] Such appear-

---

[161] There are several ECJ decisions about these formal requirements, see in particular *Salotti v. RÜWA*, case 24/76, [1976] ECR 1831; *Segoura v. Bonakdarian*, case 25/76, [1976] ECR 1851; *Russ v. Nova*, case 71/83, [1984] ECR 2417; *Berghoefer v. ASA*, case 221/84, [1985] ECR 2699; *Iveco Fiat v. Van Hool*, case 313/85, [1986] ECR 3337; *Powell Duffryn v. Petereit*, case C-214/89, [1992] ECR I-1745; *MSG v. Gravières Rhénanes*, case C-106/95, [1997] ECR I-911; *Trasporti Castelleti v. Trumpy*, case C-159/97, [1999] ECR I-1597; *Coreck v. Handelsveem*, case C-387/98, [2000] ECR I-9337. Some of these decisions have become partly obsolete due to the subsequent changes in the wording of the Brussels rules.

[162] *Trasporti Castelletti v. Trumpy*, case C-159/97, [1999] ECR I-1597.

[163] *Elefanten Schuh v. Jacqmain*, case 150/80, [1981] ECR 1671.

[164] See, for example, Briggs & Rees, *Civil Jurisdiction*, pp. 53-55; Byrne, *The European Union*, pp. 144-147; Czernich & Tiefenthaler, *Die Übereinkommen*, pp. 156-160; Dashwood, Hacon & White, *A Guide*, pp. 130-132; Donzallaz, *La Convention*, vol. III, pp. 1150-1177; Gaudemet-Tallon, *Compétence*, pp. 119-123; Geimer & Schütze, *Europäisches Zivilverfahrensrecht*, pp. 419-433; Hartley, *Civil Jurisdiction*, p. 76; Kaye, *Civil Jurisdiction*, pp. 1116-1131; Lasok & Stone, *Conflict*, pp. 268-270; Layton & Mercer (eds.), *European Civil Practice*, vol. I, pp. 743-755; Nielsen, *International privat- og procesret*, pp. 209-212; Pålsson, *Brysselkonventionen*, pp. 205-207; Philip, *EU-IP*, pp. 84-85; Rauscher (ed.), *Europäisches Zivilprozessrecht*, pp.

ance gives the court jurisdiction unless it would be contrary to the rules on exclusive jurisdiction in Article 22. Incompatibility with an existing exclusive choice-of-court agreement[165] or with the mandatory provisions on jurisdiction in weak-party disputes[166] does not preclude tacit prorogation. It is irrelevant whether the defendant's behaviour is the result of his conscious acceptance of the jurisdiction of the court or is caused by his ignorance of the applicable jurisdictional rules. The latest moment in the proceedings when jurisdiction may be contested is not specified in the Regulation, which seems to mean that it is to be determined by the procedural rules of the forum country. National rules of the Member State of the forum govern tacit choice of court also when the defendant is not domiciled in any Member State, as Article 24 does not constitute an exception from Article 4. Nevertheless, the rules on exclusive jurisdiction in Article 22 must be respected even under such circumstances.

3.3.6   Some General Jurisdictional Issues

The circumstances serving as connecting factors pursuant to the Regulation's jurisdictional rules in principle are to be examined as they are at the time of the initiation of the proceedings, although there are some exceptions. A competent court does not lose its jurisdiction on account of subsequent changes (the principle of *perpetuatio jurisdictionis*, for example, if the defendant moves to another Member State while the case is pending), but subsequent changes can turn an incompetent court into a competent one (for example, if the defendant moves to the forum country after the proceedings have started but before the case is dismissed due to lack of jurisdiction).

Another important question is whether the Regulation's jurisdictional rules are applied at the court's own initiative or merely if they are invoked by at least one of the parties.[167] It follows from Article 25 that the exclusive jurisdictional rules of Article 22 must be applied *ex officio*. The exclusive rules must be observed by all judicial instances on their own initiative, including such appellate instances that under their national procedural law are allowed to examine

---

281-290; Rognlien, *Luganokonvensjonen*, pp. 212-213; Rozehnalová & Týč, *Evropský justiční prostor*, pp. 277-281; Schlosser, *EuGVÜ*, pp. 119-121.

[165] *Spitzley* v. *Sommer*, case 48/84, [1985] ECR 787.

[166] See section 3.3.3 *supra*.

[167] See, for example, Briggs & Rees, *Civil Jurisdiction*, pp. 138-140; Byrne, *The European Union*, pp. 148-150; Czernich & Tiefenthaler, *Die Übereinkommen*, pp. 160-168; Dashwood, Hacon & White, *A Guide*, pp. 132-134; Gaudemet-Tallon, *Compétence*, pp. 255-260; Geimer & Schütze, *Europäisches Zivilverfahrensrecht*, pp. 433-441; Kaye, *Civil Jurisdiction*, pp. 1214-1216; Layton & Mercer (eds.), *European Civil Practice*, vol. I, pp. 756-769; Nielsen, *International privat- og procesret*, pp. 212-214; Pålsson, *Brysselkonventionen*, pp. 208-209; Philip, *EU-IP*, pp. 96-98; Rauscher (ed.), *Europäisches Zivilprozessrecht*, pp. 291-298; Rognlien, *Luganokonvensjonen*, pp. 214-219; Rozehnalová & Týč, *Evropský justiční prostor*, pp. 282-284; Schlosser, *EuGVÜ*, pp. 121-123.

jurisdictional grounds only upon the request of a party.[168] On the other hand, Article 24[169] makes it clear that in principle the court must not apply the Regulation's non-exclusive jurisdictional rules of its own motion if the defendant enters an appearance without contesting jurisdiction. Article 26 deals with a third conceivable situation, namely, where the rules on exclusive jurisdiction do not apply and the defendant, domiciled in another Member State, does not enter an appearance at all. Pursuant to Article 26(1), the court, even under such circumstances, must examine of its own motion whether it has jurisdiction under the Regulation. Nevertheless, the absent defendant runs a serious risk of a default judgment being given against him, due to the fact that the court may have to rely mainly on the one-sided information provided by the plaintiff. It is, therefore, important that Article 26(2) obliges the court to stay proceedings so long as it is not shown that the absent defendant, who is domiciled in another Member State, has been able to receive the document instituting the proceedings in sufficient time to enable him to arrange for his defense, or that all necessary steps have been taken to this end. Article 26(3-4) refers in this context also to Article 19 of the EC Regulation on the Service in the Member States of Judicial and Extrajudicial Documents in Civil or Commercial Matters,[170] alternatively to the corresponding provisions in Article 15 of the 1965 Hague Convention on the Service Abroad of Judicial and Extrajudicial Documents in Civil or Commercial Matters. If the defendant is domiciled in the Member State of the forum or in a non-member state, Article 26(1) does not apply and the national procedural law of the forum Member State applies instead.

Another, albeit related, question is whether the court can find itself competent or lacking jurisdiction on the basis of facts and circumstances other than those invoked by the parties. This question is not answered by the Regulation itself, and probably is left to be decided by the national procedural law of the Member State of the forum, with the exception of Articles 25 and 26(1) (see *supra*) where the courts probably are both entitled and obliged to consider all relevant facts, whether invoked by a party of not.

The Regulation wishes to avoid competing parallel proceedings and contains, therefore, in Article 27 a rule on *lis pendens*.[171] It provides that where

---

[168] *Duijnstee v. Goderbauer*, case 288/82, [1983] ECR 3663.

[169] See section 3.3.5 *supra*.

[170] See section 11.1 *infra*.

[171] See, for example, Bogdan, *Ny Juridik* 2004, no. 3, pp. 53-62; Briggs & Rees, *Civil Jurisdiction*, pp. 140-153; Byrne, *The European Union*, pp. 150-164; Czernich & Tiefenthaler, *Die Übereinkommen*, pp. 168-176; Dashwood, Hacon & White, *A Guide*, pp. 136-138; Donzallaz, *La Convention*, vol. I, pp. 521-579; Gaudemet-Tallon, *Compétence*, pp. 260-274; Geimer & Schütze, *Europäisches Zivilverfahrensrecht*, pp. 444-462 and 470-472; Hartley, *Civil Jurisdiction*, pp. 76-78 and in 54 I.C.L.Q. 815-821 (2005); Isenburg-Epple, *Die Berücksichtigung*; Kaye, *Civil Jurisdiction*, pp. 1216-1233; W. Kennett in Fentiman *et al.* (eds.), *L'espace*, pp. 103-126; Lando, *Essays Pålsson*, pp. 105-122; Layton & Mercer (eds.), *European Civil Practice*, vol. I, pp. 770-797 and 813-815; Nielsen, *International privat- og procesret*, pp. 214-217; Pålsson, *Brysselkonventionen*,

proceedings involving the same cause of action and the same parties are brought in the courts of different Member States, then any court other than the court first seized is obliged to stay its proceedings until the court first seized establishes whether it has jurisdiction. If the court first seized finds itself to have jurisdiction (which does not mean that the court must have made a formal ruling about its jurisdiction, as it suffices in most cases that nobody objected against it), then other courts must decline to deal with the dispute. It seems that the requirement that both proceedings must be between the same parties can be dispensed with when it is established that, with regard to the subject-matter of the two disputes, a party in one of the cases has identical and indissociable interests with a party in the other case, for example, when a carrier is sued in one Member State by the owner of the cargo and in another Member State by that owner's insurer.[172] The requirement in Article 27 that both proceedings must involve the same cause of action sometimes can be considered fulfilled even when the two proceedings, based on the same legal relationship, deal with different types of demands, for example, when one party sues in one Member State for a declaration that a contract is invalid or inoperative while the other party sues in another Member State for the enforcement of the same contract. In such a case, in the words of the ECJ, the same question of whether the contract is binding "lies at the heart of the two actions".[173] The ECJ also has made it clear that the terms "the same cause of action" and "the same parties" in Article 27 have an autonomous meaning, which is independent of the laws in force in the Member States, so that the distinction drawn in a Member State between an action *in personam* and an action *in rem* is not material for the interpretation of Article 27.[174] It is important to note that in order to determine whether the two proceedings have the same cause of action, account is taken only of the claims of the respective plaintiffs and not of the defences raised by the defendants (for example a set-off).[175]

The decision to stay the proceedings on the ground of *lis pendens* shall be made of the court's own motion, thus even if none of the parties requests it. This applies regardless of the domicile of the parties or the basis of the first seized court's jurisdiction, thus even in a case where the defendant is not domiciled in a Member State and the court first seized based its jurisdiction on its own national jurisdictional rules pursuant to Article 4.[176] It is possible, albeit not

---

pp. 213-220; Philip, *EU-IP*, pp. 98-100; Rauscher (ed.), *Europäisches Zivilprozessrecht*, pp. 299-308 and 313-314; Rognlien, *Luganokonvensjonen*, pp. 220-223; Rozehnalová & Týč, *Evropský justiční prostor*, pp. 285-291; Schlosser, *EuGVÜ*, pp. 123-129.

[172] See *Drouot* v. *CMI*, case C-351/96, [1998] ECR I-3075.

[173] *Gubisch* v. *Palumbo*, case 144/86, [1987] ECR 4861 (see in particular point 16 of the judgment).

[174] *Tatry*, case C-406/92, [1994] ECR I-5439.

[175] See *Gantner* v. *Basch*, case C-111/01, [2003] ECR I-4207. Cf. also *Mærsk* v. *de Haan*, case C-39/02, [2004] ECR I-9657.

[176] *Overseas Union* v. *New Hampshire Ins.*, case C-351/89, [1991] ECR I-3317.

probable, that an exception from Article 27 can be made when the court, which was seized later than the court first seized, has exclusive jurisdiction pursuant to Article 22.[177]

The ECJ has held that the rule in Article 27 cannot be derogated from on the ground that the court first seized is excessively slow.[178] This unfortunately means that the *lis pendens* rule can be abused by a person who, facing the threat of being sued in a Member State, quickly initiates competing proceedings in another Member State, which has no jurisdiction but where it will take considerable time before the lack of jurisdiction results in the case being dismissed. It is not permitted to fight such or similar abuse by means of an anti-suit injunction, ordering the abusing party to terminate the proceedings in another Member State, as the ECJ is of the view that the Regulation forbids the courts in one Member State to pass judgment on the jurisdiction of courts in other Member States.[179]

The *lis pendens* rule applies regardless of whether the proceedings in the court first seized have international implications or are purely domestic. To what extent proceedings initiated in a non-member state have the effect of *lis pendens* is not governed by the Regulation, and is to be decided by the national law of the Member State where the *lis pendens* effect is to materialize. It is reasonable to assume that such effect will only be given to those proceedings taking place in a non-member country that are expected to result in a decision which will be recognized and enforced in the Member State in question.

Even when the above-mentioned prerequisites of *lis pendens* are not fulfilled, two actions may be so closely connected with one another that it is expedient to hear and adjudicate them together in order to avoid the risk of irreconcilable judgments. When such related actions are pending in the courts of different Member States, any court other than the court first seized may (but is not obliged to) stay its proceedings in accordance with Article 28(1).[180] At the first instance stage of the proceedings, the courts other than the court first seized may, upon the application of one of the parties, also decline jurisdiction if the court first seized has jurisdiction and its law permits the consolidation of the

---

[177] Cf. *Overseas Union* v. *New Hampshire Ins.*, case C-351/89, [1991] ECR I-3317; *Gasser* v. *MISAT*, case C-116/02, [2003] ECR I-14693.

[178] *Gasser* v. *MISAT*, case C-116/02, [2003] ECR I-14693.

[179] *Turner* v. *Grovit*, case C-159/02, [2004] ECR I-3565. See Hartley, 54 *I.C.L.Q.* 821-823 (2005).

[180] See, for example, Briggs & Rees, *Civil Jurisdiction*, pp. 154-159; Byrne, *The European Union*, pp. 165-166; Czernich & Tiefenthaler, *Die Übereinkommen*, pp. 176-179; Dashwood, Hacon & White, *A Guide*, pp. 138-139; Donzallaz, *La Convention*, vol. I, pp. 580-602; Gaudemet-Tallon, *Compétence*, pp. 274-279; Geimer & Schütze, *Europäisches Zivilverfahrensrecht*, pp. 462-469; Kaye, *Civil Jurisdiction*, pp. 1233-1242; Layton & Mercer (eds.), *European Civil Practice*, vol. I, pp. 797-811; Nielsen, *International privat- og procesret*, pp. 217-218; Pålsson, *Brysselkonventionen*, pp. 220-223; Philip, *EU-IP*, pp. 100-102; Rauscher (ed.), *Europäisches Zivilprozessrecht*, pp. 309-313; Rognlien, *Luganokonvensjonen*, pp. 223-224; Schlosser, *EuGVÜ*, pp. 129-132.

proceedings (Article 28(2)). In order to establish the necessary relationship between the two actions, *i.e.* the risk of irreconcilable judgments, it suffices according to the ECJ that they would involve the risk of conflicting decisions, even if there were no risk of giving rise to mutually exclusive legal consequences. Thus, two separate actions brought against the same shipowner by two different cargo owners and concerning two separate but identical contracts have been held by the ECJ to be sufficiently related for the purpose of Article 28.[181]

It follows from the above that it is of great importance to be able to establish which of the parallel proceedings was the first to start, *i.e.*, which court was seized first. The determination of the court first seized might cause difficulties, as different national legal systems hold different views about the point in time when a court is deemed to be seized of a case. For example, in some Member States, the court is seized when the plaintiff's document initiating the proceedings is lodged with the court, while in other Member States the time of service of the document on the defendant is decisive. This is the reason why Article 30 of the Regulation contains its own autonomous solution, although it is based in part on the national law of the Member State of the court seized. Pursuant to the main rule in Article 30(1), a court shall normally be deemed to be seized at the time when the document instituting the proceedings is lodged with the court, provided that the plaintiff subsequently has not failed to take the steps he was required to take to have service effected on the defendant. However, if according to the procedural law of the Member State of the court in question the document has to be served on the defendant before being lodged with the court, then pursuant to Article 30(2) the time when the document is received by the authority responsible for the service is decisive, provided that the plaintiff has not subsequently failed to take the steps he was required to take to have the document lodged with the court as well. Article 30 does not quite clearly specify what will happen if the plaintiff is slow in taking the steps required of him, but it is natural to assume that the court is not considered seized unless the plaintiff has fulfilled all the requirements under national law, including that the service has taken place within the prescribed time limits.

The courts of a Member State having jurisdiction to adjudicate the substance of a dispute can also decide on provisional, including protective, measures, for example, a provisional sequestration of assets. Such measures, however, also can be applied for in the courts of another Member State pursuant to its national law on such measures (Article 31).[182] This request can be made even when the

---

[181] *Tatry*, case C-406/92, [1994] ECR I-5439.

[182] See, for example, H. Born in Fentiman *et al.* (eds.), *L'espace*, pp. 269-276; Byrne, *The European Union*, pp. 167-169; Czernich & Tiefenthaler, *Die Übereinkommen*, pp. 180-183; Dashwood, Hacon & White, *A Guide*, pp. 140-141; Donzallaz, *La Convention*, vol. I, pp. 603-649; Gaudemet-Tallon, *Compétence*, pp. 245-253; Geimer & Schütze, *Europäisches Zivilverfahrensrecht*, pp. 472-492; Hess, *Einstweiliger Rechts- schutz*; Kaye, *Civil Jurisdiction*, pp. 1132-1208; Layton & Mercer (eds.), *European Civil Practice*, vol. I, pp. 816-840; Marmisse & Wilderspin, *Rev.crit.d.i.p.* 1999 pp. 669-683; Newton, *The Uniform Interpretation*,

jurisdiction of every court of every Member State to deal with the substance of the dispute is validly excluded by an arbitration clause.[183] Although the wording of Article 31 is formulated in a very wide manner, the ECJ has interpreted it rather restrictively, mainly because it lays down an exception to the jurisdictional system set up by the Regulation.[184] For example, the ECJ has held that the application of Article 31 presupposes a genuine connecting link between the measure sought and the territory of the requested Member State, such as the presence in that territory of assets subject to the measure sought.[185] It appears that in order to be "provisional, including protective", the requested measure must either preserve the *status quo* until the decision on the substance of the dispute or, if the *status quo* is not preserved (for example, because the measure forces the defendant debtor to make an interim payment in anticipation of the final decision), it must guarantee that the *status quo* can be restored if the plaintiff is unsuccessful as regards the substance of his claim.[186] A measure ordering the hearing of a witness for the purpose of enabling the applicant to decide whether his case is well-founded enough to be brought to a court is not intended to preserve a factual or legal situation and, therefore, is not covered by Article 31.[187] The substantive prerequisites of the measure, such as the existence of an actual need to protect the assets from a serious risk of being consumed or misappropriated, are governed by the national law of the Member State where the measure is requested.

3.4 The Recognition and Enforcement of Foreign Judgments

For the purposes of the Regulation, judgments are defined in Article 32 as "any judgment given by a court or tribunal of a Member State, whatever the judgment may be called, including a decree, order, decision or writ of execution, as well as the determination of costs or expenses by an officer of the court". Both decisions on the merits of a dispute and decisions on provisional measures are included, but a decision of a court of a Member State, recognizing or granting exequatur to a judgment made in a non-member country,

---

pp. 281-372; Pålsson, *Brysselkonventionen*, pp. 223-228; M. Pertegás in Fentiman *et al.* (eds.), *L'espace*, pp. 277-289; Philip, *EU-IP*, pp. 103-106; Rauscher (ed.), *Europäisches Zivilprozessrecht*, pp. 315-333; Rognlien, *Luganokonvensjonen*, pp. 226-227; Rozehnalová & Týč, *Evropský justiční prostor*, pp.292-293; Schlosser, *EuGVÜ*, pp. 133-138; Schulz, *ZEuP* 2001 pp. 805-836.

[183] *Van Uden* v. *Deco-Line*, case C-391/95, [1998] ECR I-7091.

[184] *St.Paul Diary* v. *Unibel*, case C-104/03, [2005] ECR I-3481.

[185] *Van Uden* v. *Deco-Line*, case C-391/95, [1998] ECR I-7091; *Mietz* v. *Intership*, case C-99/96, [1999] ECR I-2277.

[186] *Van Uden* v. *Deco-Line*, case C-391/95, [1998] ECR I-7091; *Mietz* v. *Intership*, case C-99/96, [1999] ECR I-2277.

[187] *St.Paul Diary* v. *Unibel*, case C-104/03, [2005] ECR I-3481.

is not.[188] A requirement which is not mentioned in Article 32, probably because it is considered self-evident, is that the judgment must fall within the scope of the Regulation as defined in Article 1 ("civil and commercial matter", etc.).[189] Another requirement appears to be that the judgment must have been rendered in accordance with the rules governing procedure in contradictory matters and that the defendant must have been summoned and given the opportunity to be heard.[190] The nationality and domicile of the parties in principle are irrelevant, and it makes no difference whether the court that gave the judgment based its competence on the jurisdictional rules in the Regulation or on its own national jurisdictional rules applicable pursuant to Article 4.[191] It is, subject to some exceptions (see *infra*), equally irrelevant whether the court applied the jurisdictional rules correctly or not. The dispute resolved by the judgment does not have to be of an international nature at all, as the Regulation's rules on recognition and enforcement apply even to judgments on disputes having a purely domestic character.

The Regulation differentiates between recognition (Articles 33-37) and enforcement (Articles 38-52) of judgments given in another Member State. The two aspects, however, are inter-related, in particular as Article 45, dealing with the grounds for refusing enforcement, is a mere reference to the grounds for refusing recognition in Articles 34 and 35.

Recognition under the Regulation means normally that the foreign judgment is given the same effects of *res judicata* as it has in the Member State of its origin.[192] To the same extent as in the Member State from which it originates, the judgment is considered to have settled the dispute, and prevents a re-examination of its substance in new proceedings between the same parties with regard to the same cause of action. A judgment which does not have such effects in the Member State where it was given, for example, a judgment on a maintenance obligation which can be amended or replaced at any time due to changed circumstances, will not be given more far-reaching effects in other Member States either.

A judgment given in a Member State is recognized in the other Member States automatically, *i.e.* without any special exequatur procedure being required. The sole requirement imposed by Article 53(1) of the Regulation is that the party seeking recognition shall produce a copy of the judgment which satisfies the conditions necessary to establish its authenticity. The production of a certified translation may be required (Article 55(2)), but no legalization or other similar formality (Article 56). These rules are the same regardless of whether the party seeking enforcement is a national of and/or is domiciled in a Member State or not.

---

[188] *Owens Bank* v. *Bracco*, case C-129/92, [1994] ECR I-117.

[189] See section 3.2 *supra*.

[190] Cf. *Denilauler* v. *Couchet Frères*, case 125/79, [1980] ECR 1553.

[191] See, however, the very special exception in Article 72.

[192] *Hoffmann* v. *Krieg*, case 145/86, [1988] ECR 645.

The issue of recognition arises usually either as a bar to initiation of new proceedings concerning the same cause of action between the same parties, or as an incidental question relevant for the outcome of a dispute adjudicated in the recognizing state, for example, when a defendant sued for payment allegedly due under a contract invokes a foreign judgment declaring the contract in question to be null and void. Such "incidental recognition" of a foreign judgment, expressed merely among the grounds of the decision and not in the conclusion or the court order itself, does not as such normally oblige other courts in the same Member State to recognize the same judgment in another context. The risk of the same foreign judgment being recognized for one purpose while being refused recognition for another purpose is not great, but it exists. Waiting for an incidental recognition also may force the parties to live in a protracted state of uncertainty as to whether the judgment will be recognized or not. Article 33(2) of the Regulation makes it, therefore, possible for any interested party to apply for a separate declaratory decision stipulating once and for all purposes that the foreign judgment is recognized, even though such separate decision is never a compulsory requirement for recognition. The procedure to be used for the purpose of obtaining the decision is in principle the same as that used to obtain a declaration of enforceability (see *infra*). It should be noted that the party opposing the recognition has no corresponding right under the Regulation to apply for a separate decision, albeit it may be able to apply for a negative declaratory judgment in accordance with national procedural law.

The recognition both can and must[193] be refused on the grounds listed exhaustively in Articles 34 and 35.[194] The most general reason for refusal is the traditional *ordre public* exception in Article 34(1), *i.e.* when recognition would be manifestly contrary to the public policy of the Member State in which recognition is sought.[195] This ground for refusal of recognition is intended to be used as a last resort in very exceptional situations only, and the Member States do not have a total freedom to define their public policy as they wish. To begin with, the fact that in the eyes of the recognizing court the judgment is wrong

---

[193] The refusal is mandatory; see *Italian Leather* v. *WECO*, case C-80/00, [2002] ECR I-4995.

[194] An additional, non-mandatory ground for refusal is the rather special provision in Article 61 concerning some judgments given in a civil matter in connection with criminal proceedings where the defendant failed to appear and had no opportunity to arrange for his defence. See *Rinkau*, case 157/80, [1981] ECR 1391; *Krombach* v. *Bamberski*, case C-7/98, [2000] ECR I-1935.

[195] See, for example, Bogdan, *SvJT* 2001 pp. 329-339; Briggs & Rees, *Civil Jurisdiction*, pp. 321-323; Czernich & Tiefenthaler, *Die Übereinkommen*, pp. 196-198; Dashwood, Hacon & White, *A Guide*, pp. 148-149; Donzallaz, *La Convention*, vol. II, pp. 397-449; Gaudemet-Tallon, *Compétence*, pp. 321-330; Geimer & Schütze, *Europäisches Zivilverfahrensrecht*, pp. 542-554; Hartley, *Civil Jurisdiction*, p. 89; Kaye, *Civil Jurisdiction*, pp. 1437-1449; Lasok & Stone, *Conflict*, pp. 299-301; Layton & Mercer (eds.), *European Civil Practice*, vol. I, pp. 879-891; Matscher, *IPRax* 2001 pp. 428-436; Moura Ramos, *YearbPIL* 2000 pp. 25-39; Newton, *The Uniform Interpretation*, pp. 373-436; Pålsson, *Brysselkonventionen*, pp. 250-252; Philip, *EU-IP*, p. 109; Rauscher (ed.), *Europäisches Zivilprozessrecht*, pp. 351-361; Rognlien, *Luganokonvensjonen*, pp. 236-238; Rozehnalová & Týč, *Evropský justiční prostor*, pp. 307-308; Schlosser, *EuGVÜ*, pp. 152-157.

as to its substance and conclusion is not a sufficient reason for invoking public policy, not even if the incorrectness is manifest (see Article 36).[196] Secondly, Article 35(3) states explicitly that the test of public policy must not be applied to the rules relating to jurisdiction, which means, for example, that a judgment given in another Member State must be recognized even if due to Article 4 it was given on the basis of a national jurisdictional ground deemed exorbitant in the Member State where recognition is sought.[197] Thirdly, the ECJ may review the limits within which the courts of a Member State can have recourse to their public policy and it can find an excessive use thereof to be contrary to the Regulation.[198] According to the ECJ, recourse to the public policy clause presupposes that the recognition of the foreign judgment would be at variance to an unacceptable degree with the legal order of the state in which recognition is sought, because of a manifest breach of a rule of law regarded as essential in the legal order of that state or of a right recognized as being fundamental within its legal order. For example, a violation of the right to be effectively defended by a lawyer, guaranteed by the European Convention for the Protection of Human Rights and Fundamental Freedoms, has been found to constitute a legitimate reason for refusing recognition.[199] Finally, the use of the public-policy clause is precluded where the recognition is objected to because of a reason which is regulated in one of the more specific provisions in Articles 34 and 35.[200]

The first of these specific provisions is Article 34(2), which stipulates that a judgment given in another Member State must be refused recognition if the court in which recognition is sought establishes that the judgment has been given in default of appearance and the defendant has not been served with the document instituting the proceedings in sufficient time and in such a way as to enable him to arrange for his defence, unless the defendant failed to commence proceedings to challenge the judgment when it was possible for him to do so.[201]

---

[196] *Renault* v. *Maxicar*, case C-38/98, [2000] ECR I-2973.

[197] *Krombach* v. *Bamberski*, case C-7/98, [2000] ECR I-1935.

[198] *Renault* v. *Maxicar*, case C-38/98, [2000] ECR I-2973.

[199] *Krombach* v. *Bamberski*, case C-7/98, [2000] ECR I-1935.

[200] *Hoffmann* v. *Krieg*, case 145/86, [1988] ECR 645; *Hendrikman* v. *Magenta*, case C-78/95, [1996] ECR I-4943.

[201] Cf. *Klomps* v. *Michel*, case 166/80, [1981] ECR 1593; *Pendy* v. *Pluspunkt*, case 228/81, [1982] ECR 2723; *Debaecker* v. *Bouwman*, case 49/84, [1985] ECR 1779. See also, for example, Braun, *Der Beklagten-schutz*; Briggs & Rees, *Civil Jurisdiction*, pp. 323-324; Byrne, *The European Union*, pp. 175-185; Czernich & Tiefenthaler, *Die Übereinkommen*, pp. 198-204; Dashwood, Hacon & White, *A Guide*, pp. 149-154; Donzallaz, *La Convention*, vol. II, pp. 450-472; Gaudemet-Tallon, *Compétence*, pp. 330-340; Geimer & Schütze, *Europäisches Zivilverfahrensrecht*, pp. 554-571; Hartley, *Civil Jurisdiction*, pp. 89-92; Kaye, *Civil Jurisdiction*, pp. 1449-1482; Lasok & Stone, *Conflict*, pp. 301-307; Layton & Mercer (eds.), *European Civil Practice*, vol. I, pp. 892-917; Newton, *The Uniform Interpretation*, pp. 437-518; Pålsson, *Brysselkonventionen*, pp. 243-247; Philip, *EU-IP*, pp. 109-110; Rauscher (ed.), *Europäisches Zivilprozessrecht*, pp. 361-371; Rognlien, *Luganokonvensjonen*, pp. 238-239; Rozehnalová & Týč, *Evropský justiční prostor*, pp. 309-312; Schlosser, *EuGVÜ*, pp. 157-166.

The question whether the judgment in fact was given in default of appearance of the defendant may sometimes give rise to considerable doubts, for example, when the defendant, who in the main proceedings was seemingly represented by a lawyer, claims that the lawyer lacked the authority to act on his behalf[202] or that the lawyer defended him against criminal charges only but not as regards to the civil claim for damages that was adjudicated in the same proceedings[203].

Another ground for refusing recognition is irreconcilability with another judgment.[204] This problem arises normally when the foreign judgment is irreconcilable with a judgment given in a dispute between the same parties in the Member State in which recognition is sought (Article 34(3)), but recognition is barred also by irreconcilability with an *earlier* judgment given in a third Member State or even in a non-member country involving the same cause of action and between the same parties, provided that the earlier judgment in question is recognized in the Member State where recognition is sought (Article 34(4)). The ECJ has held that the foreign judgment's irreconcilability with a court-approved settlement between the parties does not constitute a cause for refusal of recognition, notwithstanding the fact that the settlement was reached before a court in the country where enforcement is sought and is enforceable there, the reason being that a court settlement does not constitute a judgment within the meaning of Article 34(3-4).[205] It is important to note that the local or third-country judgment in question does not have to deal with the same issue as the judgment whose recognition is under scrutiny; in fact it may deal with a matter falling totally outside the scope of the Regulation. For example, a judgment made in another Member State ordering a spouse to pay maintenance to the other spouse will be refused recognition if it is irreconcilable with a local judgment (or a recognized earlier third-country judgment) pronouncing the divorce or invalidity of the same marriage.[206] It seems that recognition will be refused also

---

[202] See *Hendrikman v. Magenta*, case C-78/95, [1996] ECR I-4943, where the defendant was not considered to have been validly represented and the judgment therefore was treated as having been given in default.

[203] See *Sonntag v. Waidmann*, case C-172/91, [1993] ECR I-1963, where the defendant was considered to have been represented because his lawyer had not clearly declined to appear for the purposes of the civil-law claim.

[204] See *Italian Leather v. WECO*, case C-80/00, [2002] ECR I-4995. See also, for example, Briggs & Rees, *Civil Jurisdiction*, pp. 325-326; Byrne, *The European Union*, pp. 185-188; Czernich & Tiefenthaler, *Die Übereinkommen*, pp. 204-207; Donzallaz, *La Convention*, vol. II, pp. 473-500 and 519-527; Gaudemet-Tallon, *Compétence*, pp. 340-350; Geimer & Schütze, *Europäisches Zivilverfahrensrecht*, pp. 571-576; Hartley, *Civil Jurisdiction*, pp. 92-93; Kaye, *Civil Jurisdiction*, pp. 1482-1492 and 1498-1501; Lasok & Stone, *Conflict*, pp. 307-310; Layton & Mercer (eds.), *European Civil Practice*, vol. I, pp. 917-926 and 930-933; Pålsson, *Brysselkonventionen*, pp. 247-250; Philip, *EU-IP*, pp. 111-112: Rauscher (ed.), *Europäisches Zivilprozessrecht*, pp. 371-373; Rognlien, *Luganokonvensjonen*, pp. 239-241; Rozehnalová & Týč, *Evropský justiční prostor*, pp. 312-313; Schlosser, *EuGVÜ*, pp. 166-168.

[205] *Solo Kleinmotoren v. Boch*, case C-414/92, [1994] ECR I-2237.

[206] *Hoffmann v. Krieg*, case 145/86, [1988] ECR 645.

if the judgment debt has been erased by a judicial or other similar debt-adjust-ment scheme organized or recognized in the Member State where recognition or enforcement is sought, irrespective of whether such a scheme amounts to proceedings between the same parties.[207] Irreconcilability with an arbitration award is not mentioned in Article 34, but should reasonably be given the same effects as irreconcilability with a court judgment.

Finally, a judgment can and must be refused recognition pursuant to Article 35 if it was given in violation of the Regulation's mandatory jurisdictional rules on insurance disputes, consumer disputes or exclusive jurisdiction,[208] or if the Member State where recognition is sought has, prior to the entry into force of the Regulation, undertaken *vis-à-vis* a third country not to recognize judgments given against defendants domiciled in that third country on the basis of the exorbitant jurisdictional grounds listed in Annex I to the Regulation. In other situations, it makes no difference whether the court that gave the judgment really had jurisdiction pursuant to the Regulation or not, since its jurisdiction must not be reviewed. In addition, even in those rare cases where review of jurisdiction is permitted, the reviewing court is bound by the findings of fact on which the court of the Member State of origin based its jurisdiction, for exam-ple, that the disputed tenancy agreement dealt with a temporary tenancy for not more than six consecutive months (see Article 22(1) para. 2). It deserves to be noted that Article 35 does not mention, among the grounds for refusing recogni-tion, a violation of the mandatory jurisdictional rules on employment disputes; the reason is that in such disputes it is normally the employee who initiates the proceedings and non-recognition of the resulting judgment therefore would normally constitute a disadvantage to the weaker party.

It is not a necessary precondition of recognition that the judgment is final, but if in the Member State of its origin the judgment is challenged by ordinary appellate review, the court in the Member State where recognition is sought may – but is not obliged to – stay the proceedings in order to wait for the outcome of the appeal (Article 37). "Ordinary appeal" is defined by the ECJ as any appeal that forms part of the normal course of an action and which constitutes a proce-dural development that any party must reasonably expect. More specifically, the ECJ held that this means any appeal which may result in the annulment or the amendment of the judgment, provided that the lodging of the appeal is bound to a period which is laid down by the law and starts to run by virtue of that same judgment.[209]

In contrast to recognition, enforcement presupposes that the judgment given in another Member State has, upon the application of a party, been declared enforceable by a special declaratory decision (exequatur) of a court in the

---

[207] Cf. *Coursier* v. *Fortis*, case C-267/97, [1999] ECR I-2543, concerning the effects of a court-supervised liquidation in the country of the origin of the judgment.

[208] See sections 3.3.3 and 3.3.4 *supra*.

[209] *Industrial Diamonds* v. *Riva*, case 43/77, [1977] ECR 2175.

Member State where enforcement is sought (Article 38),[210] unless the judgment is a European Enforcement Order[211]. Articles 38-56 contain several important, but rather technical, provisions regarding the exequatur procedure. This procedure is exclusive in the sense that the judgment creditor cannot use any alternative way of obtaining enforcement, for example, by suing again for a new judgment in the country where enforcement is to take place if for some reason a new action to him seems to be more expedient or more economical than the exequatur proceedings.[212]

The competent courts in the various Member States to which applications for exequatur must be submitted are enumerated in Annex II to the Regulation (the appellate instances are listed in Annexes III and IV). The exequatur procedure, to the extent it is not regulated by the Regulation itself, is governed by the law of the Member State where enforcement is sought.[213] The party applying for a declaration of enforceability must produce, in addition to a copy of the judgment, a special certificate, which is issued upon request by the court or other competent authority in the Member State where the judgment was given, although the production of the certificate can be dispensed with. A standard form for the certificate is found in Annex V to the Regulation. A certified translation of the documents may be required, but not additional legalization or other similar formality (Articles 54-56). No charge or fee calculated by reference to the value of the matter at issue may be levied in the proceedings (Article 52). All this applies even if the applicant is domiciled in and a citizen of a non-member state.

Pursuant to Article 41, a judgment which is enforceable in the Member State where it was given has to be declared enforceable in the other Member States immediately on the completion of the formalities, without any review (not even a review from the point of view of public policy is permitted). In fact, the party against whom enforcement is sought is not even entitled to make any submissions at this stage. However, the resulting exequatur decision is served on him and he may lodge an appeal against it; no actual enforcement measures other than protective measures may be taken in the meantime (Article 47(3)). The time for appeal is according to Article 43(5) relatively short, namely one month after the exequatur was served on the party against whom enforcement is sought, but the time is extended to two months if that party is domiciled in another Member State (it remains thus one month if that party is domiciled in a non-member state, irrespective of how distant). The exequatur decision gives the applicant automatically the power to proceed to protective measures, see Article 47(2).[214] The appeal against a decision granting exequatur may succeed only on one of the grounds for refusing recognition specified in Article 34, 35 and 61

---

[210] In the United Kingdom, exequatur is replaced by a registration for enforcement, see Article 38(2).

[211] See section 4.1 *infra*.

[212] See *de Wolf* v. *Cox*, case 42/76, [1976] ECR 1759.

[213] See *Carron* v. *Germany*, case 198/85, [1986] ECR 2437.

[214] See *Capelloni* v. *Pelkmans*, case 119/84, [1985] ECR 3147.

(see *supra*). If exequatur is refused, it is the applicant who is entitled to lodge an appeal. It must be stressed that the Regulation regulates merely the procedure for obtaining an order of exequatur and does not deal with the subsequent execution itself, which is governed totally by the domestic law of the country in which execution is sought, including the remedies available for contesting execution.[215]

Similar to recognition (cf. *supra* about Article 37), it is not a pre-condition for obtaining exequatur that the judgment has become final in the Member State where it was given (provided it is enforceable there[216]), but Article 46 makes it under certain conditions possible for the court to which an appeal against an exequatur is lodged to stay the exequatur proceedings if an ordinary appeal has been lodged against the judgment in the Member State of origin or if the time for such an appeal has not yet expired.

A special régime applies to authentic instruments (private documents which in the Member State where they originate have become enforceable due to participation by a public authority,[217] such as certain agreements authenticated by a Notary Public) and court settlements made or approved in another Member State (Articles 57 and 58). The Regulation does not require that such instruments and settlements should be recognized and given the effect of *res judicata*,[218] but they can be enforced after having been declared enforceable in accordance with the procedures provided for in the Regulation, on the condition that they are produced together with a certificate issued on a standard form in Annex V (court settlements) or VI (authentic instruments). Such certificate is issued by the authorities of the country of origin upon the request of any interested party. Declaration of enforceability may be refused only if enforcement would be manifestly contrary to the public policy of the Member State where enforcement is sought, which means that the other grounds for refusing recognition and enforcement in Articles 34 and 35 cannot be used. The fact that the Member State where enforcement is sought does not permit authentic instruments in corresponding matters in its own legal system, as such, cannot legitimize the use of the public policy exception.

---

[215] See *Deutsche v. Brasserie du Pêcheur*, case 148/84, [1985] ECR 1981; *Hoffmann v. Krieg*, case 145/86, [1988] ECR 645.

[216] Cf. *Coursier v. Fortis*, case C-267/97, [1999] ECR I-2543.

[217] The involvement of a public authority is essential, see *Unibank v. Christensen*, case C-260/97, [1999] ECR I-3715. See also Czernich & Tiefenthaler, *Die Übereinkommen*, pp. 253-258; Dashwood, Hacon & White, *A Guide*, pp. 179-180; Donzallaz, *La Convention*, vol. II, pp. 272-322 and 928-941; Gaudemet-Tallon, *Compétence*, pp. 387-392; Geimer & Schütze, *Europäisches Zivilverfahrensrecht*, pp. 696-709; Kaye, *Civil Jurisdiction*, pp. 1681-1687; Lasok & Stone, *Conflict*, pp. 324-325; Layton & Mercer (eds.), *European Civil Practice*, vol. I, pp. 1035-1050; Leutner, *Die vollstreckbare Urkunde*; Pålsson, *Brysselkonventionen*, pp. 274-278; Philip, *EU-IP*, p. 123; Rauscher (ed.), *Europäisches Zivilprozessrecht*, pp. 454-469; Rognlien, *Luganokonvensjonen*, pp. 268-272; Rozehnalová & Týč, *Evropský justiční prostor*, pp. 334-336; Schlosser, *EuGVÜ*, pp. 227-231.

[218] Cf. *Solo Kleinmotoren v. Boch*, case C-414/92, [1994] ECR I-2237.

CHAPTER 4

Instruments Complementary to the Brussels I Regulation

4.1   European Enforcement Order for Uncontested Claims

One serious drawback of the enforcement procedure set up in the Brussels I Regulation[1] is the requirement of exequatur, *i.e.*, the need for approval in each individual case by a court of the Member State where the enforcement is to take place. The exequatur procedure causes both delays and expenses that particularly appear to be unwarranted in those cases where the judgment concerns a claim which has not been contested by the defendant debtor. As pointed out by the Commission,[2] it seems to be an increasing problem that creditors are compelled to go to courts not in order to obtain a decision on a contentious question of fact or law but merely to obtain an enforceable title that can be forcibly executed against a debtor who is unwilling to pay his debt which is not in dispute. Under such circumstances, the only reasonable requirement at the recognition and enforcement stage should be that the debtor had been properly informed about the court action filed against him and given fair opportunity to contest the claim. Requiring exequatur proceedings and other obstacles standing in the way of an inexpensive and rapid enforcement provide recalcitrant debtors of uncontested claims with an incentive to withhold payment without any legitimate reason.

The EC Regulation No 805/2004 of 21 April 2004 creating a European Enforcement Order for Uncontested Claims,[3] which applies from 21 October 2005 to judgments given after its entry into force on 21 January 2005, is an independent legal instrument of EC law. However, it is obviously intended to function as a complement to the Brussels I Regulation, mainly by introducing an alternative, simplified enforcement procedure with regard to uncontested claims irrespective of the amount. It does not limit itself to enforcement though, as it simplifies also the recognition of judgments regarding such claims.

In view of the mutual trust in the administration of justice in the Member States, the Regulation authorizes the court making the judgment regarding an uncontested claim to issue, in addition to the judgment itself, a standardized certificate showing that all conditions imposed by the Regulation are fulfilled. Such certificate enables the judgment, thus certified as a European Enforcement Order, to be enforced in the other Member States without the need for any declaration of enforceability and to be recognized there without any possibility of opposing the recognition (Article 5).

---

[1]   See section 3.4 *supra*.

[2]   See COM(2004)173 final, at pp. 4-5.

[3]   OJ 2004 L 143 p. 15. The Annexes to the Regulation have been replaced by Regulation No 1869/2005 of 16 November 2005, OJ 2005 L 300 p. 6. See also d'Avout, *Rev.crit.d.i.p.* 2006 pp.1-48; Kohler, *Zeitschrift für Schweizerisches Recht* 2005 pp. 276-282; Péroz, *Clunet* 2005 pp. 637-676; Stadler, *IPRax* 2004 pp. 2-11; Stein, *IPRax* 2004 pp. 181-191; Wagner, *IPRax* 2002 pp. 75-95 and in *IPRax* 2005 pp. 189-200.

The term "European Enforcement Order" appears to be somewhat mislead-ing, as neither the judgment itself nor the certificate is issued by any Euro-pean institution but merely by the national court of origin of the judgment in question. The certificate is issued "upon application at any time", which means that it does not have to be issued simultaneously with the judgment itself, but can be applied for later, for example, when the judgment creditor finds out that the debtor has assets in another Member State. The certificate is issued in the language of the judgment, using a standard form annexed to the Regulation (Article 9). The certificate, in contrast to the judgment itself, is not subject to appeal, although it may be rectified or even withdrawn pursuant to the law of the Member State of origin if there is a discrepancy between the certificate and the judgment or if the certificate has been granted in violation of the conditions imposed by the Regulation (Article 10).

The scope of application of the Regulation is practically the same as that of the Brussels I Regulation, as far as the subject matter of the dispute is concerned.[4] This follows from Article 2 of the Regulation on European Enforce-ment Order, which corresponds to Article 1 of the Brussels I Regulation; the only noticeable difference is that the Regulation on European Enforcement Order excludes explicitly from its scope any matters concerning the liability of the state for acts and omissions in the exercise of its authority (acta jure imperii). This difference in the wording of the two instruments is relevant only if and to the extent such liability is deemed to be a civil or commercial matter in the first place; if this is not the case it falls beyond the scope of the Brussels I Regulation, too.[5]

Pursuant to its Article 3, the Regulation on European Enforcement Order applies to judgments, court settlements and authentic instruments "on uncon-tested claims". A claim is regarded as uncontested if the debtor has expressly agreed to it, in most cases by admission or a settlement in the course of judicial proceedings or in an authentic instrument (Article 3(1)(a and d)), or if he has refrained from objecting to it in compliance with the procedural requirements of the Member State of origin in the course of the court proceedings there (Article 3(1)(b)),[6] or if he has neither appeared nor been represented at the court hearing provided that such conduct amounts to a tacit admission under the law of the Member State of origin of the Order (Article 3(1)(c)).

---

[4] In matters relating to maintenance obligations, the Regulation's rules probably will be replaced by the proposed Regulation on Jurisdiction, Applicable Law, Recognition and Enforcement of Decisions and Cooperation in Matters relating to Maintenance Obligations, see Article 48(1) of the proposal presented by the Commission on 15 December 2005, COM(2005)649 final.

[5] Cf. *Sonntag* v. *Waidmann*, case C-172/91, [1993] ECR I-1963.

[6] Thus, it is in principle the law of the Member State of origin that decides which objections make the claim contested and therefore preclude the certification, for example, with regard to the situation where the debtor contests the claim on the sole ground that he simply does not have sufficient funds to pay the debt in question.

The Regulation applies only to claims for payment of a specific sum of money that has fallen due or for which the due date is indicated in the judgment (Article 4(2)). Demands regarding a specific performance, even if uncontested, thus, are not included. On the other hand, the certification applies also to the costs related to the court proceedings, unless the debtor, during the proceedings, has specifically objected against his obligation to bear those costs (Article 7). The certification may be partial if only a part of the judgment fulfills the conditions imposed by the Regulation (Article 8).

The certification does not presuppose that the judgment has become final, provided that it has become enforceable in the Member State of origin. If a judgment certified as European Enforcement Order is challenged by appeal or other similar procedure, then the Regulation shall also apply to the decision on the challenge, irrespective of whether that decision affirms or changes the judgment (Article 3(2)).

In order to be certified as a European Enforcement Order, the judgment must fulfill a number of additional conditions specified in Article 6. For example, it must not conflict with the Brussels I Regulation's jurisdictional rules on insurance disputes and exclusive jurisdiction. If the claim relates to a consumer contract and it is the consumer who is the debtor, the judgment must be given in the Member State of his domicile unless he expressly agreed to the claim. Thus, a French judgment against a consumer domiciled in Germany cannot be certified as a European Enforcement Order if the claim is considered uncontested merely because the consumer has never objected to it or has not appeared or been represented (see Article 3(1)(b-c)). The most important requirement is, however, that the proceedings leading to the judgment must have met the minimum procedural standards set out in Articles 12-19 of the Regulation. These minimum standards pertain mainly to the service on the debtor or his representative of documents instituting the proceedings and to the information to be contained in such documents. They must be observed only when the claim is considered uncontested by virtue of Article 3(1)(b-c), *i.e.*, they need not be complied with when the debtor has expressly agreed to the claim.

In addition to various forms of service with proof of receipt by the debtor (Article 13), the Regulation in Article 14 accepts certain forms of service even without such proof, for example, a duly attested service on persons living in the same household as the debtor or employed by the debtor or service by depositing the document in the debtor's mailbox or at a post office. Service by regular mail without proof is accepted too, but only where the debtor has his address in the Member State of origin of the Order. Service by electronic means attested by an automatic confirmation of delivery is acceptable provided that the debtor has expressly accepted this method of service in advance.

Both Article 13 and Article 14 presuppose that the debtor to be served has a known address. Service of documents on a debtor whose address is not known with certainty, such as service by advertising in a newspaper or by nailing the summons to the church door, is not sufficient for the issuing of a European

Enforcement Order certificate, but the resulting judgment nevertheless may be recognized and declared enforceable in the other Member States pursuant to the Brussels I Regulation, provided of course that all conditions imposed by that Regulation are fulfilled.

The issuing of a European Enforcement Order certificate requires, further-more, that the documents instituting the proceedings have contained the infor-mation about, *i.a.*, the amount of and reasons for the claim, the interest sought, the procedural conditions for contesting the claim (such as the prescribed time limits) and the consequences of an absence of objection (Articles 16-17).

Pursuant to Article 18, non-compliance with the procedural requirements in the Regulation can be cured in two ways. Firstly, non-compliance with the service and information requirements in Articles 13-17 is cured if the resulting judgment, together with information about the possibilities of challenging it, has been served on the debtor in conformity with Article 13 or Article 14 and the debtor, who had the possibility to challenge the judgment, has failed to do so. Secondly, non-compliance with Articles 13-14 is cured if the conduct of the debtor in the court proceedings proves that he has personally received the docu-ments in sufficient time to arrange for his defense.

Finally, the certification of a judgment as a European Enforcement Order requires that the debtor must be entitled, provided that he acts promptly, to apply for a review of the judgment if the documents were served on him by one of the methods listed in Article 14 (*i.e.*, without proof of receipt) and, without any fault on his part, the service was not effected in sufficient time to enable him to arrange for his defence, or if he was prevented from objecting to the claim by *force majeure* or other extraordinary circumstances without any fault on his part (Article 19).

It must be reiterated that the check on all these conditions is to be carried out by the court in the Member State of origin prior to issuing the European Enforcement Order certificate and not by the courts in the Member State where the enforcement is to take place; albeit the ultimate enforcement as such is governed by the law of the latter (Article 20(1)). The enforcement can (and must) be refused by the Member State where it is to take place only if the judgment is irreconcilable with an earlier judgment between the same parties and involving the same cause of action, further conditions being that the earlier judgment was made or is recognized in the Member State where enforcement is sought *and* the irreconcilability was not and could not be raised as an objection in the court proceedings in the Member State of origin of the European Enforcement Order (Article 21).

Articles 24-25 in the Regulation contain special rules for certain court settle-ments and authentic instruments, as defined in Article 4(3). Such settlements and instruments also can be certified as European Enforcement Orders, which makes them enforceable in the other Member States without the need of an exequatur. However, there is no provision in the Regulation requiring that court settlements and authentic instruments also should be recognized (*i.e.*, given the effect of *res judicata*) in the other Member States, which means that they do not preclude new adjudication on the same debt or even the enforcement of a judgment incompatible with the settlement or instrument in question.

The simplified mechanism set up for European Enforcement Orders is always optional for the creditor, who may prefer to use the system under the Brussels I Regulation instead, *i.e.*, to apply for an exequatur in the proper court in the Member State where the enforcement is to take place. It must also be noted that the Regulation creating a European Enforcement Order does not impose any legal obligation on the Member States to adapt their national procedural law, in particular the rules regarding the service of documents, to the minimum standards set out in the Regulation's Articles 12-19. However, in those cases where those standards are not met, the judgment must not be certified as being a European Enforcement Order and can only be enforced pursuant to the Brussels I Regulation. This should provide an incentive for the Member States to comply with the Regulation's minimum standards in order to make the enforcement of their decisions in the other Member States more rapid and efficient. Another thing to keep in mind is that even those Member States, which do not always comply with the minimum standards and are consequently sometimes unable to certify their judgments as European Enforcement Orders, are obliged to recognize and enforce judgments so certified in the other Member States.

4.2   Proposed European Order for Payment Procedure

Most Member States provide in their procedural law for some kind of simplified summary proceedings for uncontested claims. In May 2004, the Commission presented a proposal for a regulation that would introduce into all Member States an additional type of summary procedure, essentially governed by EC law, which would be suitable for obtaining such decisions on uncontested claims that would qualify for certification as European Enforcement Orders.[7] Even though the proposal had its legal basis in Articles 61(c) and 65(c) of the EC Treaty, it was not an instrument of PIL, as it dealt merely with issues of procedural law and the proposed procedure was intended to be used even in purely domestic situations. In response to suggestions from the European Parliament, the Commission presented in February 2006 an amended proposal,[8] radically different from the previous one. The amended proposal confines itself to cross-border cases (defined as cases in which at least one of the parties is domiciled or habitually resides in a state other than the Member State of the forum) and deals both with the purely procedural aspects of the proposed European Order for Payment procedure and with the PIL aspects thereof.

---

[7]   See the proposal, presented by the Commission on 25 May 2004, for a Regulation creating a European Order for Payment Procedure, COM(2004)173 final. See further Sujecki, *ZEuP* 2006 pp. 124-148.

[8]   See COM(2006)57 final, dated 7 February 2006.

The proposed procedure is intended to be used for uncontested pecuniary claims for a specific amount that have fallen due. The scope of the proposal is partly similar to the scope of the Brussels I Regulation;[9] the main difference is that most claims arising from non-contractual obligations are excluded. The principal features of the proposal are that the court seized of the application for a European Order for Payment issues, after a summary examination of the application's admissibility, an Order calling upon the defendant to pay or to oppose the claim. The Order is served on the defendant in accordance with specific and detailed rules, mostly inspired by the minimum standards set in Regulation No 805/2004 creating a European Enforcement Order for Uncontested Claims.[10] The Order becomes enforceable unless the defendant lodges a statement of opposition within 30 days. If the defendant lodges such a statement, the proceedings will continue in accordance with the rules of ordinary civil procedure, unless the claimant explicitly requests the termination of the proceedings. The European Order for Payment procedure is substantially simplified by the use of standard forms and representation by a lawyer is not mandatory. It serves as an additional and optional means for the claimant, who remains free to resort to any other procedure available under domestic or Community law.

Turning to PIL matters, jurisdiction is regulated in the proposed Article 6. It refers essentially to the jurisdictional rules in the Brussels I Regulation,[11] but if the defendant is a consumer, only the courts in the Member State of his domicile will have jurisdiction. Article 19 stipulates that a European Order for Payment, which has become enforceable in the Member State of origin, will be recognized and enforced in the other Member States without the need for a declaration of enforceability and without any possibility of opposing its recognition. The enforcement will be governed by the law of the Member State where it takes place (Article 21). Enforcement can and must be refused merely in certain cases of irreconcilability with an earlier decision valid in the Member State where enforcement is sought (Article 22).

4.3   Proposed European Small Claims Procedure

The existing and proposed rules of European PIL dealing with uncontested claims must not be confused with the rules, proposed by the Commission in March 2005, regarding a European procedure for small claims.[12] There are, no doubt, certain similarities between the two sets of rules, such as that they both are based on Articles 61(c) and 65(c) of the EC Treaty,

---

[9]   See section 3.2 *supra*.

[10]   See section 4.1 *supra*.

[11]   See section 3.3 *supra*.

[12]   See the proposal, presented by the Commission on 13 March 2005, for a Regulation establishing a European Small Claims Procedure, COM(2005)87 final.

are intended to complement the Brussels I Regulation, and one of their main purposes is to do away with exequatur and other requirements that are perceived as unnecessary.

Like the proposed Regulation creating a European Order for Payment Procedure,[13] the proposed Regulation establishing a European Small Claims Procedure deals both with the substance of a new small claims procedure governed by Community law and with the recognition and enforcement of decisions delivered in that procedure. Both proposals are intended to be optional for the claimants and will not force the Member States to abandon or modify their national procedures, but the proposed procedure for small claims can be used in both domestic and cross-border situations.

The proposed European Small Claims Procedure is expected to significantly simplify and speed up litigation and enforcement regarding small claims, defined as monetary or non-monetary claims of total value not exceeding 2,000 EUR. Even though it can be expected that the procedure will mostly be used by or against consumers or between two parties acting outside their trade or profession, it will be available for disputes between businessmen as well. The proposed rules will apply in civil and commercial matters with a number of exclusions similar to those in Article 1 of the Brussels I Regulation. An exclusion having no counterpart in Brussels I concerns claims based on employment law, which are not considered suitable for the European Small Claims Procedure. The procedure will be based on a wide use of standard forms and will normally be written only, without any requirement of representation by a lawyer. The judgment must be rendered within six months. The national procedural law of the Member State of the forum decides on the availability of appeal, but the judgment, notwithstanding any appeal, will be immediately enforceable. The same national procedural law also will govern all those aspects of the proceedings that are not dealt with by any of the provisions of the proposed Regulation.

Of direct interest for PIL is Article 18 of the proposed Regulation, which prescribes that a judgment delivered in a Member State in a European Small Claims Procedure will be recognized and enforceable in another Member State without the need for an exequatur decision and without any possibility of opposing the recognition and enforcement, provided that the judgment has been certified by the court of origin using a particular form. The sole ground for refusing certification is that the judgment conflicts with the jurisdictional rules of the Brussels I Regulation concerning matters relating to insurance and exclusive jurisdiction.

As to the relationship between the rules on uncontested claims and rules on small claims, it must be noted that the proposed rules on uncontested claims apply to uncontested claims irrespective of their amount, thus even to small claims. At the same time, the proposed European Small Claims Procedure seems to apply to small claims regardless of whether they are contested or not.

---

[13] See section 4.2 *supra*.

This means that the claimant in some situations will have the choice between two summary procedures governed by EC law (in addition to the summary procedures offered by the national law of the forum Member State). The rules on the recognition and enforcement mechanism in the proposed Small Claims Regulation constitute an exception, as they do *not* apply to judgments on uncontested claims within the meaning of Article 3(1) of Regulation No 805/2004.[14]

4.4 Proposed Rules on Maintenance Disputes

On 15 December 2005, the EC Commission presented a proposal for a Regulation on Jurisdiction, Applicable Law, Recognition and Enforcement of Decisions and Cooperation in Matters relating to Maintenance Obligations,[15] which is intended to replace, as far as maintenance disputes are concerned, both the Brussels I Regulation and the Regulation creating a European Enforcement Order for Uncontested Claims.

The jurisdictional rules in the proposal differ in several respects from those in the Brussels I Regulation. In addition to jurisdictional grounds corresponding to Articles 2 and 5(2) of that Regulation, Article 3 of the proposal gives jurisdiction in maintenance disputes to the court competent to entertain proceedings concerning parental responsibility under the Brussels II Regulation,[16] provided that the maintenance matter is ancillary to those proceedings. Another novelty is that a choice-of-court agreement is not accepted regarding maintenance obligations towards a child below the age of 18 and that, rather surprisingly, "tacit prorogation" based on the voluntary appearance of the defendant is not accepted if another court has been previously agreed on by an exclusive choice-of-law agreement (Articles 4 and 5 of the proposal).

When no Member State has jurisdiction pursuant to the above, then the Member State of the common nationality of the parties or, in the case of maintenance obligations between spouses or ex-spouses, the Member State of their last common habitual residence during the last year before the initiation of the proceedings will have jurisdiction according to the proposal's Article 6.

An important improvement and progress introduced by Articles 25-38 of the proposal is that maintenance judgments, as well as enforceable authentic instruments and agreements concerning maintenance, originating in a Member State in principle will be both recognized and enforced in the other Member States without any requirement of a declaration of enforceability and with very limited possibilities of opposition. In fact, the courts in the Member State where recognition or enforcement is sought will not even be allowed to refuse it because of their public policy.

---

[14] See section 4.1 *supra*.

[15] COM(2005)649 final and the Commission's commentary on the proposal in COM(2006)206 final.

[16] See section 5.3.1 *infra*.

The proposal intends, furthermore, to create a system of central authorities designated by the Member States, with the task of cooperating in various ways, for example by providing information and assistance to maintenance creditors (Articles 39-47).

4.5 Proposed Rules on Mediation in Civil and Commercial Matters

On 22 October 2004, the EC Commission presented a proposal for a Directive on Certain Aspects of Mediation in Civil and Commercial Matters.[17] Even though the proposal is based on Article 65 of the EC Treaty, the proposed rules are intended to be transposed into the mediation legislation of the Member States (except Denmark) even in respect to situations containing no cross-border elements at all.

Mediation is defined in Article 2 of the proposal as any process, however named, where two or more parties to a dispute are assisted by a third party to reach an agreement on the settlement of the dispute, regardless of whether the process is initiated by the parties, suggested or ordered by a court or prescribed by national law. Attempts by the judge to settle a dispute within the course of judicial proceedings, however, are not included.

The proposal contains a number of procedural rules concerning referrals to mediation, ensuring the quality of mediation, enforcement of settlement agreements, non-disclosure of information (such as statements or admissions made by a party in the course of the mediation) and suspension of limitation periods.

At the time of writing it is uncertain whether, and if so when, the proposals concerning the European Order for Payment Procedure, European Small Claims Procedure, maintenance disputes and mediation will be adopted. In view of the high probability that the proposals under all circumstances will be amended on many points, the above presentation is extremely brief.

---

[17]   COM(2004)718 final.

CHAPTER 5

Regulation Brussels II

5.1   The Scope and Other General Features of the Regulation

The EC Regulation No 2201/2003 of 27 November 2003,[1] concerning Jurisdiction and the Recognition and Enforcement of Judgments in Matrimonial Matters and the Matters of Parental Responsibility, repealing Regulation No 1347/2000, applies fully from 1 March 2005, when it replaced, as stated in its heading, a previous Regulation on roughly the same subject from 2000[2]. The purpose of the Regulation, commonly known as Brussels II, is to fill some parts of the gap created by the exclusion of most areas of family law from the field of application of the Brussels I Regulation. The Brussels II Regulation deals with two such areas, namely some matrimonial matters and some matters relating to parental responsibility. Like the Brussels I Regulation, Brussels II is a double instrument, dealing with both the jurisdiction of courts and the recognition and enforcement of the resulting decisions. The question of applicable substantive legal system, on the other hand, remains unregulated.[3]

As far as matrimonial matters are concerned, Article 1(1)(a) states that the Regulation applies in civil matters relating to "divorce, legal separation or marriage annulment". Disputes concerning, for example, the validity of a marriage ceremony thus are not included. Disputes about issues such as the division of matrimonial property or other ancillary matters are also excluded, as they do not concern the dissolution as such of the matrimonial ties. When the Regulation speaks of divorce, legal separation or marriage annulment, it has in mind traditional marriages only, thus not other similar legal institutions such as registered partnerships of same-sex couples existing in some of the Member States. It is not quite clear whether the Regulation applies to same-sex marriages, which have now been introduced in the Netherlands, Belgium and Spain; even though in the legal terminology of their respective countries these family formations are called "marriages", it is far from obvious that a mere choice of words in some Member States should be decisive for the interpretation of concepts of Community law, where the ECJ usually prefers an autonomous approach.[4]

---

[1]   OJ 2003 L 338 p. 1.

[2]   See EC Regulation No 1347/2000 of 29 May 2000, OJ 2000 L 160 p. 19. This Regulation in turn to a large extent was based on an EC Convention which never entered into force but was commented on by a semi-official explanatory report prepared by Alegría Borrás, se OJ 1998 C 221 p. 27. The Borrás Report continues to be useful whenever the wording of the new Brussels II Regulation (sometimes called Brussels IIa or Brussels II bis) corresponds to that of the Convention. See also, for example, Ancel & Muir Watt, *Rev.crit.d.i.p.* 2005 pp. 569-605; Boele-Woelki, *ZfRV* 2001 pp. 121-130; Busch, *IPRax* 2003 pp. 218-222; Gaudemet-Tallon, *Clunet* 2001 pp. 381-445; Gruber, *IPRax* 2005 pp. 293-300; Jänterä-Jareborg, *YearbPIL* 1999 pp. 1-36 and 2002 pp. 67-82; Pirrung, *ZEuP* 1999 pp. 834-848; Schack, *RabelsZ* 2001 pp. 615-633.

[3]   See, however, the summary description in section 9.3 *infra* of the conflict rules proposed by the Commission on 17 July 2006, COM(2006)399 final.

[4]   See, *e.g.*, Pintens, *Liber Memorialis Petar Šarčević*, pp. 335-344.

Article 1(1)(b) stipulates that the Regulation applies also in civil matters relating to "the attribution, exercise, delegation, restriction or termination of parental responsibility". The concept of parental responsibility is defined very extensively in Article 2(7) as meaning all rights and duties relating to the person or the property of a child which are given to a natural or legal person by judgment, by operation of law or by an agreement having legal effect. A more detailed specification is found in Article 1(2), pursuant to which parental responsibility may, in particular, include matters dealing with rights of custody, rights of access, guardianship, curatorship and similar institutions, designation and functions of any person in charge of the child's person or property or representing or assisting the child, placement of the child in a foster family or in institutional care and protection of the child's property. An important limitation to be kept in mind when reading this list of partly overlapping matters is that the Regulation deals with civil matters only, so that, for example, the placement of a child in an institution is not included to the extent it constitutes a measure under administrative law. Matters such as the establishment of paternity, adoption, the name of the child, emancipation (a court decision declaring a minor to be legally competent as an adult), trusts, succession, and measures taken as a result of criminal offences committed by children are excluded as well (Article 1(3)). Disputes regarding maintenance obligations towards children also are excluded, as they are governed by the Brussels I Regulation.[5] On the other hand, the Brussels II Regulation applies to matters of parental responsibility with regard to all children, irrespective of whether they are born in or out of wedlock and whether the parental responsibility is based on biological parenthood or on adoption.

The term "court" is used in the Brussels II Regulation in a much more extensive sense than in the Brussels I Regulation. In Brussels II, the term "court" means any authority with jurisdiction in the above-mentioned matrimonial or parental matters (Article 2(1)). For example, Swedish welfare authorities, which are basically municipal administrative organs, must be considered "courts" when they are approving parental agreements on custody or access (visitation) rights. A similarly wide meaning is given also to the terms "judge" and "judgment" (Article 2(2 and 4)).

The Regulation in principle is intended to supersede earlier conventions between the Member States on the matters governed by the Regulation, although there are some exceptions (Articles 59-63). The Regulation does not apply in relation to Denmark (Article 2(3)).

---

5   See section 3.3.2 *supra*.

5.2 Marriage Dissolution

5.2.1 Jurisdiction

Article 3(1) enumerates several alternative connecting factors that serve as bases for jurisdiction in divorce, separation or annulment matters. They have equal standing, which means that they are not listed in any particular order of priority. They determine merely which Member State has jurisdiction, without deciding on the locally competent court there. Jurisdiction lies with the courts of the Member State where the spouses are habitually resident, *or* where the spouses were last habitually resident and one of them still resides, *or* where the respondent is habitually resident, *or* where either of the jointly applying spouses is habitually resident, *or* where the applicant is habitually resident if he resided there for at least a year immediately before the application was made, *or* where the applicant is habitually resident if he resided there for at least six months immediately before the application and is a local national, *or* where both spouses are nationals.[6] Furthermore, the court in which divorce, separation or annulment proceedings are pending also has jurisdiction to examine a counterclaim (Article 4), and a court that has given a judgment on a legal separation also has jurisdiction to convert that judgment into a divorce in accordance with the law of the forum (Article 5).

It is worth pointing out that the Regulation does not limit its application to EU citizens residing within the EU. It provides for jurisdiction even in relation to other parties, whenever the situation and the Member State of the forum are interconnected in a manner corresponding to at least one of the above-mentioned alternative jurisdictional grounds specified in the Regulation. For example, when Article 3(1) provides for divorce, separation or annulment jurisdiction of the Member State where the respondent is habitually resident, this includes even those cases where both spouses are nationals of a non-member state and the applicant habitually resides in a non-member state.

Pursuant to Article 6, the jurisdictional rules described above, to a large extent, are exclusive, because a spouse who is a habitual resident and/or a national of a Member State may be sued in another Member State only in accordance with those rules. Article 7 gives Member States some residual jurisdiction according to their own national jurisdictional rules, but this requires, in addition to the respondent being neither a national nor a habitual resident of any Member State, that the respondent cannot be sued in any Member State according to Articles 3-5. When exercising this residual jurisdiction and applying their national jurisdictional rules, the courts must treat applicants who are local habitual residents but citizens of another Member State as if they were local citizens

---

[6] As far as the UK and Ireland are concerned, nationality is replaced with their concept of "domicile", which lies in some respects closer to nationality than to habitual residence, see Article 3(2).

(Article 7(2)), which is of particular importance whenever the national jurisdictional rules give local citizens preferential treatment with regard to jurisdiction.

Most of the jurisdictional rules in Article 3 are based on the concept of habitual residence, which is not defined in the Regulation. It is possible that the concept of domicile, as defined in Article 59 of the Brussels I Regulation,[7] can be used by analogy for the interpretation of habitual residence in the Brussels II Regulation as well, although it also could be argued that habitual residence in the Brussels II Regulation should be given an autonomous interpretation of its own. In any case, it is clear that the term "domicile" in the special rules pertaining to the United Kingdom and Ireland (Articles 3(1)(b) and 3(2) of the Brussels II Regulation) has a meaning that differs from the meaning of domicile in the Brussels I Regulation, as well as from the habitual residence in the other provisions of the Brussels II Regulation.

The Regulation contains also some general jurisdictional provisions, such as rules about *lis pendens* and provisional measures (Articles 16-20), which are similar, albeit not identical, to the corresponding rules in the Brussels I Regulation. Provisional measures can hardly be used in divorce, separation and annulment proceedings and are intended only for disputes regarding parental responsibility.

It deserves to be mentioned that in July 2006 the Commission submitted a proposal for some changes in the jurisdictional rules described above.[8] In particular, it suggests that the parties be given a possibility to choose the competent court in proceedings relating to divorce and legal separation (not marriage annulment). This freedom of choice, however, will be confined to courts in countries with which the spouses have a close connection by virtue of any of the grounds of jurisdiction listed in Article 3, the last common habitual residence for a period of at least three years, or the nationality (in the case of the United Kingdom and Ireland, the "domicile") of one of the spouses.

5.2.2 Recognition

A divorce, separation or marriage annulment judgment given in a Member State is recognized for all purposes, including civil-status records and re-marriage, in the other Member States without the need of any special recognition procedure (Article 21). Whether the Member State producing the judgment actually had jurisdiction pursuant to the Regulation is not decisive for recognition.[9] Decisions as to the invalidity of a marriage, taken by Catholic

---

7 See section 3.3.1 *supra*.

8 See the Commission's proposal of 17 July 2006 for a Regulation Amending Regulation No 2201/2003 as regards Jurisdiction and Introducing Rules concerning Applicable Law in Matrimonial Matters, COM(2006)399 final.

9 An exception is made in Article 59(1)(d) for Finnish and Swedish judgments, due to these countries' wish to continue to apply in their mutual relations the Nordic Convention of 1931 comprising International Private Law Provisions on Marriage, Adoption and Guardianship in place of the Regulation.

ecclesiastical authorities under treaties concluded by the Holy See (the Vatican) with some Member States (Italy, Malta, Portugal and Spain), are also recognized in all Member States in accordance with Article 63.[10]

The issue of recognition of a marriage dissolution is normally raised as an incidental or preliminary question in connection with such matters as the right to re-marry, maintenance, inheritance or division of matrimonial property, but any interested party may apply for a generally binding, independent decision confirming for all purposes that the judgment is or is not recognized (Article 21(3-4)).

Recognition will be refused, pursuant to Article 22, if it would be manifestly contrary to the public policy (*ordre public*) of the Member State where recognition is sought, *or* if the judgment was given in default of appearance and the respondent had not been served documents in sufficient time and in a satisfactory way (unless he has accepted the judgment unequivocally, for example, by re-marrying), *or* if the judgment is irreconcilable with a local judgment or an earlier judgment given in a third state but recognized in the Member State where recognition is sought.

The test of public policy is limited in two important respects. First, it must not be applied to the jurisdiction of the court of origin (Article 24) and, secondly, the recognition must not be refused merely because the divorce, separation or annulment would not be allowed in a corresponding case by the law of the Member State where recognition is sought (Article 25). This means that Malta, which is at present the only Member State not permitting divorce, must not refuse to recognize a Swedish divorce granted on the basis of a simple request by the spouses, whereas Sweden must recognize Maltese legal separations although such separations do not exist in the Swedish legal system. The Regulation, however, does not provide any guidance as to the legal effects to be given to, for example, a recognized legal separation when the matrimonial property regime, maintenance or inheritance is governed by a legal system which does not have any rules on such separation or any other corresponding legal phenomenon.

5.3 Parental Responsibility

5.3.1 Jurisdiction

The principal ground for jurisdiction in matters of parental responsibility is the habitual residence of the child in the Member State of the forum (Article 8). It is irrelevant whether the child is a national of a Member State, a third country or even stateless.

There are some exceptions though. If a child moves lawfully from one Member State to another, the courts of the country of the child's former habitual

---

[10] As amended by Regulation No 2116/2004 of 2 December 2004, OJ 2004 L 367 p. 1.

residence retain, for a period of three months, jurisdiction to modify a judgment on access rights issued there before the move, provided that the holder of access rights continues to reside in that country (Article 9). The holder of access rights thus has the possibility to obtain, in his own country of residence, a decision adapting his access rights to the new circumstances after the child has been moved to another Member State. Such adaptation, for example, may result in less frequent but longer access periods. Article 9 restricts to some extent the possibilities of the parent having sole custody (and consequently in principle authorized to move the child) to avoid jurisdiction of the country of the child's habitual residence regarding access rights by moving the child to another Member State. This does not apply, however, if the access-rights holder chooses to participate in proceedings before the courts of the country of the child's new habitual residence, irrespective of whether he initiated such proceedings himself or participates as defendant without contesting the jurisdiction of those courts.

In accordance with Article 12, which bears the somewhat misleading heading "Prorogation of Jurisdiction", the courts of a Member State have jurisdiction regarding parental responsibility also in some other situations, such as in connection with divorce, separation or annulment proceedings initiated by virtue of Article 3, or even in other proceedings (such as a paternity litigation) where the child has a substantial connection with the forum state. This requires that the jurisdiction be accepted expressly or otherwise unequivocally by all the parties and is in the interest of the child. Article 12(4) stipulates that when the child resides habitually in a third state which is not a party to the 1996 Hague Convention on Jurisdiction, Applicable Law, Recognition, Enforcement and Cooperation in respect of Parental Responsibility and Measures for the Protection of Children, then jurisdiction of a Member State under Article 12 is in the child's interest, "in particular if it is found impossible to hold proceedings in the third state in question". Regarding the requirement of a substantial connection between the child and the Member State of the forum, Article 12(3) provides that such connection can be deemed to exist in particular when one of the holders of parental responsibility is habitually resident in that Member State or when the child is a citizen of that Member State.

The mere presence of the child is sufficient for jurisdiction according to Article 13, but only if the child's habitual residence cannot be ascertained and no jurisdiction can be determined based on Article 12. This applies also to children that are refugees or internationally displaced. Further, if no Member State has jurisdiction pursuant to Articles 8-13, the Regulation permits residual jurisdiction on the basis of the national jurisdictional rules of the forum (Article 14).

Article 15 creates a system making it possible to transfer, by way of exception, parental responsibility disputes from the courts of a Member State having jurisdiction by virtue of the Regulation to another Member State whose courts are better placed to hear the case, provided that the child has a particular connection with the latter state and the transfer is in the best interests of the child. The

requirement of the child's particular connection with a Member State is considered met if that state is the present or former habitual residence of the child, the
country of the child's nationality, the habitual residence of a holder of parental
responsibility, or – if the case concerns the protection of the child's property
– the place where that property is located. The transfer, which must not take
place if *all* parties oppose it, can be requested by a party or be decided upon the
court's own initiative or upon the application from a court of another Member
State with which the child has a particular connection as defined above. The
transferring court must set a time limit by which the court of the other Member
State has to be seized, and it will continue to exercise jurisdiction unless the
latter court accepts within six weeks of being seized to take on the case. This
possibility of transferring the proceedings to a foreign court, which is better
placed to hear the case, is reminiscent of the doctrine of *forum non conveniens*,
which is normally not adhered to on the European Continent and is not accepted
in the context of the Brussels I Regulation.[11]

The general jurisdictional provisions in Articles 16-20 (*lis pendens, etc.*) apply
in matters of parental responsibility as well.

In Articles 10 and 11, the Regulation contains some special jurisdictional
rules regarding cases of child abduction, which is defined as the wrongful
removal or retention of a child. In order to be considered wrongful, the removal
or retention must be in breach of the rights of custody in the Member State
where the child was habitually resident immediately before the removal or
retention, and those rights actually must have been exercised, jointly or alone,
or would have been exercised if the abduction had not taken place (Article 2(11)).
Joint exercise of custody rights includes all those situations where one holder of
parental responsibility is not authorized to decide on the child's place of residence without the consent of the other.

The main idea behind the rather complicated rules in Article 10 on jurisdiction in cases of child abduction is that the courts of the country of origin should
retain their jurisdiction for the time needed by the deprived parent to obtain
the return of the child on the basis of the 1980 Hague Convention on the Civil
Aspects of International Child Abduction. The retention of jurisdiction by the
courts of the country of origin persists until the child has acquired habitual residence in another Member State *and* certain additional conditions are fulfilled;
namely, *either* that each person having custody acquiesces in the removal or
retention *or* that the child has resided in that other Member State for at least
one year after the person(s) having custody found out or should have found
out about its whereabouts and the child has become settled in its new environment and at least one of the following further conditions is met: a request for
the return of the child has not been timely lodged or has been withdrawn or the
custody proceedings in the country where the child resided before the abduction have been closed in accordance with Article 11(7) due to the passivity on the

---

[11]   See section 3.3.1 *supra*.

part of the deprived parent (see *infra*) or have resulted in a custody judgment not requiring the return of the child.

The relatively detailed rules about the return of abducted children in Article 11 aim at making the 1980 Hague Convention more efficient and expeditious, for example, by imposing short time limits on the courts in the requested Member State (except under exceptional circumstances, the judgment must be made within six weeks after the application) and by further restricting their possibilities to refuse to return the child. Thus, the return of the child cannot be refused on the basis of Article 13(b) of the Hague Convention (grave risk that the return would expose the child to physical or psychological harm or otherwise place the child in an intolerable situation), if it is established that adequate arrangements have been made to secure the protection of the child after its return, such as a placement in a foster home. Another addition to the rules of the Hague Convention is that the return of the child cannot be refused unless the person requesting it has been given an opportunity to be heard. The abducted child also must be given the opportunity to be heard during the proceedings, unless it would be inappropriate in regard to the child's age or degree of maturity.

The most important novelty regarding the return of abducted children is found in Article 11(6-8) of the Regulation. If a court in the requested Member State decides, on the basis of Article 13 of the Hague Convention, that the child shall not be returned, the decision and other relevant documentation must immediately, directly or through a central authority, be forwarded to the competent court of the Member State from which the child has been abducted. This court has to receive the documentation within one month of the date of the non-return order. The court or the central authority must, in turn, notify the parties and invite them to make submissions, for example, to initiate custody proceedings if such proceedings are not pending already. If no submissions are received within three months of the date of notification, the court will close the case (Article 11(7)), which means that the child may remain in the Member State to which it has been abducted. If the case is not closed and the proceedings result in a judgment requiring the return of the child, this judgment will be recognized and enforceable in other Member States, including the country to which the child has been abducted, normally without any declaration of enforceability and without any possibility of opposing its recognition (see Articles 40 and 42), notwithstanding that the courts there have previously decided that the child should not be returned. This means that the courts in the Member State where the child was habitually resident immediately before the abduction have the final say in the matter. The system obviously is based on a very high degree of trust and confidence between the Member States, and it seems that it probably will put an end to cross-border child abductions within the EU.

5.3.2   Recognition and Enforcement

In contrast to divorces, separations and annulments, some judgments regarding parental responsibility, in particular judgments on custody and access rights, are capable of being not only recognized but also of being enforced.

The rules on the recognition of judgments concerning parental responsibility (Articles 21-27) are the same as or similar to the rules on the recognition of divorces, separations and annulments, although in Article 23 there are some additional grounds for refusing recognition, for example, that the judgment was made without the child having been given an opportunity to be heard as required by fundamental principles of procedure in the Member State in which recognition is sought, or that the judgment was made without an opportunity to be heard having been given to a person claiming that the judgment infringes his parental responsibility. Irreconcilability with another judgment, strangely enough, is accepted as a ground for refusal only if that other judgment deals with parental responsibility, which seems to mean, for example, that a custody or access judgment made in another Member State in principle must be recognized even if it is irreconcilable with a local adoption or a paternity decision pursuant to which the person relying on the foreign judgment is not related to child at all (adoption and paternity judgments do not seem to deal with parental responsibility as defined in Art. 1 of the Regulation). It is possible that a solution to this problem has to be sought in the public policy exception. If the decision involves the placement of a child in institutional care or with a foster family in another Member State, it will not be recognized there unless the special procedure laid down in Article 56 has been complied with, which normally means that the central authority of the requested Member State, designated pursuant to Article 53, must have consented to such placement.[12]

A judgment given in another Member State must not be reviewed as to its substance (Article 26), but this does not prohibit a new judgment making changes in parental responsibility due to changed circumstances, at least to the extent that such changes are permitted under the law of the Member State of the origin of the judgment.

While recognition requires no special procedure, the enforcement of a judgment on the exercise of parental responsibility only can take place after the judgment has been declared enforceable in the Member State where it is to be enforced (Article 28). It is not necessary that the judgment has become final in its country of origin, provided it is enforceable there. The procedure for obtaining exequatur (Articles 30-36) reminds one of the corresponding procedure under the Brussels I Regulation, but there are some differences. One such difference is that the Brussels II Regulation does not suspend the actual enforcement during the time specified for an appeal against the exequatur decision and until

---

[12]   See section 5.3.3 *infra*.

any such appeal has been determined.[13] It seems, however, that the Member State where enforcement is sought has the possibility to impose this type of suspension by its national law, as both the procedure for applying for exequatur and the enforcement itself are governed by the law of the Member State where the enforcement is to take place (Articles 30(1) and 47)).

According to Article 48, the courts of the Member State where a judgment on the right of access is to be enforced may make practical arrangements for organizing the exercise of that right, if such arrangements are necessary but have not been provided for sufficiently in the judgment itself. The essential elements of the judgment, however, must be respected. For example, the enforcement of a foreign judgment on a parent's access rights has to abide by the judgment's instructions that the access can only be exercised in the presence of a third person or under the condition that the parent in question deposits his passport or provides a financial guarantee. Enforcement is not precluded by the mere fact that the judgment grants an access right of a type that is not known in the Member State where the enforcement is to take place, for example, the right of a parent to speak to the child on the phone or chat with the child on the Internet at certain specified points in time.

Two types of judgments under certain circumstances are enforceable even without exequatur, namely judgments on the right of access (Article 41) and some judgments on the return of an abducted child (Article 42). Such decisions are recognized and enforceable in another Member State without the need for a declaration of enforceability and without any possibility of opposing recognition. This requires, however, that the judge who delivered the judgment has issued a special certificate on the appropriate standard form attached to the Regulation (Annexes III and IV), attesting that certain conditions have been complied with, such as that the parties concerned and the child have been given an opportunity to be heard. In addition, if the judgment is on the right of access and was given in default, the certificate can be issued only if the person defaulting either accepted the decision unequivocally or had been served with the document which instituted the proceedings in sufficient time and in such a way as to enable that person to arrange for his defense. If the judgment is on the return of an abducted child, the certificate can only be issued under the additional condition that the court has taken into account the reasons for and evidence underlying the non-return order made pursuant to Article 13 of the Hague Convention of 1980.[14]

Authentic instruments and agreements between the parties, which are enforceable in the Member State of origin, both are recognized and declared enforceable under the same conditions as judgments (Article 46). This is an important difference in comparison with the corresponding provision in the

---

[13]   Cf. Article 47(3) of the Brussels I Regulation.

[14]   Cf. section 5.3.1 *supra* on Article 11(6-8) of the Regulation.

Brussels I Regulation,[15] which only speaks of enforceability of such instruments and agreements, not of their recognition.

5.3.3   Cooperation between Central Authorities

In addition to provisions on jurisdiction and recognition/ enforcement, the Brussels II Regulation contains a special chapter on cooperation between central authorities of the Member States in matters of parental responsibility (Articles 53-58). According to these rules, each Member State shall designate one or more central authorities to assist with the application of the Regulation, for example, by communicating information on national laws and procedures, collecting and exchanging information on specific cases, assisting holders of parental responsibility in obtaining recognition and enforcement of decisions, facilitating mediation between such holders, and providing information and assistance pertaining to cross-border placement of children. A request for assistance, which is free of charge, can be submitted by any holder of parental responsibility to the central authority of the Member State of his or the child's habitual residence.

In particular, Article 56 states that where a court in a Member State contemplates the placement of a child in institutional care or with a foster family in another Member State whose law requires some form of public intervention for domestic cases of child placement, it must consult the central authority or other authority having jurisdiction in the latter Member State, and the placement must not be ordered unless the competent authority in the requested Member State consents to it. If the law of the Member State where the child is to be placed requires no public intervention for domestic placements, the central authority there at least must be informed about the placement decision. If the procedure laid down in Article 56 has not been complied with, the placement decision will not be recognized.[16]

---

[15]   Cf. section 3.4 *supra* about Articles 57 and 58 of the Brussels I Regulation.

[16]   See Article 23(g) and section 5.3.2 *supra*.

CHAPTER 6

Some Other EC Instruments on Jurisdiction

Scattered and fragmentary provisions on jurisdiction of courts and recognition and enforcement of judgments are found in some other EC instruments. In contrast to the Brussels Regulations I and II, most of these instruments are binding even for and in relation to Denmark, due to the fact that their legal basis is found in other provisions of the EC Treaty than its Title IV.

Some of these instruments deal with disputes concerning industrial or intellectual property, for example, Regulation No 40/94 of 20 December 1993 on the Community Trade Mark,[1] whose Articles 90, 93 and 94 stipulate that the Brussels/Lugano rules apply with certain modifications to proceedings relating to Community trade marks. Other relevant jurisdictional provisions can be found, for example, in Articles 101 and 102 of Regulation No 2100/94 of 27 July 1994 on Community Plant Variety Rights[2] and in Articles 79, 82 and 83 of Regulation No 6/2002 of 12 December 2001 on Community Designs[3].

Another example is Articles 5 and 6 of Directive No 96/71 of 16 December 1996, concerning the Posting of Workers in the Framework of the Provision of Services,[4] requiring the Member States to ensure that adequate procedures are available to workers for the enforcement of their rights under the Directive. In particular, the workers may institute judicial proceedings in the Member State where they are or have been posted (Article 6), but this does not deprive them of their right to institute such proceedings in another Member State having jurisdiction pursuant to the Brussels/Lugano rules.

Regulation No 2271/96 of 22 November 1996, protecting against the Effects of the Extra-territorial Application of Legislation Adopted by a Third Country and Actions Based Thereon or Resulting Therefrom,[5] is intended to counteract the effects of the extra-territorial application of certain foreign legislation, such as embargos imposed by the USA, affecting the activities of natural and legal persons in the Member States. Article 6 of the Regulation provides that proceedings for compensation for damage caused by such extra-territorial application can be instituted at a court having jurisdiction on the basis of the Brussels jurisdictional rules, as well as in the courts of any Member State where the defendant holds assets. Jurisdiction based on the presence of the defendant's assets, normally forbidden by the Brussels/Lugano rules, thus is made available in these cases, irrespective of whether it is accepted in the national jurisdictional rules of the Member State of the forum.

Directive No 98/27 of 19 May 1998 on Injunctions for the Protection of Consumers' Interests[6] also deserves to be mentioned. A number of EC directives

---

[1]   OJ 1994 L 11 p. 1.

[2]   OJ 1994 L 227 p. 1.

[3]   OJ 2002 L 3 p. 1.

[4]   See OJ 1997 L 18 p. 1 and section 9.1 *infra*.

[5]   OJ 1996 L 309 p. 1.

[6]   OJ 1998 L 166 p. 51. See Bogdan, [1998] *Consumer L.J.* 369-375.

contain provisions intended to protect the collective interests of consumers,[7] for example, by obliging the Member States to forbid the use of misleading advertising or unfair terms in consumer contracts. These provisions do not regulate contractual relationships between an individual consumer and an individual undertaking, but rather deal with restraining orders and financial sanctions (fines) against misbehaving enterprises in the interest of consumers in general. Nevertheless, to the extent the matter can be classified as civil or commercial, the jurisdiction of courts and the recognition and enforcement of judgments is governed by the Brussels I Regulation.[8] As the infringement normally originates in the Member State where the infringing enterprise is domiciled and/or from which it acts, this usually leads to the result that the courts of that state have jurisdiction on the basis of Articles 2 or 5(3) of the Brussels I Regulation, whereas the courts of the affected market also have jurisdiction pursuant to the same Regulation's Article 5(3).[9] Another effect of the Brussels rules is that the resulting injunction is recognized and enforceable in all Member States. However, in some Member States the measures taken against infringements of collective consumer interests are mainly of public-law nature, for example, in Sweden where the proceedings normally are initiated by the Consumer Ombudsman (a state instrumentality) and the resulting fines are paid to the state treasury. This probably makes the Brussels rules inapplicable. A Swedish

---

[7] See Directive No 84/450 of 10 September 1984 relating to the Approximation of the Laws, Regulations and Administrative Provisions of the Member States concerning Misleading Advertising, OJ 1984 L 250 p. 17; Directive No 85/577 of 20 December 1985 to Protect the Consumer in respect of Contracts Negotiated Away from Business Premises, OJ 1985 L 372 p. 31; Directive No 87/102 of 22 December 1986 for the Approximation of the Laws, Regulations and Administrative Provisions of the Member States concerning Consumer Credit, OJ 1987 L 42 p. 48 (as amended); Directive No 89/552 of 3 October 1989 on the Coordination of Certain Provisions Laid down by Law, Regulation or Administrative Action in Member States concerning the Pursuit of Television Broadcasting Activities, OJ 1989 L 298 p. 23 (as amended); Directive No 90/314 of 13 June 1990 on Package Travel, Package Holidays and Package Tours, OJ 1990 L 158 p. 59; Directive No 92/28 of 31 March 1992 on the Advertising of Medicinal Products for Human Use, OJ 1992 L 113 p. 13; Directive No 93/13 of 5 April 1993 on Unfair Terms in Consumer Contracts, OJ 1993 L 95 p. 29; Directive No 94/47 of 26 October 1994 on the Protection of Purchasers in respect of Certain Aspects of Contracts relating to the Purchase of the Right to Use Immovable Properties on a Timeshare Basis, OJ 1994 L 280 p. 83; Directive No 97/7 of 20 May 1997 on the Protection of Consumers in respect of Distance Contracts, OJ 1997 L 144 p. 19; Directive No 1999/44 of 25 May 1999 on Certain Aspects of the Sale of Consumer Goods and Associated Guarantees, OJ 1999 L 171 p. 12; Directive No 2000/31 of 8 June 2000 on Certain Legal Aspects of Information Society Services, in particular Electronic Commerce, on the Internal Market, OJ 2000 L 178 p. 1; Directive 2002/65 of 23 September 2002 concerning the Distance Marketing of Consumer Financial Services, OJ 2002 L 271 p. 16; Directive 2005/29 of 11 May 2005 concerning Unfair Business-to-consumer Commercial Practices in the Internal Market, OJ 2005 L 149 p. 22.

[8] See Chapter 3 *supra*.

[9] *Verein für Konsumenteninformation* v. *Henkel*, case C-167/00, [2002] ECR I-8111.

injunction consequently at present is probably not recognized and enforced in the home country of the enterprise,[10] which makes it essential that the courts of that country consider themselves to have jurisdiction to deal with the Swedish Consumer Ombudsman's action. This is where Directive No 98/27 steps in. It does not provide for the recognition and enforcement of foreign injunctions and similar measures; it rather focuses on extending the jurisdiction of the Member State of the infringing behaviour's origin and making it encompass even that behaviour's adverse effects in consumer markets in the other Member States.

Pursuant to Article 4(1) of the Directive, each Member State is obliged to take the measures necessary to ensure that, in the event of an alleged infringement originating in that Member State, any qualified entity from another Member State affected by that infringement can bring proceedings against the enterprise in question. According to Article 2(1), each Member State also must designate those of its courts or administrative authorities that are competent to rule on and take measures against infringements originating in the country. The action may be brought by a "qualified entity", which may be, for example, an independent public body such as the Swedish Consumer Ombudsman or an organization whose purpose is to protect collective consumer interests in accordance with the criteria laid down by its national law (Article 3). Each Member State communicates, upon the request of its qualified entities, their name and their purpose to the Commission (Article 4(2)), which publishes the list of such qualified entities in the Official Journal of the European Union (Article 4(3)).

The Directive does not make the jurisdiction of the Member State where the infringement originates exclusive and does not restrict in any way the jurisdiction of the Member States affected by the infringement. Furthermore, the Directive does not contain any conflict rule determining the national substantive law, which should be applied to the infringement. On the contrary, Article 2(2) stipulates explicitly that the Directive is without prejudice to the rules of private international law, "thus leading normally to the application of either the law of the Member State where the infringement originated or the law of the Member State where the infringement has its effects". This formulation is so weak that it actually imposes no restrictions whatsoever on the conflict rules of the Member States. The Rome Convention on the Law Applicable to Contractual Obligations of 1980[11] cannot be used, since it only covers contractual obligations such as those between an individual consumer and an individual undertaking.

---

[10] However, financial penalties imposed by a Member State due to offences committed by violating obligations arising from an instrument adopted under the EC Treaty, including penalties for violations of national laws implementing EC directives on consumer protection, in the future normally will be recognized and enforced in the other Member States pursuant to Council Framework Decision No 2005/214/JHA of 24 February 2005 on the Application of the Principle of Mutual Recognition to Financial Penalties, OJ 2005 L 76 p. 16. The Member States are obliged to comply with this Framework Decision by 22 March 2007.

[11] See Chapter 7 *infra*.

However, the proposed Rome II Regulation, dealing with the law applicable to non-contractual obligations, seems to apply to some of the situations where a consumer organization demands an injunction or claims damages as the result of the defendant's fraudulent advertising, his use of unfair contract terms, *etc.*[12] A special directive applies in the field of electronic commerce.[13]

There is also a Regulation[14] dealing with the cooperation, in matters concerning intra-Community infringements, between the competent authorities in the Member States designated as responsible for the enforcement of the laws that protect consumers' interests. Article 2 of this Regulation states expressly that the Regulation does not affect the Community rules on PIL, in particular, rules related to court jurisdiction and applicable law. The same Article provides also that the Regulation is without prejudice to Directive 98/27 described above. The Regulation makes it possible for a Member State to request assistance of the authorities of another Member State, including measures to be initiated in accordance with Directive 98/27, in order to bring about the cessation or prohibition of intra-Community infringements in a proportionate, efficient and effective way.

---

[12] See Chapter 8 *infra.*

[13] See section 9.2 *infra.*

[14] See Regulation No 2006/2004 of 27 October 2004 on Cooperation between National Authorities Responsible for the Enforcement of Consumer Protection Laws, OJ 2004 L 364 p. 1.

CHAPTER 7

The Rome Convention

7.1 The Scope and Other General Features of the Convention

In the PIL of most of the EU Member States, the most important conflict rules regarding contracts are found in the Convention on the Law Applicable to Contractual Obligations, opened for signature in Rome on 19 June 1980 and commonly called the Rome Convention or Rome I Convention.[1] The Convention entered into force in 1991 after having been ratified by seven Member States (in this context denoted Contracting States). Since then, it was joined by all of the remaining pre-2004 Member States. A convention on the accession of the ten new (2004) Member States to the Rome Convention was signed in April 2005 and is expected to be effective relatively soon,[2] although the process has started to convert the Rome Convention into an EC Regulation (Rome I Regulation).[3]

One of the principal purposes of the Convention is to neutralize, at least to some extent, the effects of the forum shopping made possible by the Brussels rules on jurisdiction and recognition and enforcement of judgments,[4] as the advantages of a tactical choice of court are diminished when the choice is between courts using the same conflict rules.

The text of the Convention has been drawn in the official languages of all of the Contracting States and all of the linguistic versions are, at least in theory, equally authentic. The interpretation of an international instrument, which exists in so many equally authentic linguistic versions, may be problematic. Pursuant to Article 18, the interpretation and application of the Convention has to be done having regard to its international character and to the desirability of achieving uniformity. Even though the Convention as such is not part of EC law in the strict sense, by virtue of special protocols it is subject to the authoritative interpretation by the ECJ.[5] The provisions on the ECJ's authority to interpret the Convention entered into force on as late as 1 August 2004 and have not led to any judgments so far, but there is a certain amount of case law emanating from the national courts of the Contracting States. There is also a great amount of legal writing about the Convention. Of particular importance for the interpretation is the semi-official report written by professors Mario Giuliano and Paul

---

[1] The most recent consolidated wording of the Convention is found in OJ 2005 C 334 p. 1.

[2] The text of the Convention on the accession of the new Member States to the Rome Convention is found in OJ 2005 C 169 p. 1.

[3] See the Commission's proposal in COM(2005)650 final and section 7.7 *infra*.

[4] See Chapter 3 *supra*.

[5] OJ 1998 C 27 pp. 47 and 52. It is noteworthy that the Convention is not an instrument of EC law of the type referred to in Article 68(1) of the EC Treaty and that preliminary rulings of the ECJ on the interpretation of the Convention pursuant to the protocols can be requested not only by courts against whose decisions there is no judicial remedy under national law, but even by other courts of the Contracting States when acting as appellate courts.

Lagarde, published in 1980 in the Official Journal of the European Communities.[6]

The Convention, according to its Article 1(1), applies in the courts of the Contracting States whenever a choice between the laws of different countries has to be made with regard to contractual obligations, *i.e.* whenever it has to be decided which law(s) shall be applied to a particular contractual issue. The term "countries" denotes in this context even territorial units other than states, provided they have legal systems of their own, such as Scotland as opposed to England and Wales (Article 19), although the courts in such units are not bound to apply the Convention to conflicts between the laws of the different units within their own state. This means, for example, that a conflict between Danish law and the law of the Faroe Islands shall be solved by Swedish courts applying the Convention, whereas Denmark is free to decide that its courts will solve the same problem pursuant to some other conflict rules. However, the Convention does not prohibit Denmark from using the Convention on a voluntary basis even for such internal conflicts of law, and Denmark in fact has chosen to do so.[7]

The Convention applies in principle even to contracts that do not have international character, *i.e.*, those contracts where all elements are connected with one single country only, regardless of whether that is a foreign country or the country of the forum. Even such single-country contracts sometimes can make it necessary for the court to address issues of applicable law, for example, if one of the parties to a purely domestic Mexican contract moves subsequently to Germany and is sued by the other party in a German court for a claim based on that contract. The determination of the law applicable to a single-country contract might seem to be a very simple task, as all connecting factors point to the same legal system, so that it is actually irrelevant which connecting factor is deemed to be decisive. However, the issue of the applicable legal system becomes somewhat problematic if the parties to a single-country contract have agreed on the application of the law of another country.[8]

In contrast to the Brussels I and Brussels II Regulations, which divide jurisdiction between Member States only and deal only with the recognition and

---

[6] OJ 1980 C 282 p. 1. See also, for example, Bogdan, *TfR* 1982 pp. 1-49; Czernich & Heiss, *Das Europäische Schuldvertragsübereinkommen*; B. Dutoit in von Hoffmann (ed.), *European Private International Law*, pp. 39-65; Fletcher, *Conflict*, pp. 147-185; Foyer, *Clunet* 1991 pp. 601-631; Gaudemet-Tallon, *Rev.trim.dr.eur.* 1981 pp. 215-285; Juenger, *RabelsZ* 1982 pp. 57-83; Junker, *RabelsZ* 1991 pp. 674-696; Kassis, *Le nouveau droit*; Kaye, *The New Private International Law*; Lagarde, *Rev.crit.d.i.p.* 1991 pp. 287-340; Lando, 24 C.M.L.R. 159-214 (1987); Martiny, *ZEuP* 1993 pp. 298-305, 1999 pp. 246-270, 2001 pp. 308-328 and 2003 pp. 590-628; Pålsson, *Romkonventionen*; Plender & Wilderspin, *The European Contracts Convention*; Rammeloo, *Das neue EG-Vertragskollisionsrecht*; Reithmann & Martiny (eds.), *Internationales Vetragsrecht*; Rozehnalová & Týč, *Evropský justiční prostor*, pp. 29-166; Strömholm, *Upphovsrätt*, pp. 303-361; Villani, *La Convenzione*.

[7] See Philip, *EU-IP*, pp. 130-131.

[8] See Article 3(3) and section 7.2 *infra*.

enforcement of judgments given in a Member State, the conflict rules in the Rome Convention apply, without any requirement of reciprocity, in relation to every legal system in the world, regardless of whether it is the law of a Contracting State or not (Article 2). The territorial limits of the scope of the Convention thus are of importance merely for deciding whether the courts of the forum country are obliged to apply the Convention (*i.e.*, whether the forum country is a Contracting State), but not for deciding whether the Convention must be applied in relation to a particular foreign legal system. Within the scope of application of its rules, the Convention is comprehensive and does not leave any residual space for autonomous national conflict rules of the Contracting States.

As many cross-border commercial disputes are adjudicated by arbitrators, it is important to note that these are not bound formally to abide by the Convention's rules, as an arbitral tribunal is not an organ of any of the Contracting States. However, it is not unusual that the tribunal, often composed of arbitrators from different countries, decides to follow the conflict rules of the country where it has its seat, in which case the Convention's rules become applicable when the arbitral tribunal carries out its work in a Contracting State. It also happens that arbitrators decide to apply the "most appropriate" legal system and use the Rome Convention as a source of inspiration and an authoritative codification of what is deemed appropriate in modern European PIL.

The Convention contains no definition of "contractual obligation", but it appears that an extensive interpretation of this concept is intended, including one-sided obligations such as suretyship or donation. Delimitation problems can, nevertheless, arise in relation to non-contractual obligations[9] and the effects of a contract *vis-à-vis* third parties, such as the creditors (the contract's effects *in rem*).

Some contract-related questions and some types of contractual obligations, furthermore, are excluded from the scope of the Convention by its Article 1(2).[10] To begin with, the exclusion applies to questions involving the status or legal capacity of natural persons (with the exception of Article 11[11]), obligations arising out of a matrimonial property relationship or other family relationships, wills and successions (Article 1(2)(a-b)).[12] This means, for example, that agreements

---

[9]   It is probable, but far from certain, that this delimitation will follow the existing case law of the ECJ regarding Articles 5(1) and 5(3) of the Brussels I Regulation, see section 3.3.2 *supra*. See also Pålsson, *Romkonventionen*, pp. 32-33; M. Pertegás in Meeusen, Pertegás & Straetmans (eds.), *Enforcement*, pp. 175-190; Philip, *EU-IP*, pp. 128-129.

[10] See, for example, Kassis, *Le nouveau droit*, pp. 483-490; Lasok & Stone, *Conflict*, pp. 348-355; Nielsen, *International privat- og procesret*, pp. 491-494; Pålsson, *Romkonventionen*, pp. 34-37; Philip, *EU-IP*, pp. 133-135; Plender & Wilderspin, *The European Contracts Convention*, pp. 59-84; Rozehnalová & Týč, *Evropský justiční prostor*, pp. 46-53;

[11] See section 7.6 *infra*.

[12] It should be noted that the family-law exception in the Rome Convention is similar, but not identical, to the corresponding exception in the Brussels I Regulation. See section 3.2 *supra* and M. Bogdan in Meeusen, Pertegás & Straetmans (eds.), *Enforcement*, pp. 211-223.

concerning the marital property regime (including pre-nuptial agreements and agreements on the division of matrimonial property after the dissolution of the marriage), agreements on custody or parental access rights, and agreements dividing an inheritance are excluded. An agreement on payment of maintenance is beyond the scope of the Convention if it relates to a maintenance obligation based on family ties, whereas it is within that scope if pertains to maintenance payments to a former employee or voluntary maintenance payments to a distant relative. A contract of sale between a husband and wife is excluded to the extent that it is subject to special provisions of family law, but not with regard to the usual issues of the law on sales, such as a dispute about the quality of the object sold, *etc.*

Among the other exclusions, the obligations arising out of the negotiable character of bills of exchange, checks, promissory notes and other negotiable instruments deserve a special mention (Article 1(2)(c)). Negotiability means that a proper transfer of the instrument to a person acting in good faith passes a good title to the property or value represented by the instrument, whatever the title of the transferor may have been. As far as bills of exchange and checks are concerned, conflict rules are found in two Geneva Conventions from 1930 and 1931, which have been ratified by many, albeit not all, of the EC Member States. The underlying transaction, for example, a contract of sale stipulating that payment has to be made by a bill of exchange, is not excluded from the scope of the Rome Convention.

Arbitration agreements and agreements on the choice of court are excluded by Article 1(2)(d) irrespective of whether they are embodied in separate instruments or mere clauses within a larger contract. The validity and effects of such agreements are regulated partly by the New York Convention on the Recognition and Enforcement of Foreign Arbitral Awards of 1958 and by Article 23 of the Regulation Brussels I.[13]

Questions governed by company law, such as the creation, legal capacity, internal organization and winding up of companies and other similar entities, as well as the personal liability of their directors and members, are excluded pursuant to Article 1(2)(e), while other company-related agreements (for example, contracts on the sale of shares or contracts between future shareholders on the founding of a company) are not excluded, unless the matter concerns some issues very intimately connected with company law, such as the question of whether the company's shares are transferable.

The authority of agents to bind their principals, which is of great importance for the validity of many commercial contracts, is excluded by Article 1(2)(f) and so is the authority of an organ of a company or other entity to represent it *vis-à-vis* third parties. Questions regarding the constitution of trusts and the

---

[13] See section 3.3.5 *supra.*

relationship between settlors, trustees and beneficiaries of a trust are excluded by Article 1(2)(g).[14]

According to Article 1(2)(h), questions regarding evidence and procedure, with the exception of special presumptions of law and rules on the burden of proof stipulated in contract law (see Article 14), in principle are excluded also. Pursuant to Article 1(3), the same is true of contracts of insurance covering risks situated within the EC Member States. Whether a risk is situated within the EC is decided by application of the internal law of the Contracting State of the forum. The gap created by the exclusion of insurance contracts is largely filled by the special EC directives in the insurance field.[15] The exclusion of insurance contracts does not apply to contracts of re-insurance.

The Convention contains a couple of articles dealing with some of the general problems of PIL, in particular on the exclusion of *renvoi* (Article 15) and on the non-application of foreign law when its application *in casu* would be manifestly incompatible with the public policy (*ordre public*) of the forum (Article 16). The non-acceptance of *renvoi*, expressed by the stipulation that the application of the law of any country specified by the Convention means the application of the rules of law in force in that country other than its rules of PIL, makes no real difference when the applicable law is that of another Contracting State, as the relevant conflict rules in that state are in principle the same as those in the Contracting State of the forum.

Even though the Convention is silent on this point, it can be assumed that, with the possible exception of Article 7,[16] it deals in principle with private-law matters only and does not prescribe the application of purely public-law provisions, such as exchange regulations or trade embargoes.[17] The matter is

---

[14] Article 1(2)(g) covers not merely traditional trusts as known in the legal systems of the common-law world, but also similar institutions under continental laws exhibiting the same characteristics. Certain guidance can be found in Article 2 of the 1985 Hague Convention on the Law Applicable to Trusts and on their Recognition, where "trust" is defined as the legal relationship created – *inter vivos* or on death – by a person, the settlor, when assets have been placed under the control of a trustee for the benefit of a beneficiary or for a specified purpose. According to the same Article 2, the characteristic features of a trust are that the assets constitute a separate fund and are not a part of the trustee's own estate, the title to the trust assets stands in the name of the trustee or in the name of another person on behalf of the trustee, and the trustee has the power and the duty, in respect of which he is accountable, to manage, employ or dispose of the assets in accordance with the terms of the trust and the special duties imposed upon him by law.

[15] See section 9.1 *infra*. As the application of these insurance directives is extended to the whole EEA (European Economic Area, including not only the EC but also Iceland, Norway and Liechtenstein), it seems reasonable to interpret Article 1(3) of the Rome Convention to exclude even contracts of insurance covering risks situated in these three countries.

[16] See section 7.5 *infra*.

[17] See, for example, Kassis, *Le nouveau droit*, p. 460; Nielsen, *International privat- og procesret*, p. 540; Pålsson, *Romkonventionen*, pp. 109-113; Philip, *EU-IP*, pp. 176-177.

disputed but it is submitted that it hardly would be appropriate to treat such public-law rules in the same way as rules of private law, for example, by allowing the parties to avoid or opt in exchange regulations by exercising their right to choose the law applicable to the contract.[18] This does not mean that foreign public-law measures should be ignored though. For instance, they must be taken into account if and to the extent their factual consequences are relevant according to the law governing the contract. Thus, a trade embargo, under certain circumstances, may constitute a *force majeure* that makes performance impossible, and that impossibility, pursuant to the law applicable to the contract, may discharge the obliged party of its duty to perform. It should not matter, in such a case, whether the embargo was enacted by the country of the forum, the country whose law governs the contract, or a third country, as long as it makes performance impossible and that impossibility has certain legal consequences according to the law governing the contract in question.

The Convention does not answer the question of whether its conflict rules (and thus also the law applicable pursuant to these rules) can and must be applied at the court's own initiative or only if invoked by a party. It could be argued that this question is left to be decided by the national law of the Contracting State of the forum, but the Convention's special relationship with EC law speaks in favor of application *ex officio*, which will probably prevail once the Convention is replaced with an EC Regulation.

Article 20 of the Convention gives precedence to EC law, both existing and future, as well as to those national laws of the Member States that have been harmonized in implementation of EC directives. There are several national conflict rules harmonized by directives concerning, for example, consumer contracts and individual employment contracts.[19] Similarly, the application of other conventions to which a Contracting State is, or becomes, a party is not affected (Article 21). For example, some Contracting States (Belgium, Denmark, Finland, France, Italy and Sweden) are parties to the 1955 Hague Convention on the Law Applicable to the Sale of Goods, which means that contracts covered by that instrument are in those countries in principle excluded from the application of the Rome Convention. Article 1(1)(a) of the United Nations Convention on Contracts for the International Sale of Goods (CISG) also makes it possible to avoid, in some situations, the conflict rules of the Rome Convention, because it makes the CISG applicable to sales contracts between parties whose places of business are in different states parties to the CISG, regardless of the conflict rules in the country of the forum.[20] Among other relevant conventions, it is possible to mention the Convention on the Grant of European Patents (the European Patent Convention), concluded in 1973,[21] which contains in Article 60(1)

---

[18] See section 7.2 *infra.*

[19] See section 9.1 *infra.*

[20] It should be noted that pursuant to special reservations the CISG at present does not apply to intra-Nordic trade.

[21] 1065 United Nations Treaty Series 199.

some conflict rules regarding the right to inventions made by employees within the framework of their employment contract.

A special Protocol to the Rome Convention allows the Nordic Contracting States (Denmark, Finland and Sweden) to retain, in their maritime laws, certain conflict rules resulting from Nordic legislative cooperation even though they have not become formalized in any convention.[22]

It must also be noted that Article 23 opens certain possibilities for a Contracting State to adopt, in regard to any particular category of contracts (thus not in regard to contracts in general), new conflict rules deviating from the Convention, but only after having gone through a special communication and consultation procedure enabling the other Contracting States to block the adoption of the new rule for a period of two years. As pointed out above, the Rome Convention does not prohibit subsequent accessions by a Contracting State to other conventions, but Article 24(1) prescribes that the same procedure as under Article 23 must be used, albeit with the two-year period reduced to one year, if a Contracting State wishes to become a party to another multilateral convention principally aiming to lay down PIL rules concerning matters governed by the Rome Convention. If the other convention is not principally an instrument of PIL, it can be ratified without such procedure even if it comprises some conflict rules relating to contracts. There are some additional situations where the communication and consultation procedure need not be followed but, in view of the forthcoming conversion of the Convention into an EC Regulation, there is no need to discuss them here.

The Convention is not intended to have retroactive effect. Pursuant to Article 17, it applies to contracts made after the date on which it entered into force for the forum country, which means that under many years to come the courts of the Contracting States will have to deal also with older contracts to which the Convention does not apply. As the date of the Convention's entry into force is not the same for all Contracting States, the same contract may be subject to the Convention in some Contracting States while being considered to fall outside its scope in other such States. However, the Convention does not prohibit the Contracting States from using, on a voluntary basis, its conflict rules even in respect of older contracts. Some Contracting States, for example Denmark, started to apply the Convention's rules several years before it entered into force. The Contracting States are similarly free to extend the application of the Convention's rules to situations and questions that are excluded from its scope, provided of course that such extension does not collide with other international commitments of the Contracting State involved.

---

[22] OJ 1998 C 27 p. 44.

7.2   Party Autonomy

The Convention recognizes the well-established principle of party autonomy, *i.e.* the right of the parties to conclude a legally binding agreement with one another on the legal system applicable to their contract (Article 3),[23] although there are certain restrictions[24].

The Convention does not impose any particular requirements regarding the form of choice-of-law agreements, but it accepts that such requirements can be imposed by the applicable national law (see the reference in Article 3(4) to Art. 9). The national formal requirements, however, must not be contrary to Article 3(1), which stipulates that the choice can be either explicit or demonstrated with reasonable certainty by the terms of the contract or other circumstances. Such other circumstances, for example, may be that the contract uses certain legal terms that are taken from a particular legal system or that it is a long-standing practice between the parties to use a particular legal system. The choice may be expressed indirectly and it may even depend on some future circumstance, for example, if the parties agree that the law of the country of the (future) defendant shall be applied (such choice, which has the disadvantage of leaving the parties uncertain about which law they have to follow, is sometimes made in order to discourage future litigation). The choice of a court or of arbitration proceedings in a particular country, on the other hand, does not necessarily imply a choice of the substantive legal system to govern the contract, although it may constitute an indication which, if considered together with other circumstances, can demonstrate a tacit choice of law. In any case, the choice must be a real choice, so that a hypothetical reasoning about which law the parties would probably have chosen if they had made a choice is not sufficient.

The freedom of choice of the parties is not limited to legal systems having some natural connection with the contract. The parties can in fact choose any existing legal system they wish, for instance, a system with widely known and particularly developed rules for the type of contract involved (such as English law for contracts of carriage of goods by sea), a legal system they perceive as "neutral" (for example, Swedish law is sometimes chosen in contracts within the American-Russian trade), or simply a legal system they both happen to be familiar with. According to the traditional view, the freedom of choice is limited to existing legal systems, and the chosen system is applied "alive", *i.e.* including changes and developments that have taken place after the choice was made, unless the chosen legal system's own transitional provisions make such new rules inapplicable to older contracts. References to *"lex mercatoria"*, "Roman

---

[23] See, for example, Kassis, *Le nouveau droit*, pp. 347-371; Nielsen, *International privat- og procesret*, pp. 498-504; Pålsson, *Romkonventionen*, pp. 43-53; Philip, *IP-EU*, pp. 136-143; Plender & Wilderspin, *The European Contracts Convention*, pp. 87-107; Rozehnalová & Týč, *Evropský justiční prostor*, pp. 56-78.

[24] See, for example, section 7.4 *infra* about the restrictions with regard to certain consumer contracts and individual employment contracts, and section 7.5 *infra* about the overriding mandatory rules.

law", "French law as it was on 1 January 1990" or various private or semi-official compilations of rules (the Lando Commission's Principles of European Contract Law, the Unidroit Principles of International Commercial Contracts, *etc.*), according to the traditional view, can serve merely as contractual terms that are only valid to the extent the parties enjoy freedom of contract pursuant to the legal system governing the contract, *i.e.*, to the extent the matter is not regulated by mandatory rules of that legal system. The same seems to be true when the parties attempt to exclude all legal systems and agree to subject their contract exclusively to its own provisions (so-called self-regulating contracts): such agreement is probably valid only within the framework of the freedom of contract allowed by the law applicable to the contract in question. There is, however, an increasing support for the opinion favoring the right of the parties to choose freely among both state and private sets of rules, without any limitation as to their type and age.

For many of the Contracting States, it was a radical departure from previous conflict principles that the Convention admits that different parts of a contract can be governed by different legal systems. The parties can achieve such *dépeçage* (splitting) by choosing different legal systems for different parts of the contract or by limiting their choice of applicable law to a part only of the contract (Article 3(1)). *Dépeçage* can be useful in particular in those cases where the contract is composed of parts that could survive as separate agreements, for example, a licence contract concerning copyright in several countries or a contract with a multinational bank whereby a client opens several accounts in several countries. The wording of Article 3(1) permits, however, *dépeçage* also in other respects, such as a choice of different legal systems for different types of legal problems, for example, the choice of one law for the material validity of the contract, another law for its interpretation, a third law for consequences of breach, *etc.* To the extent the parties have agreed on *dépeçage* leading to the application of mutually incompatible rules, and no way can be found to reconcile them by reasonable interpretation, their choice will probably have to be disregarded.

The choice of law, in most cases, is made in connection with the conclusion of the contract, but the parties, at any later time, may agree to subject the contract to a law other than that which previously governed it, regardless of whether the previously governing law resulted from a choice-of-law agreement or from the application of conflict rules used in the absence of choice[25]. Such subsequent choice in principle is valid, but it cannot adversely affect the rights of third parties (for example, of a guarantor) or prejudice the contract's formal validity (Article 3(2)). Whether a contract, which is formally invalid when it is concluded, can become valid with retrospective effect by virtue of a subsequent choice of law is less certain. A practically useful form of choice of law made after the conclusion of the contract is that the parties, for reasons of procedural

---

[25] See section 7.3 *infra*.

convenience and economy and in view of a pending or imminent litigation, agree on the application of the *lex fori*. It happens in court proceedings that the question of applicable law is not raised at all but both parties refer to provisions of the *lex fori* in their pleadings. Such behavior, under certain circumstances, may be interpreted as a tacit but conscious choice of law, which must be distinguished from the situation where the references to provisions of *lex fori* reflect rather the ignorance of the parties about PIL. In the latter case, the court faces the question of whether it should apply, upon its own initiative, the Convention's conflict rules on the determination of the law applicable in the absence of party autonomy.[26]

As has been pointed out already,[27] the Convention applies in principle even to contracts where all elements are connected with the same single country. This gives rise to the question whether the parties to such single-country contracts enjoy full party autonomy and are free to choose the law of another country. Article 3(3) provides that choice of law must not prejudice, in such cases, the application of mandatory rules of the only country with which the contract is connected. This means that in such situations the choice of another law is given effect, but only within the framework of the freedom of contract allowed by the substantive law of that country. This is true even if in addition to choosing a foreign legal system the parties have agreed to submit their future disputes to a foreign court, because such a choice of court does not by itself turn the contract into an international one. It has been asserted that the freedom of choice in these cases does not constitute true party autonomy in the PIL sense, but is merely an expression of the freedom of contract offered by the substantive law of the only country with which the contract is connected, and that the law of that country governs in fact the contract in spite of the choice-of-law clause. This is, however, only partially correct, because it seems that the mandatory rules of the legal system chosen by the parties must also be treated as mandatory, although only to the extent that they do not contradict the mandatory rules of the single country with which the contract is connected. As could be expected, there are borderline cases where it is difficult to decide whether the contract should be treated as a single-country contract or not. For example, there may be good practical reasons to permit an importer of goods to subject, by a choice-of-law clause, his purely domestic contracts with his domestic customers to the same foreign law that governs his contracts with his foreign suppliers.

A problem that is related to Article 3(3) but is not dealt with by the Convention concerns the mandatory rules of the EC Member States harmonized by EC directives. As a contract involving two Member States is not connected with one country only, the parties seem to enjoy full party autonomy, unrestricted by Article 3(3). This might appear to make it possible for them to avoid, simply by choosing the law of a non-member country, mandatory rules imposed by

---

[26] See section 7.1 *supra*.

[27] See section 7.1 *supra*.

EC directives, even though all connecting factors point to EC Member States. The problem could be solved by treating the whole EC as one country with regard to mandatory rules imposed by EC directives, but this would require an amended wording of or an addition to Article 3(3). Some of the EC directives in the consumer field contain provisions protecting consumers against possible adverse effects of the choice of the law of a non-member country when the contract has a close connection with the territory of the Member States, for example, Article 6(2) of the Directive on Unfair Terms in Consumer Contracts.[28] In addition, the ECJ has held in the case of *Ingmar* v. *Eaton Leonard Technologies* that Directive No 86/653 of 18 December 1986 on the Coordination of the Laws of the Member States relating to Self-employed Commercial Agents[29] comprises a similar, albeit merely tacitly implied, restriction of party autonomy[30]. The consumer directives and the *Ingmar* judgment restrict party autonomy even when the contract has a significant connection with a non-member country, which means that they go much further than Article 3(3), which covers merely those cases where the contract is purely domestic and has no relevant connection at all with another country. In fact, one of the parties to the contract in the *Ingmar* case was an American company, but the ECJ held that the mandatory rules imposed by the EC directive in question must be respected whenever the commercial agent carries on his activity in a Member State, even if his principal is established in a non-member country and a clause of the contract stipulates that the contract is to be governed by the law of that non-member country.[31]

The validity of a choice-of-law clause, even if it complies with the rules of PIL described above, can be challenged on the grounds of substantive contract law, for example, if it was made under the influence of coercion or fraud, if one or both of the parties lacked the capacity to make a valid agreement, or if the clause does not fulfill certain formal requirements imposed by national law. The existence and validity of the choice-of-law clause in these respects is governed by the law determined in accordance with the same conflict rules that are provided in the Convention for contracts in general (Article 3(4)). Consequently, the validity of a choice-of-law clause with regard to coercion or fraud is governed by the law chosen by that very same clause, and the chosen law may even be decisive for the formal validity of that clause. Theoretically, this might appear to be an illogical vicious circle, but it has not given rise to any difficulties in practice. The permissibility and validity of the choice-of-law clause from the viewpoint of PIL,

---

[28] See section 9.1 *infra*.

[29] OJ 1986 L 382 p. 17.

[30] Case C-381/98, [2000] ECR I-9305.

[31] It should be noted that the ECJ, at the time of the *Ingmar* judgment, did not have the authority to interpret and apply the Rome Convention and that the outcome of the case was compatible with the Convention's Article 20 on the precedence of Community law (*in casu* the restriction of party autonomy implied in the EC directive in question).

for example, the possibility of choosing a legal system having no natural connection with the contract, is governed exhaustively by the Convention itself (Article 3), without recourse to any national PIL.

7.3 Applicable Law in the Absence of Choice

Surprisingly enough, the parties to contracts of an international nature make use relatively seldom of their freedom to choose the applicable law. The reasons are manifold, ranging from ignorance of PIL to reluctance to burden contractual negotiations with an additional potential cause of disagreement. Whatever the reason, the limited use of party autonomy increases the practical importance of the Convention's conflict rules determining the applicable law in the absence of choice by the parties.[32]

Pursuant to Article 4(1), which on its face might look as if it were the main rule, the contract, in the absence of a valid choice by the parties, is governed by the law of the country with which it is most closely connected. Even here there is some space for *dépeçage*, but in contrast to Article 3(1) a part of the contract can only be governed by a law different from the rest "by way of exception" and provided that the part in question is "separable". The meaning of the last-mentioned condition is far from clear; one possible interpretation is that the severed part of the contract must be capable of constituting a meaningful separate contract, while a more permissive view is that separable simply means that the splitting must not lead to the application of mutually irreconcilable rules.

In order to identify the country with which an individual contract is most closely connected, the courts have to take account of all kinds of circumstances, such as the habitual residence and nationality of the parties, the place of contracting, the agreed upon place of performance, the language and currency used in the contract, the agreement of the parties on judicial or arbitral proceedings in a certain country, *etc.* The Giuliano/Lagarde Report complicates things somewhat by suggesting that in order to determine the country with which the contract is most closely connected it is also possible to take account of factors, which supervened after the conclusion of the contract.[33] This is rather surprising, as it would be hardly appropriate to allow one of the parties to influence the determination of the applicable law retroactively by one-sided actions, for example, by moving to another country.

The evaluating, comparing and counter-balancing of the various connecting factors in each individual case (the so-called individualizing method) often

---

[32] See, for example, Kassis, *Le nouveau droit*, pp. 285-327; Nielsen, *International privat- og procesret*, pp. 504-514; Pålsson, *Romkonventionen*, pp. 53-69; Philip, *EU-IP*, pp. 144-149; Plender & Wilderspin, *The European Contracts Convention*, pp. 109-133; Rammeloo, *Das neue EG-Vertragskollisionsrecht*, pp. 285-335; Rozehnalová & Týč, *Evropský justiční prostor*, pp. 79-93.

[33] See OJ 1980 C 282 p. 20.

would make the applicable law very difficult to predict. Article 4(2-4) introduces, therefore, three presumptions making the task of determining the applicable law easier and the result more predictable. For most practical purposes, these presumptions function as the real main rules, but it is important to keep in mind that they are mere presumptions and that they can and should be disregarded in those – relatively rare – cases where it appears from the circumstances as a whole that the contract is connected more closely with another country (Article 4(5)). It is disputed, both among legal writers and in the court practice in the Contracting States, whether the three presumptions can and should be disregarded only in those cases where the preponderance in favor of another country is manifest, or even whenever the connection with another country is merely slightly stronger. The wording of Article 4(5) seems to support the latter interpretation, although this makes the presumptions much weaker and the applicable law much more difficult to predict.

The most important presumption is found in Article 4(2), pertaining to contracts in general, with the exception of contracts on rights in immovable property or to use immovable property, contracts for the carriage of goods, and certain weak-party contracts. Contracts generally are presumed to be most closely connected with the country where the party who is to effect the performance, which is characteristic of the contract, has his habitual residence (in the case of a juridical person, its central administration), at the time of conclusion of the contract. However, most international contracts are entered into in the course of the trade or profession of the party effecting the characteristic performance, in which case the habitual residence or central administration is replaced by the principal place of business or, where the performance is to be effected through another place of business, the country in which that other place of business is situated.

The concept of characteristic performance, which stems originally from Swiss PIL, is not defined in the Convention itself, but the Giuliano/Lagarde Report explains it by stating the following:[34]

> Identifying the characteristic performance of a contract obviously presents no difficulty in the case of unilateral contracts. By contrast, in bilateral (reciprocal) contracts whereby the parties undertake mutual reciprocal performance, the counter-performance by one of the parties in a modern economy usually takes the form of money. This is not, of course, the characteristic performance of the contract. It is the performance for which the payment is due, i.e. depending on the type of contract, the delivery of goods, the granting of the right to make use of an item of property, the provision of a service, transport, insurance, banking operations, security, etc., which usually constitutes the centre of gravity and the socio-economic function of the contractual transaction.

---

[34] See OJ 1980 C 282 p. 20.

The performance that takes place in kind (the specific performance) is characteristic of the contract in the sense that it characterizes (classifies) it as, for example, sale of goods or provision or services. The preference given by the Convention to the law of the party effecting the characteristic performance can be explained mainly by the fact that such performance is normally much more complicated from the legal point of view than the relatively simple payment of money. Furthermore, the party effecting the characteristic performance is often an enterprise selling goods or providing services on a large scale. Reasons of efficiency and economy speak in favor of the application of the same legal system to all such transactions performed by the same enterprise, irrespective of the individual customer, and this legal system must reasonably be the law of the country of that enterprise. On the other hand, the presumption has been criticized for favoring the application of the laws of the developed countries exporting goods and services rather than of the laws of the developing nations. Also, it has been argued that it distorts competition, because the offers made by competing suppliers of goods and services from different countries may be difficult to compare if they are based on different legal systems. Such and other similar drawbacks, however, often can be remedied to some extent by the use of party autonomy.[35]

The presumption in Article 4(2) must be disregarded if the characteristic performance cannot be determined, for example, in respect of a currency exchange transaction between two banks where both parties perform by paying money, a contract on cooperation by exchanging information, or a swap of goods against services (Article 4(5)). The application of Article 4(2) becomes particularly complicated when the contract in question is "mixed", i.e., where the same party performs both in money and in kind. For example, a contract between an author and his publisher may provide that the publisher will pay certain royalties, but it may impose on him a number of other obligations as well, with regard to marketing, publication of new editions, taking measures to protect the author's copyright, etc. In some such cases, it may be so difficult to determine which party provides the performance characteristic of the contract that pursuant to Article 4(5) the presumption must be disregarded and the country with which the contract is most closely connected must be determined in accordance with Article 4(1), i.e., by evaluating and comparing the various connecting factors pertaining to the individual contract under scrutiny. It can be argued that the same should apply when the habitual residence, etc. of the party effecting the characteristic performance is unknown to the other party at the time of the conclusion of the contract, for example, when a purchase of an object from an anonymous seller takes place at a public auction.

A different presumption is stipulated in Article 4(3) for contracts regarding a right in immovable property or a right to use immovable property (this presumption thus does not apply to, for example, a contract concerning repairs

---

[35] See section 7.2 *supra*.

to be done on a building). It seems that the concept of "a right in immovable property or a right to use immovable property" is somewhat wider than the concept of "rights *in rem* in immovable property or tenancies of immovable property" in Article 22(1) of the Brussels I Regulation.[36] It is presumed that such contracts are most closely connected with the country where the immovable property is situated, although there are good reasons to disregard the presumption when the contract is about a short-term lease and none of the parties resides habitually in the country where the immovable property is situated.[37]

The third and last presumption, found in Article 4(4), concerns contracts for the carriage of goods, including single-voyage charter-parties and other contracts the main purpose of which is the carriage of goods (thus not, for example, a bare-boat lease of a ship or a contract for the carriage of passengers). This presumption leads to the law of the country of the principal place of business of the carrier (who is normally identical with the party effecting the characteristic performance), but only if the place of loading, the place of discharge, or the principal place of business of the consignor also is situated there. If none of these additional conditions is fulfilled, then neither Article 4(4) nor the general presumption in Article 4(2) can be used and the applicable law has to be determined by the individualizing method pursuant to Article 4(1). The fact that many carriers use registrations (flags) of convenience, and have their registered principal place of business in a country having no real relationship with their activities, makes the main presumption in Article 4(2) inappropriate with regard to contracts on carriage of goods. Also, it should be noted that carriage of goods, in some respects, is subject to regulation by international conventions unifying or harmonizing substantive law, which makes the PIL issue less relevant. To the extent such conventions even contain explicit or tacit conflict rules, they enjoy priority in relation to the Rome Convention (see Article 21).[38] It can be added that Article 4(4) applies even to carriage of goods involving the use of a negotiable bill of lading, even though questions arising out of the negotiable character of such documents are excluded from the scope of the Rome Convention.[39]

7.4   Weak-party Contracts

The Convention contains two special articles on weak-party contracts, namely Article 5 on certain consumer contracts and Article 6 on individual employment contracts. Certain provisions on such contracts are found also in Article 9(5) concerning the formal validity of consumer contracts and in some EC directives[40].

---

[36] See section 3.3.4 *supra*.

[37] Cf. Article 22(1) of the Regulation Brussels I, section 3.3.4 *supra*, and Article 9 of the Timeshare Directive, section 9.1 *infra*.

[38] With regard to Denmark, Finland and Sweden, see the special protocol in OJ 1998 C 27 p. 44.

[39] See Article 1(2)(c) and section 7.1 *supra*.

[40] See section 9.1 *infra*.

Article 5 applies to contracts the object of which is the supply of goods or services (thus not, for example, sales of real property) to a person (the consumer) for a purpose outside his trade or profession, as well as contracts for the provision of credit for that purpose.[41] As far as the provision of credit is concerned, the provider does not have to be the same person who provides the goods or services. For example, a bank loan is within the scope of Article 5 even if it is provided for the purpose of financing the purchase of a car from an independent car dealer. On the other hand, a bank loan for financing the purchase of a house is excluded, because houses are neither goods nor services as understood in Article 5.

Although there is no explicit stipulation to that effect in Article 5, it is considered to apply only when the consumer's counterpart is a businessman acting within his trade or profession. This means that a contract between two persons, both acting outside of their trade or profession, is not included. Nevertheless, it is possible that Article 5 applies exceptionally even to contracts between private individuals, for example, if the party selling goods or providing services deliberately or negligently created the impression that it acted in a business or professional capacity, *e.g.* by pretending to charge value-added tax. On the other hand, Article 5 probably does not apply when the businessman, acting in good faith, had reasons to believe that he was supplying goods or services to another businessman, for instance, when his counterpart, who was in fact a consumer, claimed to be a businessman in order to be allowed to make a purchase at a wholesale price.[42] A sale of goods by a consumer *to* a businessman, for example, a sale of an inherited stamp collection to a professional stamp dealer, is certainly excluded. If Article 5 is of no avail, the law applicable to the contract has to be ascertained with the help of the general conflict rules in Articles 3 and 4 of the Convention.[43]

The weaker party, *i.e.* the consumer, is protected by Article 5 mainly against a disadvantageous use of party autonomy.[44] Article 5 stipulates that a choice of law made by the parties does not deprive the consumer of the protection afforded to him by the mandatory rules of the law of the country of his habitual residence. Further, the contract, in the absence of party autonomy, is governed

---

[41] See, for example, Kassis, *Le nouveau droit*, pp. 334-342; Klauer, *Das europäische Kollisionsrecht*; Larsson, *Konsumentskydd*; Morse, 41 I.C.L.Q. 1-21 (1992); Lasok & Stone, *Conflict*, pp. 380-384; Nielsen, *International privat- og procesret*, pp. 515-520; Pålsson, *Romkonventionen*, pp. 70-81; Philip, *EU-IP*, pp. 150-156; Plender & Wilderspin, *The European Contracts Convention*, pp. 137-157; Puurunen, *ZEuP* 2003 pp. 789-816; Rammeloo, *Das neue EG-Vertragskollisionsrecht*, pp. 360-382; Rozehnalová & Týč, *Evropský justiční prostor*, pp. 94-100; G. Straetmans in Meeusen, Pertegás & Straetmans (eds.), *Enforcement*, pp. 315-322.

[42] Cf. *Gruber v. Bay Wa AG*, case C-464/01, [2005] ECR I-439, concerning the corresponding problem arising in connection with Article 15 of the Regulation Brussels I (see section 3.3.3 *supra*).

[43] See sections 7.2 and 7.3 *supra*.

[44] See also section 9.1 *infra* about Article 6(2) of Directive No 93/13 on Unfair Terms in Consumer Contracts and other similar provisions in consumer directives.

by the law of the country of the consumer's habitual residence; this is not a mere presumption but a definite conflict rule that cannot be set aside by showing that the contract is more closely connected with another country. Of course, the substantive provisions of the law of the country of the consumer's habitual residence are not necessarily more advantageous for the consumer than the law of his counterpart, but it is usually an important advantage from the consumer's point of view to be able to follow a legal system which he knows or which is easily accessible to him. Article 5 reasonably must be understood to have in mind the consumer's habitual residence at the time of the conclusion of the contract, so that subsequent changes of his residence should be without effect in this respect.

It would be obviously inappropriate to extend such far-reaching protection to all consumer contracts, for example, those concluded by a Swedish tourist when shopping in a regular supermarket in Spain, where the shopkeeper cannot even be expected to be aware of the consumer's habitual residence. The protection accorded by Article 5 applies therefore in three situations only. First, it applies if the conclusion of the contract was preceded by a specific invitation, addressed to the consumer in the country of his habitual residence, or by advertising in that country, *and* the consumer has taken in that country all the steps necessary on his part for the conclusion of the contract. Secondly, the protection applies if the other party or his agent received the consumer's order in the consumer's country. Thirdly, the protection applies if the contract is for the sale of goods (thus not, for example, for the provision of services) and the consumer traveled from his country to another country and gave his order there, provided the journey was arranged by the seller for the purpose of inducing the consumer to buy.

These seemingly simple rules can give rise to many problems of interpretation. For example, advertising on satellite TV channels or in periodicals with international coverage probably can be considered to constitute advertising in all countries to which it directs itself, while it is questionable whether advertising on the borderless Internet constitutes advertising in the consumer's country merely because the consumer can access it from there. Article 5 does not seem to require that the consumer has actually placed his order on the basis of the invitation or advertising in his country. The requirement that the consumer must have acted in his own country seems to mean, for example, that he is deprived of the protection accorded to him by the mandatory rules of his own law if he mails a coupon, published in a newspaper in his country, during a short visit abroad. Another doubtful issue is whether a mere subsidizing of ticket prices or a distribution of free bus or railway tickets amounts to arranging the consumer's journey.

Contracts of carriage and contracts for services to be supplied to the consumer exclusively in a country other than that of his habitual residence (for example, a direct booking of hotel accommodation or of a language course in a foreign country) – with the exception of package tours combining travel and accommodation – are excluded from Article 5, which means that the main conflict rules in Articles 3 and 4 apply to them in full.

The special rules on individual[45] employment contracts in Article 6,[46] designed to protect the employee who is normally the weaker party, are in part similar to Article 5. Thus, the choice of law made by the parties to an individual employment contract does not have the result of depriving the employee of the protection afforded to him by the mandatory rules of the law, which would be applicable in the absence of choice. On the other hand, the last-mentioned law is not designated by a firm conflict rule but by two somewhat softer rules, in practice functioning as presumptions, which have to be disregarded when it appears from the circumstances as a whole that the contract is more closely connected with another country. According to the first presumption, to the extent the employment contract is not governed by the law chosen by the parties, it is governed by the law of the country in which the employee habitually carries out his work.[47] It seems that the rule has in mind the habitual place of work at the time of the dispute rather than at the time of the conclusion of the contract.[48] Article 6 stipulates explicitly that the habitual place of work is decisive even if the employee works temporarily in another country.[49] Whether the employment in another country is temporary sometimes may be difficult to ascertain, especially as it is disputed whether there is an absolute maximum time limit for temporariness. The second presumption, dealing with situations where the employee does not habitually carry out his work in any one country, prescribes that under such circumstances the contract will be governed by the law of the country of the employer's place of business through which the employee was engaged. A typical example of this situation is a traveling salesman with a sales district consisting of several countries. For the interpretation of Article 6, some guidance can probably be found in the case law concerning similar formula-

---

[45] Collective agreements concluded by an employer or an association of employers with a trade union, as well as contracts regarding the services of an independent contractor, thus are excluded from the scope of application of Article 6. However, generally applicable collective agreements in some countries are treated as laws regulating individual employment relations and, thus, they may have to be taken into account when the law of such a country has been chosen by the parties to an individual employment contract or applies to that contract due to Article 6(2).

[46] See, for example, Kassis, *Le nouveau droit*, pp. 342-346; Lasok & Stone, *Conflict*, 384-385; Liukkunen, *The Role*; Morse, 41 *I.C.L.Q.* 1-21 (1992); Nielsen, *International privat- og procesret*, pp. 521-525; Pålsson, *Romkonventionen*, pp. 82-90; Philip, *EU-IP*, pp. 156-159; Plender & Wilderspin, *The European Contracts Convention*, pp. 159-181; M.V. Polak in Meeusen, Pertegás & Straetmans (eds.), *Enforcement*, pp. 323-342; Rammeloo, *Das neue EG-Vertragskollisionsrecht*, pp. 382-417; Rozehnalová & Týč, *Evropský justiční prostor*, pp. 101-105.

[47] For seamen, this probably means the law of the country of the ship's flag.

[48] This difference in comparison with Article 5 (see *supra*) can be explained by the fact that a consumer can change his habitual residence by a unilateral decision, while a change of the habitual place of work presupposes normally at least an acceptance by both parties.

[49] See, however, the provisions of Directive No 96/71 of 16 December 1996 concerning the Posting of Workers in the Framework of the Provision of Services (section 9.1 *infra*).

tions in the Brussels/Lugano rules (today mainly in Article 19 of the Brussels I Regulation).[50]

It must be stressed that Articles 5 and 6 do not prohibit or invalidate party autonomy in consumer and employment contracts. The choice of law by the parties is recognized and normally valid, but it is not allowed to deprive the consumer or employee of the protection under the mandatory rules of the law that otherwise would govern the contract. This applies even if the dispute is adjudicated by a court in the Contracting State whose law has been chosen by the parties. As the chosen law on some points may offer consumers or employees a more far-reaching protection than the law that would apply in the absence of choice, Articles 5 and 6 shift the balance radically in favor of the consumer or employee, who seems to get the benefit of both legal systems. It is disputed whether this means that the consumer or employee merely can choose between the two legal systems in their totality or can even mix them ("pick cherries out of the cake") by combining the most advantageous rules of both of them (such as when a consumer claiming damages for breach of contract invokes the mandatory time limitation rules in the country of his habitual residence while relying on the chosen legal system's rules on the amount of compensation). If such combining is allowed, the mandatory provisions of both legal systems will have to be treated as mandatory to the benefit of the consumer or employee, although if they are mutually incompatible, the mandatory rules in the law that would govern in the absence of choice seem to prevail due to Articles 5 and 6 of the Convention. Such cumulation of advantages would give the consumer or employee more protection than any of the legal systems involved considers reasonable and in the end, it would probably make choice-of-law clauses disappear from consumer and individual employment contracts. Consumer and employment contracts normally are formulated by the consumer's or employee's counterpart (the businessman or the employer), who cannot be expected to include a clause that works one-sidedly in favor of the consumer or employee only.

7.5 Overriding Mandatory Rules

Article 7 of the Convention carries in English the heading "Mandatory Rules", but it does not deal with all mandatory provisions (*i.e.*, provisions that cannot be derogated from by contract) but merely with a small group among them, namely those mandatory rules that are intended, in the country of their origin, to be applied irrespective of which law is otherwise applicable to the contract.[51] It is thus not the Convention itself, but rather each individual national

---

[50] See section 3.3.3 *supra*.

[51] See, for example, Kassis, *Le nouveau droit*, pp. 443-475; Lasok & Stone, *Conflict*, pp. 372-380; Nielsen, *International privat- og procesret*, pp. 536-540; Pålsson, *Romkonventionen*, pp. 114-126; Philip, *EU-IP*, pp. 178-185; Plender & Wilderspin, The European Contracts Convention, pp. 183-201; Rozehnalová & Týč, *Evropský justiční prostor*, pp. 135-151.

legal system, that decides whether a particular rule of that system belongs to this group. The concept of such rules is related to the exception of public policy (*ordre public*), with the difference that the general exception of public policy (Article 16) requires an examination of the applicable foreign law before it is refused application, whereas Article 7 builds on the assumption that some rules are so important and sensitive from the point of view of the country adopting them that they are intended to be applied by that country, regardless of the contents of the law which is applicable pursuant to the Convention. Such rules are sometimes referred to as "overriding mandatory rules", "rules of positive *ordre public*" or "rules of immediate application";[52] the last-mentioned term reflects that these rules are applicable directly, without having to go through the normal conflict treatment and procedures. This does not necessarily mean that these mandatory rules are overriding under all circumstances, as their overriding nature may be limited to certain situations having a particularly close connection with their country, but they are intended to be applied in at least some cases where the normal rules of PIL point to another legal system. One problem that arises in this context is that it is often difficult to identify the overriding mandatory rules, as their nature normally is not explicitly stated in their wording but depends rather on a more-or-less speculative interpretation of the intentions of the national legislator in question.

Overriding mandatory rules of *lex fori* are dealt with in Article 7(2), which provides that the Convention does not restrict the application of the rules of the forum country in a situation where they are intended to be mandatory irrespective of the law otherwise applicable to the contract. This is not particularly controversial and, as mentioned above, can be regarded as related to the traditional exception of public policy.

Article 7(1) is much more controversial and some Contracting States (Germany, Ireland, Luxembourg, Portugal and United Kingdom), in fact, in accordance with Article 22(1), have reserved the right not to apply it. It stipulates that when applying the law of a country, effect may be given to the mandatory rules of another country with which the situation has a close connection, if and to the extent those rules are intended to be applied whatever the applicable law may be otherwise. Article 7(1) thus has in mind overriding mandatory rules belonging to a legal system which is neither *lex fori* (overriding mandatory rules of *lex fori* are the object of Article 7(2) described above) nor the law governing the contract, but rather a third legal system with a close (but not necessarily closest) connection with the situation. This third legal system may be the law that would govern the contract if the parties had not chosen another law, but it may be any other closely related law, for example, the law of the party who does not effect the performance which is characteristic of the contract. The determination in connection with Article 7(1) of whether, and if so under which circumstances, a particular foreign rule is intended to be of an overriding

---

[52] The French text of the Convention uses the term *lois de police*.

mandatory nature is obviously even more difficult than interpreting, in connection with Article 7(2), the intentions of the legislator in the court's own country. Furthermore, it is far from clear which connection between the situation and the country of origin of the rules is close enough for the purposes of Article 7(1). Finally, even if it is assumed in an individual case that the connection is close enough and that the rule under scrutiny is intended to be mandatory in the sense of Article 7(1), the outcome remains uncertain, as Article 7(1) does not require but merely allows that effect be given to the overriding mandatory rules in question. Article 7(1) attempts to mitigate this unpredictability by adding that in considering whether to give effect to these rules, regard must be had to their nature and purpose and to the consequences of their application or non-application, but such general and vague formulations are hardly of any real assistance in individual cases.

It appears that Article 7 is intended to refer to overriding mandatory rules irrespective of whether they are of public-law or private-law nature. This seems to follow from *i.a.* the examples given in the explanatory report on the Convention.[53] On the other hand, even though the Court of Justice of the European Communities has not yet had the opportunity to express its view on the matter, there is strong support for the view that public-law rules in principle are not automatically contemplated by the other conflict rules in the Convention.[54] Therefore, it is somewhat surprising that Article 7(1) speaks only of overriding mandatory rules of countries other than that whose law applies to the contract, because this may lead to the rather absurd conclusion that overriding mandatory rules of public-law nature of third countries are given more effects than corresponding rules in the legal system governing the contract. There are, therefore, good reasons to apply Article 7(1) by analogy even to public-law provisions of the legal system, which applies to the contract in accordance with the Convention's conflict rules. Foreign rules of public-law nature, nevertheless, normally will be refused effect due to their "nature and purpose". An example of a foreign rule of public law that can be expected to be given effect pursuant to Article 7(1) is a foreign trade embargo implementing an international collective action in which even the forum country participates.

7.6   The Scope of the Applicable Law

A non-exhaustive list of issues governed by the law applicable to the contract is found in Article 10(1) of the Convention. It includes the interpretation, performance, consequences of breach, termination, and consequences of nullity of the contract. The Convention comprises, furthermore, several special conflict provisions on, *i.a.*, material validity (Article 8), formal validity (Article

---

[53]   See the Giuliano/Lagarde Report in OJ 1980 C 282, in particular footnote 40 on p. 46.

[54]   See section 7.1 *supra.*

9), incapacity (Article 11), voluntary assignment (Article 12), subrogation (Article 13), burden of proof (Article 14), *etc.*[55]

With regard to interpretation (Article 10(1)(a)), the law governing the contract, for example, will be decisive for whether ambiguous formulations are to be interpreted to the disadvantage of the party that has formulated them. Another interpretation issue is whether the contract is to be interpreted literally (the traditional common-law method) or rather keeping in mind the intentions of the parties and the contract's purpose (the traditional Continental approach), although such alleged differences in interpretation methods should not be overestimated. International contracts often are written in the English language, and it is not uncommon that the parties "borrow" certain formulations from documents based on English or American law even when the contract is not connected with any English-speaking country and the parties have no intention of subjecting it to the legal system of any such country. An attempt should be made to establish whether the parties intended such "borrowed" clauses to have the meaning they have in their country of origin or according to the law governing the contract (or conceivably a third legal system).

Considering the performance of the contract (Article 10(1)(b)), the Giuliano/ Lagarde Report mentions the following matters falling within the scope of the applicable law:[56] the diligence with which the obligation must be performed, conditions relating to the place and time of performance, the extent to which the obligation can be performed by a person other than the party liable, the conditions as to performance of the obligation both in general and in relation to certain categories of obligations (joint and several obligations, alternative obligations, divisible and indivisible obligations, pecuniary obligations), the conditions relating to the discharge of the debtor who has made the payment (where performance consists of the payment of a sum of money), the appropriation of the payment, the receipt, *etc.* Article 10(2) adds that in relation to the manner of performance and the steps to be taken in the event of defective performance, "regard shall be had" to the law of the country in which the performance takes place. This means that although the substantive aspects of the performance are governed by the law applicable to the contract, minor modalities can (but do not necessarily have to) follow local laws, for example, regarding the question of whether the payment of a debt due on a Sunday or a bank holiday may be postponed until the next working-day. The borderline between the substantive aspects and modalities of performance is, however, sometimes rather unclear. The question of whether a monetary debt expressed in a foreign currency can be discharged by payment in local legal tender at the current rate of exchange

---

[55] See, for example, Kassis, *Le nouveau droit*, pp. 405-435; Nielsen, *International privat- og procesret*, pp. 525-536; Pålsson, *Romkonventionen*, pp. 91-109; Philip, *EU-IP*, pp. 166-176; Plender & Wilderspin, *The European Contracts Convention*, pp. 205-230; Rozehnalová & Týč, *Evropský justiční prostor*, pp. 106-121 and 152-157.

[56] See OJ 1980 C 282 pp. 32-33.

may be perceived as a mere modality if the local currency is freely convertible, while being a substantive issue of decisive importance if the local currency is not convertible or is subject to export restrictions and an unrealistic official exchange rate.

Among the consequences of breach to be governed by the law applicable to the contract, Article 10(1)(c) mentions explicitly the assessment of damages in so far as it is not considered to be a mere question of fact, but is governed rather by rules of law. This is of importance for such issues as the validity of a contractual clause on standard amounts of damages agreed in advance, or the statutory imposition of maximum limits of damages. Other examples of consequences of breach are the right of the other party to declare the contract cancelled, the right to demand a price reduction, or the right to demand new performance. Consequences of an anticipated future breach also are governed by the legal system applicable to the contract. On the other hand, the court is not obliged to apply that law to the extent it provides for consequences of breach that are incompatible with the procedural law of the forum, for example, when the *lex fori* does not make it possible to order specific performance.

The various ways of termination (extinguishing) of contractual obligations (Article 10(1)(d)) include such matters as time-limitation and set-off. Even Ireland and the United Kingdom, where traditionally time-limitation used to be considered a procedural matter governed by the *lex fori*, thus today are obliged to treat it as a matter of substantive law, governed by the law applicable to the contract. Termination of obligations by a one-sided declaration of set-off is somewhat more problematic, because the two opposing obligations may be governed by different legal systems and the Convention does not specify which of them is to be applied; it is also possible to argue that such set-off should be permitted if it is allowed by any of the two legal systems, or only if it complies with both of them. One of the two obligations also may be of a non-contractual nature, for example, a claim for compensation arising out of a tort. A voluntary set-off agreement is subject to its own law, to be determined by applying the general conflict rules of the Convention.

Among the consequences of nullity of the contract (Article 10(1)(e)), one may mention the restitution of performances and/or compensation. Article 22 permits, however, the Contracting States to reserve the right not to apply the law governing the contract to such remedies, because, in some countries (*e.g.*, the United Kingdom), they are considered traditionally to be of procedural rather than contractual nature.

The material validity of a contract or a contractual provision, pursuant to Article 8(1), is determined by the law that would govern it under the Convention if the contract or provision were valid. The material validity concerns not only the validity of the substantive contents of the contract but even whether the contract has been validly created with regard to such issues as the mechanism of offer and acceptance and the effects of coercion, fraud or mistake. Article 8(1) could give rise to difficulties if one party claimed that the other party had become bound by a contract due to its passivity, for example, by not having expressly rejected an offer. If the offer contained a choice-of-law clause refer-ring to an exotic legal system requiring such explicit rejection, the passive party could find itself bound, as the effects of its passivity would be determined by the law chosen in the offer. Article 8(2) provides, therefore, that a party may rely upon the law of the country of its own habitual residence to establish that it did not consent to the contract, if it appears from the circumstances that it would not be reasonable to determine the effect of its conduct in accordance with Article 8(1). Article 8(2) applies regardless of whether the party in question is a natural person, a company or other similar legal entity: although it is probable that the test of reasonableness will normally result in a greater protection for natural persons, especially when they act outside of their trade or profession.

Article 9 contains detailed conflict rules concerning the validity of contracts with regard to formal requirements, *i.e.*, legal requirements pertaining to the external manifestation on the part of a person expressing the will to be legally bound, such as a handwritten signature, registration or the presence of a Notary Public or of witnesses. The main principle is that it is sufficient for the formal validity of a contract that it satisfies the formal requirements of the law that governs the contract under the Convention but, even when the contract fails to satisfy those requirements, it is formally valid if it complies with the formal requirements of the law of the country where it was concluded (*lex loci contrac-tus*) or, if it was concluded between persons who were in different countries, the law of any of those countries (Articles 9(1-2)). If the contract was concluded by an agent on behalf of his principal, it is the presence of the agent that is relevant for the application of the rules just described (Article 9(3)). Unilateral acts relat-ing to a contract, such as a cancellation of an order or a declaration of a set-off, are formally valid if they satisfy the formal requirements of the law governing the contract or the law of the country where the unilateral act was done (Article 9(4)). All this is an expression of the ancient principle that it is sufficient for the formal validity of a legal act that it complies with the formal requirements imposed by the law of the place where the act in question was performed (the principle of *locus regit actum*, dating from those days when the person or persons wishing to make a contract or perform another legal act did not normally have access to other lawyers than the local ones). It must be repeated, however, that formal validity pursuant to the law governing the contract as such is also sufficient, although this alternative can give rise to complications when different parts of the contract are governed by different legal systems due to *dépeçage*[57] or when the parties to a formally invalid contract some time after its conclusion agree on subjecting it to another legal system[58].

Special conflict rules in Article 9(5-6) apply to formal validity of two types of contracts. First, consumer contracts entered into in one of the three situa-

---

[57] See sections 7.2 and 7.3 *supra*.

[58] See section 7.2 *supra*.

tions specified in Article 5(2)[59] are formally valid only if they satisfy the formal requirements of the country of the consumer's habitual residence, regardless of where the contract was made and whether the parties have chosen a different law to govern it. Secondly, a contract regarding a right in immovable property or a right to use immovable property must fulfill the formal requirements of the country where the property is situated, provided that those requirements are imposed by overriding mandatory rules intended to be applied irrespective of both the country where the contract was concluded and the law governing the contract as such.[60]

Legal capacity of the contracting parties who are natural persons (human beings) is, in principle, not governed by the Convention (see Article 1(2)(a)). In the PIL of most countries, this is an issue governed either by the personal law of the contracting party concerned (normally by the law of the country where that party habitually resides or of which he is a citizen), or by the law applicable to the contract as such. Article 11 modifies this by providing that in a contract concluded between persons present in the same country, a natural person who would have capacity under local law may rely on his incapacity under another legal system only if the other party was aware of this incapacity at the time of contracting or was not aware thereof as a result of his negligence. It is the natural person invoking his own incapacity under foreign law who, reasonably, must bear the burden of proof, including the proof that the other party was aware or should have been aware of this incapacity. The standard of care imposed on the other party depends naturally on the circumstances, including the importance and nature of the transaction. A seller of a house should normally be required to check the legal capacity of the buyer, including the possible PIL complications, while the same cannot be expected of the seller of a bicycle. Of course, Article 11 can be of interest only if and to the extent the PIL of the forum normally would determine the contractual capacity of the natural person in question under the law of a country other than that where the contract was concluded. Furthermore, Article 11 does not deprive one party to the contract of the possibility to invoke the invalidity of the contract due to the incapacity of the other party.

Article 12 deals with voluntary assignments of claims, for example, the situation where a businessman sells the claims he holds against his customers to his bank within the framework of a factoring arrangement. The mutual obligations of the parties to the assignment contract (the assignor and the assignee) are governed by the law applicable to that contract pursuant to the Convention's general conflict rules. On the other hand, the position of the debtor of the assigned claim (the *debitor cessus*) is governed by the law applicable to the assigned claim, for example, in matters such as whether the claim is assignable at all, the relationship between the assignee and the debtor and whether the debtor's obligations have been discharged by a payment he has made to the

---

[59] See section 7.4 *supra*.

[60] Cf. section 7.5 *supra*.

assignor after the assignment. The main purpose of this conflict rule is to make sure that the legal position of the debtor of the assigned claim is not adversely affected by the mere fact that the claim has been assigned to a new creditor. Article 12 applies irrespective of whether the assigned claim is of contractual origin or not. The assignment's effects *in rem*, in particular in relation to the creditors of the assignor and of the assignee, are not regulated by the Convention. The same is true of the negotiability of the instrument, for example, a promissory note that may have been transferred in order to execute the assignment (Article 1(2)(c)).

Subrogation, regulated in Article 13, concerns mainly the situation where a third person, who had the duty to satisfy the creditor of a contractual claim, wishes, by right of recourse, to take over and exercise the creditor's rights against the debtor. The third person in question, for example, may be a guarantor, an insurer or a co-debtor who has paid the debt. Article 13 stipulates that the right of recourse is governed by the law governing the third person's duty to satisfy the creditor, which is not necessarily the same law that is applicable to the original debt paid by the third person. It must be noted that Article 13 deals only with those situations where the third person had the duty, whether contractual or not, to satisfy the creditor; subrogation resulting from a voluntary payment of another person's debts is not covered. Another condition imposed by Article 13 is that the debt paid by the third person was of a contractual nature, although it seems reasonable to apply Article 13 by analogy even when that debt was non-contractual, for example, when compensation for a tort was paid by an insurance company which now wishes to exercise its right of recourse against the person who committed the tort. It goes without saying that the subrogation as such should not affect the legal position of the debtor of the original claim in question, which continues to be governed by the same legal system as before the subrogation.

Article 14(1) deals with certain questions concerning the burden of proof. It constitutes an exception to Article 1(2)(h), which excludes matters of evidence and procedure from the scope of the Convention. Article 14(1) provides that rules in the law of contracts of the legal system governing the contractual relationship apply even when they raise presumptions of law or determine the burden of proof, obviously in contrast to general presumptions of law and general principles on the burden of proof, which in most countries are regarded as procedural and are consequently regulated by the *lex fori*. Finally, as to the types of admissible evidence regarding the existence of a contract or another act intended to have legal effect, Article 14(2) stipulates the application of *lex fori*, but adds that other modes of proof recognized by the legal system(s) making the contract or act formally valid pursuant to Article 9 also may be used, provided they can be administered by the forum. This latter alternative is of limited importance in those Contracting States whose procedural law does not restrict the types of evidence that can be used. A liberal approach to the admissibility of proof regarding the existence of a contract, however, must not supersede the requirements concerning the contract's formal validity imposed by Article 9 (see *supra*).

7.7 Proposed Regulation Rome I

On 15 December 2005, the EC Commission presented a proposal for a Regulation on the Law Applicable to Contractual Obligations (Regulation Rome I).[61] The proposed Regulation is intended to replace the Rome Convention, which is now the only remaining Community-based PIL instrument in the form of a treaty. Even though the proposal was preceded by extensive consultations initiated by a "Green Paper" in January 2003,[62] it is far from certain how the Regulation will look like when finally adopted. The following description of the proposal deals, therefore, with its fundamental features only.

The Commission states that its proposal does not aspire to set out to establish a new set of rules, but rather to convert the existing Convention into a Community instrument. Nevertheless, the proposal introduces a substantial number of amendments, some of them quite radical, with the intention to modernize the contents of the present conflict rules on contracts and to co-ordinate them with the Brussels I Regulation and the proposed Rome II Regulation.

With regard to party autonomy,[63] one of the most important novelties in the proposal is that it gives the parties the right to choose, as the applicable law, not only the legal system of any country but also any principles and rules of the substantive law of contract recognized internationally or in the Community. According to the currently prevailing opinion, such non-state sets of rules merely can be referred to as contractual terms within the framework of the contractual freedom granted to the parties by the substantive rules of the legal system governing the contract, but cannot be used to replace that system in its totality, *i.e.*, including its mandatory rules. The proposed requirement that the chosen rules must be recognized internationally or in the Community excludes both various lesser-known private codifications and the rather imprecise *lex mercatoria*.[64] As examples of acceptable, internationally recognized bodies of rules, it is possible to mention the UNIDROIT Principles of International Commercial Contracts and the Lando Commission's Principles of European Contract Law.

---

[61] See COM(2005)650 final. See further Mankowski, *IPRax* 2006 pp. 101-113.

[62] See the Green Paper on the Conversion of the Rome Convention of 1980 on the Law Applicable to Conractual Obligations into a Community Instrument and its Modernisation, presented by the Commission on 14 January 2003, COM(2002)654 final, and the comments submitted by the Max-Planck-Institute for Foreign Private and Private International Law, *RabelsZ* 2004 pp. 1-118; Bonomi, *YearbPIL* 2003 pp. 53-97; Martiny, *ZEuP* 2006 pp. 60-95; Plender & Wilderspin, *The European Contracts Convention*, pp. 243-247; M. Wilderspin in Fuchs *et al.* (eds), *Les conflits*, pp. 173-183.

[63] See section 7.2 *supra*.

[64] See COM(2005)650 final, p. 5.

The proposal in some respects gives preferential treatment to the legal systems of the Member States, for example, by introducing a presumption that the choice of a court in a Member State – but not the choice of a court of a non-member country – implies also the choice of law of that state. Further, the choice of the law of a non-member state will not affect the application of mandatory rules of EC law applicable to the case. This restriction, intended to prevent evasion of EC mandatory rules, reminds one of Article 3(3) of the Convention (which is also retained in the proposal), but treats the whole Community as one jurisdiction and extends even to situations where the contract has connections with a non-member state but would, in the absence of choice of law, be subject to the law of a Member State. This amendment codifies, in fact, the principle applied by the ECJ in the case of *Ingmar* v. *Eaton Leonard Technologies*, decided in 2000.[65]

Another important proposed change, concerning those contracts where the applicable law has not been chosen by the parties,[66] is the replacement of presumptions in Article 4 of the Convention with fixed conflict rules for eight of the most common types of contract. For example, a contract of sale, according to the proposal, will be governed by the law of the country in which the seller has his habitual residence, a contract for the provision of services will be governed by the law of the country of the habitual residence of the service provider, and a contract relating to intellectual or industrial property rights will be governed by the law of the country in which the person who transfers or assigns the rights has his habitual residence. The law of the country appointed by these rules must be applied even when the contract under scrutiny happens to be more closely connected with another country. For contracts not falling within any of the eight categories, the proposal refers, in the first place, to the law of the country in which the party who is to perform the service[67] characterizing the contract has his habitual residence, which reminds one of Article 4(2) of the Convention but is a fixed rule rather than mere presumption. Only when the characterizing performance cannot be identified will the law of the country with which the contract is most closely connected be applicable. The replacement of presumptions with fixed conflict rules certainly would make it easier to predict the applicable law, but at the expense of flexibility.

The proposal suggests several important changes concerning conflict rules on consumer contracts.[68] For example, party autonomy will be excluded from

---

[65] Case C-381/98, [2000] ECR I-9305.

[66] See section 7.3 *supra*.

[67] Although the English version of the proposed text speaks here of "service characterizing the contract", it obviously does not have in mind contracts for the provisions of services (for which it proposes a fixed conflict rule of their own), but rather contracts not falling within any of the eight categories mentioned above. Therefore, it would be more correct to use the term "characteristic performance". Cf. the French text, which speaks of *"prestation caractéristique"*.

[68] See section 7.4 *supra*.

such contracts, which will be governed by the law of the country where the consumer has his habitual residence. This presupposes that the businessman either does business in that country or directs his business activities to it, but it will not be required any more that the consumer has done the acts needed to conclude the contract there. A radical departure from the universality of the proposed conflict rules is that these special rules will apply only in favour of consumers residing habitually in a Member State.

The proposal introduces a few novel conflict rules on some issues not covered by the Rome Convention. For example, it deals with various aspects of agency, such as the relationship between the principal and his agent, between the principal and the third party, and between the agent and the third party.

CHAPTER 8

Proposed Regulation Rome II

8.1 The Scope and Other General Features of the Proposed Regulation

The proposal for an EC Regulation on the Law Applicable to Non-contractual Obligations (the so-called Rome II Regulation) was presented by the Commission on 22 July 2003[1] and amended on 21 February 2006[2] in light of the numerous suggestions made during proceedings in the European Parliament[3] and the Council.[4] It is intended to complement both the Brussels I Regulation[5] (which deals merely with the jurisdiction of courts and recognition/enforcement of judgments, but not with the question of applicable law) and the Rome Convention[6] (which deals with applicable law, but restricts itself to contractual obligations[7]). In view of the uncertainty about how the final wording of the Rome II Regulation will look like, the following presentation is intended to describe merely the principal features of the Commission's amended proposal of 21 February 2006.

Non-contractual obligations comprise both obligations arising out of a tort/delict and obligations resulting from unjust enrichment and *negotiorum gestio* (agency without authority).[8] Furthermore, the proposed Regulation will apply not only to compensation for damage that already has arisen but also to actions to prevent future damage.[9] Like the Rome Convention, the proposed Regulation's conflict rules do not require reciprocity, and any law specified by the Regulation will be applied regardless of whether or not it is the law of a Member State (Article 2).

Pursuant to its Article 1, the proposed Regulation will apply to conflicts of law regarding non-contractual obligations in civil and commercial matters,[10]

---

[1] COM(2003)427 final. See the comments submitted by the Hamburg Group for Private International Law, *RabelsZ* 2003 pp. 1-56; Huber & Bach, *IPRax* 2005 pp. 73-84; a number of essays in Malatesta (ed.), *The Unification*; Nourissat & Treppoz, *Clunet* 2003 pp. 7-38; Posch, *Yearb.PIL* 2004 pp. 129-153; P. de Vareilles-Sommières in Fuchs *et al.* (eds), *Les conflits*, pp. 185-203.

[2] COM(2006)83 final.

[3] At first reading in plenary session on 6 July 2005, the Parliament adopted 54 amendments, see the consolidated text in document P6_TA(2005)0284.

[4] See documents 16231/04 and 16027/05.

[5] See Chapter 3 *supra*.

[6] See Chapter 7 *supra*.

[7] The 1972 draft of the Rome Convention dealt in fact also with non-contractual obligations, but that part of the project was abandoned later. See W. Posch in von Hoffmann (ed.), *European Private International Law*, pp. 87-114.

[8] See section 8.4 *infra*.

[9] Cf. Article 5(3) of the Brussels I Regulation and section 3.3.2 *supra*.

[10] The public-law schemes regarding compensation provided by states to crime victims thus are not included. The EC Directive No 2004/80 of 29 April 2004 relating to Compensation to Crime Victims (OJ 2004 L 261 p. 15) stipulates that Member States are obliged to have such schemes guaranteeing fair

excluding matters of revenue, customs or administrative law. Within civil matters, there are a number of general exclusions similar to those in the Rome Convention (issues of family law, negotiable instruments, liability under company law, trusts, *etc.*). Non-contractual obligations arising out of violations of privacy and personal rights by the media also are regrettably excluded, due to their highly controversial nature. Privacy and personal rights violations by means other than the media, such as using phone calls or letters, are covered though, but it is debatable whether, for example, defamatory statements on a private individual's website on the Internet or distributed by sending a large number of identical e-mail messages amounts to using "the media".

Article 12 of the proposal contains a non-exhaustive list of issues that are governed by the law applicable to a non-contractual obligation, *i.a.* the conditions and extent of liability, the grounds for exemption from liability, any limitation of liability and any division of liability, the existence and kinds of injury or damage for which compensation may be due, the assessment of the damage in so far as prescribed by law, the question of whether a right to compensation may be assigned or inherited, the liability for the acts of another person and the manner in which an obligation may be extinguished including time limitation. The law applicable to non-contractual obligations also governs the measures which a court has the power to exercise in order to prevent or terminate injury or damage (for example, the power to issue an injunction prohibiting certain harmful behavior), but only within the limits of the court's powers under its own procedural law. Procedure and evidence otherwise in principle are excluded from the proposed Regulation, but Article 19 provides that the law governing the non-contractual obligation will apply to presumptions of law and the burden of proof pertaining to such obligations.

Some general problems of tort law are dealt with by separate conflict rules, for example, direct action against the wrongdoer's insurer (Article 15), statutory subrogation (Article 16), and multiple liability (Article 17). A number of other articles deal with some general questions of PIL, such as overriding manda- tory rules (Article 13), exclusion of *renvoi* (Article 21), states with more than one legal system (Article 22), and public policy (Article 23). In particular, in respect to American law, it should be noted that Article 23 declares that the application of rules awarding excessive non-compensatory damages (such as exemplary or punitive damages) may be considered incompatible with the public policy of the forum. The practical value of this declaration seems to be merely that the ECJ cannot find the use of the public policy exception in such cases to be abusive.[11]

---

and appropriate compensation and that in cross-border situations involving violent intentional crimes, the compensation must be paid by the scheme of the Member State on whose territory the crime was committed, see in particular Article 12 of the Directive.

[11] Cf. *Renault* v. *Maxicar*, case C-38/98, [2000] ECR I-2973, concerning the use of the public policy excep- tion under the Brussels I Regulation, section 3.4 *supra*.

The proposed Regulation's relationship with other provisions of Community law is dealt with in Article 3, which in principle gives priority to rules in other Community instruments, especially those that lay down specific conflict rules for particular matters, lay down overriding mandatory rules, or promote the smooth operation of the internal market (for example, by implementing the country-of-origin principle with regard to the free movement of goods and services[12]). In addition, Article 24 gives priority to international conventions to which the Member State of the forum is a party at the time of adoption of the Regulation and which lay down conflict rules in relation to particular matters. However, the proposed Regulation will prevail over the 1971 Hague Convention on the Law Applicable to Traffic Accidents and the 1973 Hague Convention on the Law Applicable to Product Liability if the situation is in all respects related to Member States only.

8.2   Freedom of Choice and the General Conflict Rule

In contrast to contractual obligations, parties to a non-contractual liability dispute do not normally have the opportunity to agree on applicable law in advance. The parties, however, may wish to agree on a law of their choice after their dispute arose, for example, in order to avoid the high costs of procuring information about the otherwise applicable foreign law. According to Article 4 of the proposed Regulation, such choice will be respected provided that the choice is expressed or demonstrated with reasonable certainty by the circumstances of the case. Except in relations between businessmen, such choice can be made only after the dispute arose. Further, if all the other elements of the situation were located, at the time of the loss, in one single country other than that whose law has been chosen, the choice of the parties must not affect the application of mandatory rules of that country, and the parties' choice of the law of a non-member state must not affect the application of Community law where all the other elements of the situation were at the time of the loss located in the Community (even if not in one single Member State). In so far as the application of Community law is concerned, the whole Community thus is treated as one single country.

In respect to situations where the parties have not agreed on the law to be applied to a non-contractual obligation, the proposed Article 5(1) prescribes that the law applicable is the law of the country in which the direct damage arose or is likely to arise, irrespective of the country in which the event giving rise to the damage occurred or the indirect consequences of that event arose. This means that the proposed Regulation prefers the law of the country of the immediate resulting damage to the law of the country of the harmful act, probably because it pays more attention to compensating the victim than to influencing the

---

[12]   See section 2.2 *supra*.

behavior of the wrongdoer. If the same harmful act causes damage in several countries, or if it is likely that damage caused by the same harmful act will arise in several countries, then the main rule in Article 5(1) means that the laws of all the countries concerned have to be applied in a parallel manner to the various parts of the damage.

The proposed Article 5 contains two exceptions to the application of the law of the country of the damage. The first exception in Article 5(2) stipulates that if both the person claimed to be liable (the alleged wrongdoer) and the person sustaining direct damage (the alleged victim) have their habitual residence in the same country at the time of the damage, the law of that country will be applied. Habitual residence of companies and other legal persons is defined in Article 20 as the place of the principal establishment, unless the event giving rise to the damage occurs or the damage arises in the course of operation of a subsidiary, branch or another establishment (in which case that establishment takes the place of the habitual residence of the company or other legal person). If the damage has arisen in the course of the business activity of a natural person, the principal place of business of that person will be treated as his habitual residence.

The second exception to the application of the law of the country of the damage is found in Article 5(3) and pertains to those cases where it is clear from all the circumstances that the non-contractual obligation is manifestly more closely connected with some other country. Under such circumstances, the law of that other country is to be applied, notwithstanding the first two paragraphs of Article 5. Such manifestly closer connection in particular may be based on some pre-existing relationship between the parties, for example, a contractual or family relationship closely connected with the non-contractual obligation under scrutiny. In addition, account must be taken of the expectations of the parties regarding the applicable law.

8.3 Conflict Rules for Specific Torts

The proposed Regulation in Articles 6-9 contains a number of conflict rules pertaining to special types of delictual obligations. In accordance with the maxim *lex specialis derogat legi generali*, these special rules in principle have precedence in relation to the Regulation's general conflict rules, but at the same time, they refer to some extent to those general rules.

A conflict rule on liability arising out of a damage or risk of damage caused by a defective product (product liability) is found in Article 6, which stipulates the application of the law of the country where the victim is habitually resident at the time of the damage, unless the person alleged to be liable can show that he has not consented to the product being marketed in that country. In the last-mentioned situation, the law of the country of the habitual residence of the person claimed to be liable will be applied instead.

Non-contractual obligations arising out of unfair commercial practices are governed pursuant to Article 7 by the law of the country (countries) of the directly and substantially affected market(s). However, if the act merely affects the interests of a specific competitor, Articles 5(2) and 5(3) will apply.[13] This means, for example, that if both competitors reside in the same country, the law of that country will apply, unless the obligation is manifestly more closely connected with another country.

Cross-border environmental damage is dealt with in Article 8, which gives the claimant the right to base his claim either on the law determined by Article 5(1)[14] or the law of the country in which the event giving rise to the damage occurred (the country of the harmful act). It is not quite clear whether and to what extent the wrongdoer facing claims based on the law of the country where the environmental damage arose can rely on Article 14, according to which, regardless of the applicable law, account is to be taken "as a matter of fact, and in so far as is appropriate" of the rules of safety and conduct which were in force at the place and time of the harmful act.

Non-contractual obligations arising from an infringement of an intellectual property right (copyright, patent, trademark, etc.) are governed by the law of the country for which protection is sought (Article 9). This application of *lex loci protectionis* appears to reflect the principle of territoriality, according to which intellectual property rights in individual countries are independent of each other. A trademark infringement on the Internet, violating trademark protection in many countries at the same time, thus in the same proceedings can be subject in a parallel manner to various legal systems regarding various parts of the damage. Infringements of a unitary Community industrial property right, such as a Community trademark, however, will be governed, with regard to the whole Community, first, by Community law and second, by the legal system of the Member State in which the act of infringement was committed. Article 9 applies notwithstanding the other conflict rules of the Regulation, and thus excludes even the possibility of choosing the applicable law pursuant to Article 4.[15]

8.4   Unjust Enrichment and *Negotiorum Gestio*

The proposed conflict rules on non-contractual obligations arising out of unjust enrichment (Article 10) and out of actions performed without due authority in connection with the affairs of another person (*negotiorum gestio*, Article 11) are constructed in a similar way.   + cic Art 12

---

[13] See section 8.2 *supra*.

[14] See section 8.2 *supra*.

[15] See section 8.2 *supra*.

In the first place, if such an obligation concerns a previous relationship between the parties, for example, a previous contract closely connected with the non-contractual obligation, then the law governing that previous relationship is to be applied to the non-contractual obligation as well. If there is no such previous relationship, then the law of the country of the common habitual residence of the parties will be applied. In the absence of a common country of habitual residence, unjust enrichment will be governed by the law of the country in which the event giving rise to the enrichment substantially occurs and *negotiorum gestio* by the law of the country where the action performed without due authority took place. All this applies subject to the reservation that where it is clear from all the circumstances of the case that the non-contractual obligation manifestly is connected more closely with another country, the law of that other country has to be applied.

CHAPTER 9

Some Conflict Rules in Other EC Instruments

9.1   Weak-party Contracts

In view of the protection enjoyed by consumers pursuant to Article 5 of the Rome Convention,[1] it might seem surprising that consumers have been given additional privileges on the PIL level by some subsequent EC directives. These directives deal mainly with harmonization of the mandatory substantive consumer law of the Member States, and the PIL rules included therein appear to have been added without much reflection and without having been coordinated with the Rome Convention. This creates a risk of potential implementation difficulties.

The most important of the consumer directives in question is undoubtedly Directive No 93/13 of 5 April 1993 on Unfair Terms in Consumer Contracts,[2] whose Article 6(2) stipulates that Member States must take the necessary measures to ensure that the consumer (as defined in Article 2 of the Directive) does not lose, by virtue of the choice of the law of a non-member country as the law applicable to the contract, the protection granted by the Directive (or rather by the national rules of the Member States as harmonized by the Directive). This restriction of party autonomy applies only when the contract has a close connection with "the territory of the Member States", which makes it clear that Article 6(2) regards the whole Community as a single territory, so that it is irrelevant whether the close connection is with a single Member State or results from the accumulated connections with several Member States. Another fact worth noticing is that Article 6(2) merely protects against the effects of a non-member legal system chosen by the parties, but not against the effects of a non-member legal system, which is applicable to the contract in the absence of a choice-of-law clause. This perhaps can be explained by the fact that Article 6(2), even though it speaks of situations where the contract has a "close" connection with the EC territory and does not require "closest" connection, can be interpreted as to mean that it refers solely to those contracts which in the absence of choice of law would be governed by the law of a Member State; this interpretation may be inferred from the formulation that the choice of the law of a non-member country must not cause the consumer to "lose" the protection granted to him by the Directive. If in the absence of choice of law the contract is governed by the law of a non-member state, then the consumer does not enjoy the protection afforded by the Directive and consequently cannot "lose" that protection by the choice of law of another non-member state. The ECJ has held that Member States must not transpose the requirement of "close connection" into their national law by stipulating fixed predetermined criteria for evaluating the intensity of the connection, because the general expression in the Directive seeks to make it possible to take account of various circumstances of the particular case, although the introduction of presumptions is permitted.[3]

---

[1]   See section 7.4 *supra*.

[2]   OJ 1993 L 95 p. 29.

[3]   *Commission* v. *Spain*, case C-70/03, [2004] ECR I-7999.

It appears, consequently, that Article 6(2) of the Unfair Terms Directive is of practical importance mainly with regard to those consumer contracts that are not covered by Article 5(2) of the Rome Convention (for example, because the consumer did not take in his country all the steps necessary on his part for the conclusion of the contract[4]) but, in the absence of choice of law by the parties, would be governed by the law of a Member State.[5] Some of the Member States have implemented Article 6(2) in a more far-reaching and consumer-friendly manner than is warranted by its wording. This is permitted by the Directive's Article 8, which allows the Member States to adopt or retain more stringent provisions to ensure a maximum degree of protection for the consumer, but it is doubtful whether such extensive implementation, going beyond what the Directive requires and varying from Member State to Member State, is compatible with Article 20 of the Rome Convention, as that article gives precedence to national laws merely to the extent they are harmonized in implementation of EC instruments.

A similar, but far from identical, provision is found in Directive No 94/47 on the Protection of Purchasers in respect of Certain Aspects of Contracts Relating to the Purchase of the Right to Use Immovable Properties on a Timeshare Basis.[6] Pursuant to Article 9 of this so-called Timeshare Directive, the Member States are obliged to take the measures necessary to ensure that, whatever the law applicable may be, the purchaser is not deprived of the protection afforded by the Directive, if the immovable property concerned is situated within the territory of a Member State. As can be seen, this provision specifies very clearly the required connection with the Community (the location of the immovable property concerned), rather than referring to an unspecified "close connection". Even more interesting is that Article 9 does not confine itself to protecting the purchaser against negative effects of the choice of law by the parties; it protects the purchaser also against the law applicable in the absence of the choice of law, if that law does not correspond to the Directive's standards.

Another consumer-oriented EC directive of interest in this context is Directive No 97/7 of 20 May 1997 on the Protection of Consumers in respect of Distance Contracts,[7] whose Article 12(2) is almost identical with Article 6(2) of the Unfair Terms Directive discussed above. The same can be said about Article 7(2) of Directive No 1999/44 of 25 May 1999 on Certain Aspects of the Sale of Consumer Goods and Associated Guarantees[8] and Article 12(2) of Directive No 2002/65 of 23 September 2002 concerning the Distance Marketing of Consumer Financial Services[9].

---

[4] See section 7.4 *supra*.

[5] Cf. *Commission v. Spain*, case C-70/03, [2004] ECR I-7999.

[6] OJ 1994 L 280 p. 83.

[7] OJ 1997 L 144 p. 19.

[8] OJ 1999 L 171 p. 12.

[9] OJ 2002 L 271 p. 16.

Another type of weak-party contractual relationship is the individual employment contract, where the employee enjoys far-reaching protection on the PIL
level pursuant to Article 6 of the Rome Convention.[10] This protection, however,
was deemed insufficient and it is, therefore, complemented by Directive No 96/
71 of 16 December 1996 concerning the Posting of Workers in the Framework
of the Provision of Services.[11] The main purpose of this Directive is to prevent
"social dumping", whereby workers coming from poorer Member States, where
wages and other terms of employment are less favorable towards the employees,
would be permitted to compete with local labor force in other Member States.
The Directive applies to those situations where an undertaking established in
a Member State posts workers temporarily to the territory of another Member
State, but since undertakings established in a non-member state must not be
treated more leniently (Article 1(4)), the receiving Member State in practice is
obligated to abide by the Directive even in relation to workers coming from non-
member countries. On the other hand, the Directive does not impose any obligations on the courts in the Member State from which the workers are posted to a
foreign country, irrespective of whether that country is a Member State or not.

The main principle of the Directive is found in its Article 3(1). It requires the
Member States to ensure that, whatever the law applicable to the employment
relationship, the employer-undertaking guarantees foreign workers temporarily posted to their territory the local terms and conditions of employment in a
number of respects enumerated in Article 3(1), ranging from minimum wages
and minimum paid annual holidays to rules about health, safety and hygiene at
work. This does not prevent application of the terms and conditions of employment stipulated by the law governing the employment contract pursuant to Article 6 of the Rome Convention,[12] provided that they are not less favorable to the
posted worker than the law of the Member State where he is temporarily posted
(see Article 3(7) of the Directive). The Rome Convention is decisive also for the
determination of the legal system applicable to those labour-law issues that are
beyond the scope of the Directive, for example, the right to dismiss an employee.

The application of the labour-law rules of the Member State where the
workers are posted might seem to be difficult to reconcile with the Rome
Convention's Article 6(2), which in most cases subjects individual employment
contracts to the law of the country in which the employee habitually carries out
his work in performance of the contract, "even if he is temporarily employed in
another country". The relationship between the Posted Workers Directive and
the Rome Convention is debatable from a theoretical viewpoint, as the Directive's Preamble refers in recitals 10 and 11 to both Article 7 and Article 20 of
the Convention. Consequently, it is possible to argue that the Directive, and the

---

[10] See section 7.4 *supra*.

[11] OJ 1997 L 18 p. 1. See, for example, Liukkunen, *The Role*, pp. 167-274; Moreau, *Clunet* 1996 pp. 889-
908.

[12] See section 7.4 *supra*.

national rules issued on its basis, should enjoy priority by virtue of Article 20 of the Convention, but it also seems possible to consider Article 3(1) of the Directive to constitute a kind of supplement to the Rome Convention containing an enumeration of those labour-law rules that are to be given effect as overriding mandatory rules pursuant to the Convention's Article 7.

Mandatory rules of substantive law, intended to protect the weaker party in a contractual relationship, can be found or considered implied also in some EC directives outside of the fields of consumer and labor law. Thus, Articles 17 and 18 of Directive No 86/653 of 18 December 1986 on the Coordination of the Laws of the Member States relating to Self-employed Commercial Agents[13] guarantee that commercial agents are entitled to certain compensation after the termination of their relationship with the principal. The Directive contains, however, no explicit rule of PIL corresponding to Article 6(2) of the Unfair Terms Directive (see *supra*), restricting the right of the parties to contract out such mandatory compensation by choosing the law of a non-member state to govern their contract. Nevertheless, the ECJ held in the case of *Ingmar v. Eaton Leonard Technologies*[14] that as the purpose of the relevant provisions in the Commercial Agents Directive was to protect the freedom of establishment and the operation of undistorted competition for all commercial agents in the internal market, those provisions could not be evaded by the simple expedient of a choice-of-law clause. The commercial agent *in casu* was a company established and active in the United Kingdom, the principal was a Californian company, and the agency contract stipulated that it was governed by the law of California. The ECJ held that Articles 17 and 18 of the Directive (meaning probably rather the UK law as harmonized by these articles) had to be applied in spite of the choice-of-law clause. According to the ECJ, the purpose served by the provisions in question requires that they are applied whenever the situation is closely connected with the Community, in particular where the commercial agent carries on his activity in the territory of a Member State, irrespective of the law by which the parties intended the contract to be governed.

It might be tempting to interpret the *Ingmar* judgment so that the ECJ found Articles 17 and 18 of the Commercial Agents Directive to be such overriding mandatory rules to which the national courts of the Contracting States (*in casu* English courts) were free to give effect pursuant to Article 7(2) of the Rome Convention. Such interpretation, however, would be incorrect, mainly because at the time of the judgment the ECJ had no authority to interpret Article 7 of the Convention. Besides, Article 7(2) *permits* Contracting States to apply overriding mandatory rules, while the *Ingmar* judgment stipulated that English courts were *obliged* to give effect to the Commercial Agents Directive. Therefore, it is submitted that the judgment must reasonably be understood as to mean that the Commercial Agents Directive contains an implied, tacit provision corresponding to the explicit rule in Article 6(2) of the Unfair Terms Directive. This tacit provi-

---

[13] OJ 1986 L 382 p. 17.

[14] Case C-381/98, [2000] ECR I-9305. See also Bogdan, *SvJT* 2001 pp. 339-342.

sion of EC law enjoys precedence in relation to the Rome Convention by virtue of the Convention's Article 20.

The arguments used by the ECJ in the *Ingmar* Case (the need to protect the freedom of establishment and undistorted competition), it appears, would be equally valid in respect of almost any other mandatory rule of substantive private law which has been harmonized by an EC directive, for example, Article 5(3) of Directive No 90/314 of 13 June 1990 on Package Travel, Package Holidays and Package Tours.[15] It remains to be seen whether this means that all such harmonized mandatory rules must be interpreted to provide implicitly even protection against the choice of law of a non-member state, whenever the relationship has a sufficiently close connection with the territory of the Member States.

Finally, it should be recalled that Article 1(3) of the Rome Convention excludes from the Convention's scope those contracts of insurance which cover risks situated in the territories of the EC Member States.[16] This gap is filled by conflict rules found in two directives, namely, Article 7 of the Second Directive No 88/357 of 22 June 1988 on the Coordination of Laws, Regulations and Administrative Provisions relating to Direct Insurance Other than Life Assurance[17] and Article 32 of Directive No 2002/83 of 5 November 2002 concerning Life Assurance[18]. These conflict rules, in particular Article 7 of the 1988 Directive, have been criticized for being excessively complicated and cannot be presented here in detail,[19] but it is noteworthy that both directives stipulate that, subject to the exceptions set by the special conflict rules in the directives themselves, the Member States have to apply, even to insurance contracts covering risks situated in the EC Member States, the general rules of PIL concerning contractual relations. This means that both directives refer back, as the last resort, to the Rome Convention.

9.2 The Directive on Electronic Commerce

The EC Directive No 2000/31 of 8 June 2000 on Certain Legal Aspects of Information Society Services, in particular Electronic Commerce, in the Internal Market (Directive on Electronic Commerce)[20], due to its ambiguity, is one of the most criticized pieces of EC legislation, in particular among PIL specialists.[21]

---

[15] OJ 1990 L 158 p. 59.

[16] See section 7.1 *supra*.

[17] OJ 1988 L 172 p. 1, as amended by Directive No 92/49 of 18 June 1992, OJ 1992 L 228 p. 1.

[18] OJ 2002 L 345 p. 1.

[19] See, for example, Pålsson, *SvJT* 1993 pp. 43-63; Philip, *EU-IP*, pp. 161-165; Seatzu, *Insurance*.

[20] OJ 2000 L 178 p. 1.

[21] See, for example, Fallon & Meeusen, *Rev.crit.d.i.p.* 2002 pp. 435-490; Fezer & Koos, *IPRax* 2000 pp. 350-354; Grundmann, *RabelsZ* 2003 pp. 246-297; Halfmeier, *ZEuP* 2001 pp. 837-868; M. Hellner in Fuchs *et al.* (eds.), *Les conflits*, pp. 205-224; Spindler, *IPRax* 2001 pp. 400-411.

The main purpose of the Directive, as defined in its Article 1(1), is to contribute to the proper functioning of the internal market by ensuring the free movement of "information society services", in particular electronic commerce services, between Member States. Pursuant to Article 3(1), each Member State must ensure that electronic commerce services provided by a service provider established in its territory comply with those of its national provisions that fall within the "coordinated field". This "coordinated field" is defined very broadly and goes far beyond those areas of law that have been harmonized by EC legislation. A corollary of the obligation on the part of the country of origin to ensure that the services comply with its law is the duty of the Member States where the services are received not to restrict, for reasons falling within the "coordinated field", the freedom to provide services from another Member State (Article 3(2)), although the receiving Member States may use exceptionally a special procedure in order to take proportionate restricting measures necessary for the protection of certain public interests (Article 3(4-6)). It is highly controversial and much disputed whether this country-of-origin principle prevails in electronic commerce over the established PIL rules, for example, those in the Rome Convention.

On its face, the Directive does not deal with PIL issues at all. In fact, Article 1(4) states explicitly that "[t]his Directive does not establish additional rules on private international law nor does it deal with the jurisdiction of courts". Also, this is stated in recital 23 of the Directive's Preamble, which adds, however, that provisions of the applicable law designated by rules of PIL must not restrict the freedom to provide information society services as established in the Directive itself. This statement reveals that the relationship between the Directive and PIL is more complicated than a superficial reading of Article 1(4) might indicate. Much of the controversy is about whether and to what extent private-law issues belong to the above-mentioned "coordinated field", as defined in Article 2(h). This definition includes requirements, laid down in Member States, with which the provider of information society services has to comply in respect of i.a. his behaviour, the quality or content of the service including advertising, contracts and liability, irrespective of whether these requirements are of a general nature or are specifically designed for electronic commerce. Even though requirements applicable to goods as such, delivery of goods, and services not provided by electronic means are excluded explicitly, it is clear that some of the matters mentioned in the definition of "coordinated field" are typical private-law issues. Furthermore, recital 25 in the Preamble states that national courts, including civil courts dealing with private-law disputes, can take measures to derogate from the freedom to provide information society services, but merely in conformity with "conditions established in this Directive", which is also an indication of the fact that the courts of the Member States generally are not free to disregard the Directive's country-of-origin principle when dealing with private law.

The most important exceptions from the country-of-origin principle follow from Article 3(3) of the Directive, which stipulates that the first two paragraphs of Article 3 do not apply in the fields referred to in an Annex.[22] In view of the general exclusion of PIL from the scope of the Directive (see above), it is surprising and confusing to find the freedom of the parties to choose the law applicable to their contract among the exclusions in the Annex, which in addition refers to certain other typical matters of private law, such as contractual obligations concerning consumer contracts and formal validity of certain contracts concerning real property. If the list of exclusions in the Annex is interpreted *e contrario* to mean that other issues of private law are included in the "coordinated field", then the country-of-origin principle stipulated in the first two paragraphs of Article 3 will function as a kind of extremely broad PIL rule favoring the application, to such "coordinated" issues, of the law of the Member State where the service provider is established. The opposite – and preferable – interpretation is that the fuzziness of the concept of "coordinated field" and the abstruse wording of the Annex should be given less importance than the unequivocal statement in Article 1(4) that the Directive does not intend to establish additional rules of PIL, *i.e.* that it does not affect the application of the conflict rules enacted in the Rome Convention and other established PIL instruments.

Various Member States seem to have come to various conclusions on this point and have implemented the Directive in various ways. It remains to be seen which interpretation will win the approval of the ECJ. Similar problems in the future may arise also in connection with other instruments of EC law regulating the free movement of goods, persons, services and capital, for example, the future Directive on Services in the Internal Market.[23]

9.3   Some Other Regulations and Directives

A number of conflict rules are found in various EC regulations and directives, dealing with a variety of legal subjects. Their importance varies too. Some of them are relatively complicated and the following presentation is a mere non-exhaustive collection of references rather than a proper introduction to the contents of these rules.

The EC law has created some supra-national juridical persons, which are regulated by directly applicable EC rules rather than by the national company law of a particular Member State. These EC rules, however, are not exhaustive, and they leave substantial residual space for the application of national law, thus giving rise to PIL questions about which law should be applied. The first such instrument is Regulation No 2137/85 of 25 July 1985 on the European Economic Interest Grouping (EEIG).[24] Pursuant to Article 2(1) of this Regula-

---

[22] The Annex is found in OJ 2000 L 178 p. 16.

[23] See the Commission's proposal, COM(2004)2 final, as amended in COM(2006)160 final.

[24] OJ 1985 L 199 p. 1.

tion, the law applicable to the contract for the formation of an EEIG, as well as to its internal organization, is the internal law of the Member State in which the official address is situated, as laid down in the contract for the formation of the grouping. Article 1(2) provides that the groupings have the capacity, in their own name, to have rights and obligations of all kinds, to make contracts or accomplish other legal acts, and to sue and be sued, but it leaves it to the law of the Member State of registration to determine whether or not the grouping formally has legal personality of its own (Article 1(3)). The fact that Article 1(3) refers to the law of the country of registration, while Article 2(1) refers to the law of the country of the grouping's official address, does not reflect any real difference. As the EEIG must be registered in the Member State, in which it has its official address (Article 6), both references lead to the application of the same legal system.

Of greater practical importance than the EEIG is potentially the "European Company" (*Societas Europea* or SE company).[25] Since 8 October 2004, such companies can be founded on the basis of Regulation No 2157/2001 on the Statute for a European Company (SE).[26] The Regulation contains numerous important provisions of substantive company law of its own, but also many references to national company law. For example, Article 15(1) stipulates that the formation of an SE is governed by the law applicable to public limited-liability companies in the Member State in which the SE establishes its registered office (identical to the country of registration, Article 12). Pursuant to the more general rules in Articles 9 and 10, matters not regulated by the Regulation itself in principle are governed by the law of the Member State where the SE has its registered office (=is registered). The most interesting new feature of an SE is that it is allowed to move its registered office from one Member State to another, without the necessity of winding up and creating a new legal person. The move requires, however, a new registration and entails a change of the applicable law on points not governed by the substantive rules of the Regulation itself.

Rather similar to an SE from the PIL point of view is an SCE, founded on the basis of Regulation No 1435/2003 of 22 July 2003 on the Statute for a European Cooperative Society (SCE).[27] This Regulation can be used from 18 August 2006.

Of interest for PIL is also Directive No 2005/56 of 26 October 2005 on Cross-border Mergers of Limited Liability Companies,[28] which applies to mergers of limited liability companies "formed in accordance with the law of a Member State", provided that at least two of them "are governed by the laws of different Member States" (Article 1). Pursuant to Article 4, a company taking part in a cross-border merger must comply, regarding many aspects of the merger, with the national law to which it is subject (Article 4). The law of the

---

[25] See, for example, Magnier, *Rev.crit.d.i.p.* 2004 pp. 555-587.

[26] OJ 2001 L 294 p. 1.

[27] OJ 2003 L 207 p. 1.

[28] OJ 2005 L 310 p. 1.

Member State to whose legal system[29] the company resulting from the merger is subject determines the date on which the merger takes effect (Article 12).

With regard to cabotage transport, performed between two places within the same host Member State by a carrier established in another Member State, Article 6 of Regulation No 3118/93 of 25 October 1993 laying down the Conditions under which Non-resident Carriers May Operate National Road Haulage Services within a Member State[30] and Article 4 of Regulation No 12/98 of 11 December 1998 laying down the Conditions under which Non-resident Carriers May Operate National Road Passenger Services within a Member State[31] stipulate that the performance in principle is subject to the law of the host Member State regarding a number of issues listed in those Articles, including the rates and conditions governing the transport contract.

A mention also can be made of Article 12 in Directive No 93/7 of 15 March 1993 on the Return of Cultural Objects Unlawfully Removed from the Territory of a Member State.[32] This Directive allows the Member State, from which the cultural object was unlawfully removed, to request its return. Article 12 provides that ownership of the cultural object after its return is governed by the law of the requesting Member State. This means, for example, that a *bona fide* acquisition of ownership while the object was abroad, in particular through a purchase in good faith, is not governed by the usual conflict rule on rights *in rem* leading to the application of *lex rei sitae* (the law of the country where the object was situated at the time of the acquisition), but rather by the substantive law of the Member State from which the object had been unlawfully removed. It appears that this conflict rule is intended to preclude or restrict valid acquisitions of the object while it is unlawfully situated abroad, but the same rule may lead to the opposite effect if the substantive law of the Member State from which the object was unlawfully removed is more permissive, with regard to acquisitions of ownership, than the law of the country to which the object was taken and where it was situated at the time of the transaction under scrutiny.

Some rather special rights *in rem* are dealt with by Article 8 and Article 9(2) of Directive No 98/26 of 19 May 1998 on Settlement Finality in Payment and Securities Settlement Systems (the so-called Finality Directive).[33] In the event insolvency proceedings are opened against a participant in a clearing system for securities (paperless shares, bonds, *etc.*), the rights and obligations arising from or in connection with his participation are to be determined by the law governing that clearing system itself (Article 8).[34] Where securities are provided as

---

[29] The English text of the Directive uses misleadingly the word "jurisdiction".

[30] OJ 1993 L 279 p. 1.

[31] OJ 1998 L 4 p. 10.

[32] OJ 1993 L 74 p. 74.

[33] OJ 1998 L 166 p. 45.

[34] Cf. also Article 9 of Regulation No 1346/2000 of 29 May 2000 on Insolvency Proceedings, OJ 2000 L 160 p. 1.

collateral to participants or banks in connection with a system, and their rights with respect to the securities are legally recorded on a register in a Member State, then the determination of their rights as collateral holders is governed by the law of that Member State (Article 9(2)). Related questions are dealt with also in Article 9 of Directive No 2002/47 of 6 June 2002 on Financial Collateral Arrangements,[35] which gives the principle expressed in Article 9(2) of the Finality Directive a more general applicability by providing that a number of listed proprietary matters regarding securities, title to which is evidenced by entries in a register or account maintained by an intermediary, are governed by the law of the country in which the relevant account is maintained.[36] This is an expression of the so-called PRIMA principle (Place of Relevant InterMediary Approach), which seems now to be accepted generally even outside the EC.

The conflict rules in the Commission's proposal of 15 December 2005 for a Regulation on Jurisdiction, Applicable Law, Recognition and Enforcement of Decisions and Cooperation in Matters relating to Maintenance Obligations[37] also deserve to be mentioned. Pursuant to the main rule in Article 13 of the proposal, maintenance obligations will be governed by the law of the country where the creditor is habitually resident, but the law of the forum will apply instead if the law of the creditor's country does not enable the creditor to obtain maintenance, or if the debtor is habitually resident in the forum country and the creditor requests the application of *lex fori*. These conflict rules will, however, be disregarded when the law they designate does not enable the creditor to obtain maintenance and the maintenance obligation has a close (not necessarily the closest!) connection with another country, in particular the country of the common nationality of the parties, in which case the law of that country will be applied. Pursuant to the proposed Article 15, the maintenance debtor can, regardless of the applicable law, oppose the maintenance obligation other than towards a child, vulnerable adult, spouse or ex-spouse on the ground that there is no such obligation under the law of the country of the common nationality of the parties or, in the absence of a common nationality, under the law of the habitual residence of the debtor; in the case of maintenance obligations between spouses or ex-spouses, the opposition can be based on the law of the country with which the marriage has the closest connection. This unnecessarily complex system is further complicated by the proposed Article 14, giving the parties the right to agree on the applicable law but restricting that right in several respects, and by the proposed Article 17(2), which stipulates that whatever the contents of the applicable law, the needs of the creditor and the resources of the debtor must be taken into account when determining the amount of maintenance. It is not quite

---

[35] OJ 2002 L 168 p. 43.

[36] Cf. also Article 24 of Directive No 2001/24 of 4 April 2001 on the Reorganization and Winding up of Credit Institutions, OJ 2001 L 125 p. 15.

[37] COM(2005)649 final and the Commission's commentary on the proposal in COM(2006)206 final.

[38] COM(2006)399 final.

clear what "taking into account" means in this context. Another novel feature is that although the law designated by the proposed conflict rules is to be applied whether or not it is the law of a Member State, the public policy clause in Article 20 can be used against the application of the laws of non-member states only.

Finally, the Commission's proposal of 17 July 2006 for a Regulation Amending Regulation No 2201/2003 as regards Jurisdiction and Introducing Rules concerning Applicable Law in Matrimonial Matters[38] suggests some harmonized conflict rules in matters of divorce and legal separation (but not in matters of marriage annulment). The proposed rules are in principle intended to apply irrespective of whether they designate the law of the Member State or of a third country. The rules are in the first place based on the principle of party autonomy, although the freedom of choice of the spouses is limited to laws with which they have a close connection. The spouses may choose between the law of the country of the last common habitual residence insofar as at least one spouse still resides there, the law of the country of the nationality of either spouse,[39] the law of the country where the spouses have resided for at least five years and the law of the Member State in which the application is lodged. The choice-of-law agreement must be in writing and signed at the latest at the time the court is seized. In the absence of a valid choice, divorce and legal separation will, pursuant to the proposal, be subject to the law determined on the basis of a scale of connecting factors. In the first place, the law of the country of the common habitual residence of the spouses will be applied. Is there no such law, the last common habitual residence will be decisive insofar as one of the spouses still resides there. Failing that, the law of the country of which both spouses are nationals (or in the case of the United Kingdom and Ireland, both have their "domicile") will be applied. In the last resort, the proposal refers to the *lex fori*.

---

[39] In the case of the United Kingdom and Ireland, the law of the country of the "domicile" of either spouse.

CHAPTER 10

The Insolvency Regulation

10.1 The Scope and Other General Features of the Regulation

After almost four decades of fruitless efforts, EC Regulation No 1346/2000 on Insolvency Proceedings was adopted on 29 May 2000 and entered into force on 31 May 2002.[1] The purpose of the Regulation is neither to serve as a legal basis for supra-national, truly European bankruptcies nor (with some minor exceptions) to unify or harmonize the substantive insolvency law of the Member States, which would be a hopeless task, doomed to failure having regard to the widely different views and rules in different Member States on such matters as security interests and preferential rights. On the contrary, the Regulation's system builds totally on national insolvency proceedings and limits itself to regulating the PIL aspects thereof, primarily with regard to questions such as jurisdiction, applicable law, and recognition and enforcement. As other EC instruments enacted on the basis of Title IV of the EC Treaty, the Regulation does not apply in relation to Denmark.

The wording of the Insolvency Regulation is often far from crystal-clear and at times can be considered enigmatic. There is, so far, very little case law of the ECJ regarding its interpretation and application.[2] The contents of the Regulation is practically identical to that of the defunct EC Convention on Insolvency Proceedings of 1995,[3] which has been commented upon in an explanatory report, authored by Miguel Virgos and Etienne Schmit.[4] Although not formally binding and never published in the Official Journal, the Virgos/Schmit Report had a semi-official status with regard to the Convention and can provide important guidance as to the interpretation and application of the Regulation as well.[5]

The Regulation applies to those collective insolvency proceedings, opened or to be opened in a Member State, which entail the partial or total divestment of a debtor and the appointment of a liquidator (Article 1). This delimitation of the scope of the Regulation theoretically might cause problems of interpretation, especially since the Regulation does not even contain a definition of "insolvency", but such problems will arise very rarely since the types of national

---

[1]   See OJ 2000 L 160 p. 1. The original Annexes to the Insolvency Regulation were subsequently amended and replaced by new ones, see Regulation No 603/2005, OJ 2005 L 100 p. 1 and Regulation No 694/2006, OJ 2006 L 121 p. 1.

[2]   See, however, the decision in the matter of *Staubitz-Schreiber*, case C-1/04, [2006] ECR I-701 and *Eurofood*, case C-341/04, [2006] ECR I-0000.

[3]   The text of the Convention is found in, *i.a.*, 5 *Int.Insolv.Rev.* 171-185 (1996).

[4]   Document 6500/96 of the Council.

[5]   See also, for example, Becker, *ZEuP* 2002 pp. 287-315; Bogdan, *Sveriges och EU:s internationella insolvensrätt*; Bogdan, 6 *Int.Insolv.Rev.* 114-126 (1997); Bogdan, *Revue des affaires européennes* 2001-2002 pp. 452-459; Bureau, *Rev.crit.d.i.p.* 2002 pp. 613-679; Duursma-Kepplinger & Duursma, *IPRax* 2003 pp. 505-511; Garrido, 7 *Int.Insolv.Rev.* 79-94 (1998); Jobard-Bachellier, *Rev.crit.d.i.p.* 2002 pp. 491-507; Johnson, 5 *Int.Insolv.Rev.* 80-107 (1996); Kayser, 7 *Int.Insolv.Rev.* 95-140 (1998); Mellqvist, *EU:s insolvensförordning*; Moss et al. (eds.), *The EC Regulation*; Poillot-Peruzetto, *Clunet* 1997 pp. 757-781.

proceedings contemplated by the Regulation are exhaustively enumerated, country by country, in Annex A. This means that it is normally of limited practical interest that the Regulation does not intend to apply to proceedings that aim at the satisfaction of an individual creditor rather than of the whole collective of creditors and that the condition of at least a partial divestment of the debtor is fulfilled even when he retains the possession of his assets but does not have total freedom to dispose of them without the consent of the liquidator. These criteria, however, may be relevant as to whether the Regulation applies to, for example, provisional measures preceding the opening of proceedings listed in Annex A.[6]

A narrower sub-group among the insolvency proceedings listed in Annex A are the "winding-up proceedings" listed in Annex B, comprising only traditional bankruptcies which normally purport to realize and liquidate the assets of the debtor rather than achieve his economic survival. The Regulation does not provide any special term for or any list of those insolvency proceedings that are not of a winding-up nature (for example, compositions and reconstructions), but this group, which can be appropriately called "reconstruction proceedings", consists of all proceedings that are mentioned in Annex A but not in Annex B. There is also an Annex C, listing various types of liquidators in the various Member States, and it is worth noticing that the liquidator does not have to be a natural person but can be a "body", such as a corporation or an institution (Article 2(b)).

The Regulation covers insolvency proceedings regardless of whether the debtor is a juridical or a natural person, a businessman or a common consumer, an estate of a deceased person, *etc.* On the other hand, pursuant to Article 1(2), the Regulation does not apply to insolvency proceedings concerning insurance undertakings and credit institutions; these are governed by two subsequent EC directives, namely Directive No 2001/17 of 19 March 2001 on the Reorganisation and Winding-up of Insurance Undertakings[7], and Directive No 2001/24 of 4 April 2001 on the Reorganisation and Winding-up of Credit Institutions[8]. These directives, which cannot be described here in more detail, are inspired to some extent by the Regulation but are not based on Title IV of the EC Treaty but rather on the Treaty's provisions on the freedom of establishment. This means that they are applicable also in relation to Denmark.

The Regulation purports to complement the Brussels I Regulation, which excludes explicitly, in its Article 1, "bankruptcy, proceedings relating to the winding-up of insolvent companies or other legal persons, judicial arrangements, compositions and analogous proceedings".[9] However, the Insolvency Regulation goes far beyond filling this gap in the Brussels I Regulation, as it does not restrict itself to matters of jurisdiction, recognition and enforcement but deals also with other questions, such as the applicable law. As between

---

[6] See *Eurofood*, case C-341/04, [2006] ECR I-0000.

[7] OJ 2001 L 110 p. 28.

[8] OJ 2001 L 125 p. 15. See, for example, Galanti, 11 *Int.Insolv.Rev.* 49-66 (2002).

[9] See section 3.2 *supra.*

the Member States, the Regulation superseded a number of earlier insolvency treaties (Article 44). For example, after the entry into force of the Insolvency Regulation, the Nordic Bankruptcy Convention of 1933 ceased to apply between Finland and Sweden but continues to apply in both these countries in relation to Denmark, Iceland and Norway.

10.2 Jurisdiction

Article 3 of the Regulation governs the international jurisdiction of the Member States, without affecting the national rules regarding local jurisdiction of courts within a particular Member State.

If the centre of the debtor's main interests is situated within a Member State, that state has jurisdiction to open insolvency proceedings pursuant to Article 3(1). The Regulation does not define the concept of "main interests", but it seems probable that only economic interests are to be taken into consideration. Recital 13 in the Regulation's preamble speaks in this context of the place where the debtor conducts the administration of his interests on a regular basis and which therefore is ascertainable by third parties. There can be only one such place regarding each debtor. In the case of a company or legal person, the place of the registered office is presumed to be the centre of its main interests in the absence of proof to the contrary. According to the ECJ, this presumption can be rebutted only under very special circumstances, such as when factors that are both objective and ascertainable by third parties show that the debtor is a "letterbox" company not carrying out any business in the territory of the Member State in which its registered office is situated.[10] There is no corresponding presumption for debtors who are natural persons, but the Virgos/Schmit Report indicates that the habitual residence or main place of business normally will be given decisive weight.[11] Proceedings opened in the Member State where the debtor has the centre of his main interests are in the following called "main proceedings".[12]

The Regulation assumes, and in fact indirectly requires, that main insolvency proceedings aim at including also assets situated in the other Member States. Whether the proceedings aspire to comprise assets in non-member states as well is a question that is not answered by the Regulation, but main proceedings do usually have such ambitions pursuant to the national PIL of the country where they were opened.[13]

---

[10] See *Eurofood*, case C-341/04, [2006] ECR I-0000.

[11] See the Virgos/Schmit Report, point 75.

[12] The Regulation itself (for example, in Articles 16(2) and 17(1)) speaks of "proceedings referred to in Article 3(1)", but switches to "main proceedings" when distinguishing these proceedings from the secondary ones (see section 10.5 *infra*).

[13] Whether such extra-territorial ambitions will be accepted and recognized in the non-member country where the assets are located is a different matter, to be decided by the PIL of the non-member country in questions.

A Member State other than that where the debtor has his centre of main interests has jurisdiction to open insolvency proceedings if – and only if – the debtor possesses an establishment there (Article 3(2)). In such a case, the effects of the proceedings are merely territorial, *i.e.*, limited to the assets situated within that country, and the proceedings will normally have the character of secondary proceedings in relation to the main proceedings previously opened in another Member State. It follows from Article 3(3) that such secondary proceedings must be of the winding-up type, as it is hardly possible to reconstruct a mere establishment.

Under certain circumstances specified in Article 3(4), territorially limited insolvency proceedings may be opened in a Member State, where the debtor has an establishment, even prior to the opening of main proceedings in the Member State of the debtor's main interests. Such independent territorial proceedings can be opened in two situations only, the first one occurring when main proceedings cannot be started due to the conditions laid down by the law of the Member State of the debtor's main interests, for example, because that law does not provide for bankruptcies of natural persons who are not business-men. The second situation arises when the creditor requesting the opening of the proceedings has his domicile, habitual residence or registered office in the Member State where the debtor's establishment is situated, or when the request-ing creditor's claim arises from the operation of that establishment (it, however, must be kept in mind that these requirements pertain merely to the opening of the proceedings and that once the proceedings are opened, all legitimate credi-tors are allowed to participate irrespective of their origin or the origin of their claims). Independent territorial proceedings, which are expected to be relatively rare, in some respects are subjected to special rules (Articles 36-37), in particu-lar regarding the possibilities of a total or partial conversion of such proceedings into secondary-like proceedings after the initiation of main proceedings in the Member State of the debtor's main interests. The conversion depends mainly on the stage the independent territorial proceedings have reached before the open-ing of the main proceedings.

It is noteworthy that the presence of assets, irrespective of how substantial, in a Member State does not suffice for bankruptcy jurisdiction if the debtor has his centre of main interests in another Member State. On the other hand, the concept of establishment seems to be intended to be interpreted more exten-sively than, for example, "branch, agency or other establishment" in Article 5(5) of the Brussels I Regulation.[14] Pursuant to Article 2(h) of the Insolvency Regulation, "establishment" means any place of operations where the debtor carries out a non-transitory economic activity with human means and goods. It has been discussed whether even the centre of the debtor's main interests constitutes an establishment according to this definition, so that the applicant can choose between applying for main or territorial proceedings there, but it

---

[14] See the Virgos/Schmit Report, point 70.

must be noted that Article 3(2) speaks only of an establishment in the territory of a Member State other than where the centre of the debtor's main interests is situated, which should mean that territorial proceedings cannot be initiated in the last-mentioned country.

The localization of assets is given great weight in the Regulation. As has already been said, the effects of territorial proceedings are restricted to the property situated in the Member State where they are opened. Even main proceedings, albeit not restricted in this way, are denied certain effects in respect of assets situated in the other Member States.[15] Article 2(g) explains therefore where certain types of assets are considered to be situated. Tangible property is situated in the Member State where it is situated, which is hardly surprising and might even be a tautology. Of greater interest is that where ownership or entitlement must be entered in a public register, the property or rights are deemed to be situated in the Member State under the authority of which the register is kept, and that claims are situated in the Member State within the territory of which the obliged third party (thus not the bankrupt) has the center of his main interests.

Bankruptcy jurisdiction regarding debtors having their center of main interests in a non-member country is not governed by the Regulation and is left to be decided by the national jurisdictional rules of each Member State. Insolvency proceedings opened in a Member State concerning such debtors are not subject to the Regulation and are not entitled to recognition in the other Member States by virtue of the Regulation, although they may be recognized pursuant to the national PIL of the Member State where recognition is sought.

The Virgos/Schmit Report suggests that Article 3 regulates not merely the jurisdiction to open insolvency proceedings but even the jurisdiction to deal with actions directly derived from insolvency and in close connection with the insolvency proceedings, such as disputes about the voidability of the debtor's transactions made prior to bankruptcy or about the personal liability of managers of a bankrupt enterprise. Such disputes are not covered by the Brussels I Regulation[16] and the Report finds it therefore logical to subject them to Article 3 of the Insolvency Regulation in order to avoid "unjustifiable loopholes".[17] This extensive interpretation of Article 3, however, has no support in its wording and may give rise to complications due to the fact that these kinds of disputes in some Member States are dealt with within the framework of the bankruptcy itself while in other Member States they are adjudicated in separate proceedings.

---

[15] See section 10.3 *infra*.

[16] See section 3.2 *supra*.

[17] See the Virgos/Schmit Report, point 77.

10.3 Applicable Law

Pursuant to Articles 4 and 28 of the Insolvency Regulation, the law applicable to insolvency proceedings, both main and territorial, and their effects will be normally that of the Member State within the territory of which the proceedings are opened (*lex concursus*). This law determines the conditions for the opening of the proceedings, their conduct and their closure, in particular questions such as against which debtors insolvency proceedings may be brought, the assets which form the estate,[18] the treatment of assets acquired by the debtor after the opening of the proceedings, the respective powers of the debtor and the liquidator, the conditions under which set-offs may be invoked, the effects of the insolvency proceedings on current contracts of the debtor and on proceedings brought by individual creditors (with the exception of the effects on lawsuits pending, see *infra*), the claims which are to be lodged, the treatment of claims arising after the opening of the insolvency proceedings, the lodging, verification and admission of claims, the distribution of proceeds, the ranking of claims,[19] the rights of creditors who have obtained partial satisfaction after the opening of the proceedings by virtue of a right *in rem* or through a set-off, the conditions for and the effects of the closure of the proceedings (in particular by composition), creditors' rights after the closure of the proceedings, who is to bear the costs and expenses incurred in the proceedings, and the voidness, voidability or unenforceability of legal acts detrimental to all the creditors. These matters, enumerated in a non-exhaustive manner in Article 4(2), can be classified as typical issues of insolvency law. More general questions of private-law nature also may arise in connection with insolvency proceedings, for example, the question of whether a particular suretyship or guarantee is invalid because it was not created in writing or whether a claim lodged by a creditor is barred by time limitation, but such issues are governed by the law determined by the more general conflict rules in the forum country (such as the Rome Convention on the Law Applicable to Contractual Obligations[20]), because there are no reasons why they should be treated differently in insolvency proceedings than in other contexts.

---

[18] See, however, Article 12, which provides that Community patents, Community trade marks and any other similar rights established by Community law (for example, Community designs and Community plant variety rights) are included only in main proceedings, and not in territorial proceedings such as the secondary ones. This is obviously related to the difficulties in localizing such rights in one single Member State only.

[19] It is worth noting that Article 36 of the Commission's proposal of 15 December 2005 for a Regulation on Jurisdiction, Applicable Law, Recognition and Enforcement of Decisions and Cooperation in Matters relating to Maintenance Obligations, COM(2005)649 final, provides that maintenance claims are to be paid in preference to all the other debts, including the debts from expenses of the enforcement of maintenance decisions.

[20] See Chapter 7 *supra*.

There are a number of important exceptions from the main principle of *lex concursus*. Of particularly great interest is the protection, for the sake of security of credits, of the rights *in rem* enjoyed by secured creditors. According to Article 5, the opening of insolvency proceedings in one Member State will not affect the rights *in rem* (liens, mortgages, *etc.*) of creditors or third parties in respect of assets situated in other Member States. This is not a conflict rule in the strict sense, as it does not determine the law to be applied but rather gives the security interests in question some kind of "immunity" against the effects of the insolvency proceedings, regardless of the contents of the substantive rules of both *lex concursus* and *lex rei sitae*. Whether the security interest has been validly created is a matter of general private law; as such, it is not governed by the Regulation but rather by the general conflict rules of the forum (see *supra*).

A similar kind of immunity is stipulated in Article 6 for the right of creditors to demand the set-off of their claims against the claims of the debtor: if such a set-off is permitted by the law applicable to the insolvent debtor's claim, then it is not affected by the insolvency proceedings.[21] Article 7 grants similar immunity against the effects of bankruptcy also to the seller's rights based on a reservation of title, and to the buyer's right to acquire title,[22] provided that at the time of the opening of proceedings the asset was situated in the territory of a Member State other than the state of the opening.

The immunity under Articles 5, 6 and 7 does not extend, however, to actions for voidness, voidability or unenforceability of legal acts detrimental to all the creditors, for example, an action by the liquidator to recover assets sold cheaply by the insolvent debtor to his spouse shortly before the opening of the proceedings. Such recovery in principle is governed by the *lex concursus* (see Article 4(2)(m)), but an exception is made in Article 13 for those cases where the person who benefits from the act (for example, the person who bought the asset cheaply short time before the opening of the proceedings) proves that the act is subject to the law of another Member State and that law does not allow any means of challenging that act. This provision deserves to be criticized, since it is hardly reasonable that the law governing the contract, which may have been chosen by the bankrupt and his co-contractant,[23] can protect the contract against being challenged by third parties, such as the liquidator or the creditors harmed by the fraudulent transaction.

The Regulation contains a number of special conflict rules on certain selected issues. Thus, the effects of insolvency proceedings on contracts confer-

---

[21] This immunity is of interest only if the set-off is not permitted by the *lex concursus*, which may allow it pursuant to Article 4(2)(d).

[22] It is logical therefore that Article 7 states also that the opening of insolvency proceedings against the seller shall not constitute grounds for rescinding or terminating the sale by the buyer, if the asset sold was situated in another Member State at the time of the opening.

[23] See section 7.2 *supra* about Article 3 of the Rome Convention on the Law Applicable to Contractual Obligations.

ring the right to acquire immoveable property or to make use of such property are governed solely by the law of the Member State where the property is situated (Article 8). The effects of insolvency proceedings on the rights and obligations of the parties in relation to a payment or settlement system (netting) or in relation to a financial market in principle are governed solely by the law of the Member State applicable to that system or market, although there are some exceptions (Article 9). The effects of insolvency proceedings on employment relationships are governed solely by the law of the Member State applicable to the contract of employment (Article 10). The effects of insolvency proceedings on the right of the debtor in a registered immovable property, ship or aircraft are determined by the law of the Member State under the authority of which the register is kept (Article 11). The validity of the debtor's disposals, for consideration and after the opening of the proceedings, of immovable property, registered ship or aircraft or securities registered in a register laid down by law is similarly in principle governed by the law of the state where the immovable assets are situated or under the authority of which the register is kept (Article 14). Finally, the effects of insolvency proceedings on a pending lawsuit concerning an asset of which the debtor has been divested is governed solely by the law of the Member State in which that lawsuit is pending (Article 15).

Some of these conflict rules can be criticized for being too broad and unsophisticated. For example, Article 4(2)(e) stipulates that the effects of insolvency proceedings on current contracts to which the debtor is a party are governed by the *lex concursus*. This rule does not take into account the fundamental difference between the question whether the bankruptcy entitles the liquidator to avoid disadvantageous contracts (a typical matter of insolvency law, appropriately governed by the *lex concursus*) and the question whether the bankruptcy entitles the other party to repudiate contracts due to the anticipated inability of the bankrupt to fulfill his part of the deal (a typical issue of contract law, which should appropriately be governed by the law applicable to the contract in question).

The exceptions from the application of the *lex concursus* apply generally in favour of the laws of other Member States only, although Articles 6 and 14 do not say so explicitly. However, the Virgos/Schmit Report states that the fact that an exception rule cannot be used because there is no sufficient connection with the Member States (for example, if the above-mentioned Article 10 cannot be used because the employment contract in question is subject to the law of a non-member state) does not mean that the *lex concursus* becomes applicable pursuant to the main rule in Article 4, but rather that the Member State of the forum is free to follow its own national conflict rules.[24] An interesting difference among the conflict rules is that most of them (Articles 8, 9, 10 and 15) state that the issue under scrutiny is governed "solely" by the designated legal system, whereas other (Articles 11 and 14) omit that word, which might indicate that

---

[24] See the Virgos/Schmit Report, point 93.

in those matters the *lex concursus* should perhaps also be taken into account in some cumulative way.[25]

The Virgos/Schmit Report states that the conflict rules of the Regulation refer to the internal law of the designated Member State, excluding its rules of PIL.[26] The Regulation thus is opposed to the concept of *renvoi*. Further, the Report suggests that the provisions of the Regulation, including its conflict rules, should be applied by the court of its own motion even if they are not invoked by any of the parties concerned, although it is for the national law (obviously the *lex fori*) to determine whether the judge must himself investigate and establish the relevant facts and circumstances leading to the application of a particular rule or whether it is for the interested parties to do so.[27]

10.4   Recognition and Enforcement

It follows from Article 16 of the Regulation that insolvency proceedings opened in a Member State which has jurisdiction pursuant to Article 3 will be recognized automatically in all the other Member States[28] as from the time when the proceedings became effective in the state of the opening, although such recognition does not preclude the subsequent opening of parallel secondary proceedings in a Member State where the debtor owns an establishment.

Even proceedings opened in a Member State where the debtor merely has an establishment are entitled to being recognized in other Member States pursuant to Article 16, but it follows from their territorial character that they are recognized only regarding property situated in the Member State where they were opened. Unfortunately, the Regulation does not oblige the court opening the proceedings to state in its decision whether it based its jurisdiction on the debtor's center of main interest or merely on the presence of an establishment, but the inclusion of this information in the judgment opening the proceedings can be required by the *lex concursus*. Even though it does not follow from the text of the Regulation, the main proceedings opened by a court of a Member State must be recognized as such in the other Member States, which are not permitted to review the jurisdiction of the opening Member State,[29] for example, in connection with the recognition of the extra-territorial effects of the proceedings in question.

---

[25] See the Virgos/Schmit Report, point 130.

[26] See the Virgos/Schmit Report, point 87.

[27] See the Virgos/Schmit Report, point 47.

[28] The proceedings must be recognized by the Community institutions as well, see *Commission v. AMI*, case C-294/02, [2005] ECR I-2175, points 64-72.

[29] See *Eurofood*, case C-341/04, [2006] ECR I-0000.

Recognition means that the judgment produces, with no further formalities being required, the same effects in the other Member States as under the law of the state of the opening of the proceedings (Article 17). This includes normally the termination of the debtor's authority to dispose of the assets, as well as putting an end to judgment executions in favour of individual creditors. The liquidator appointed in the main proceedings may exercise all the powers conferred upon him by the law of the state of the opening of the proceedings even in the other Member States (unless secondary proceedings have been opened there), including the power to remove the debtor's assets from the Member State in which they are situated (Article 18). The Regulation tries in this way to avoid a situation where the authority of the same liquidator appointed in the main proceedings would vary from country to country. The recognition of the powers conferred upon the liquidator by the *lex concursus* means that a foreign liquidator may sometimes have greater powers than those that would be given to a corresponding local liquidator by the law of the Member State where the foreign liquidator is acting. On the other hand, Article 18(3) obligates the liquidator appointed in main proceedings to comply, when exercising his powers, with the local law, in particular with regard to modalities such as procedures for the realization of assets. The liquidator must be able to prove his appointment by means of a certified copy of the decision appointing him or a certificate issued by the court having jurisdiction (Article 19). The powers of a temporary administrator, preceding the opening of main proceedings, to request preservation measures to secure assets in other Member States are regulated in Article 38.

The liquidator may – but is not obliged to – request that notice of the judgment opening the proceedings be published in any other Member State in accordance with the publication procedures provided for there (Article 21). In the case of main proceedings, he also can request that the judgment be registered in the land register, the trade register or other public register kept in the other Member States (Article 22). Those Member States where the debtor has an establishment or where the register is kept may require mandatory publication or registration, but they must not make it a precondition for the recognition of the proceedings. Publication in a particular Member State, however, is relevant for the determination of whether a person, who has paid his debt there to the bankrupt instead of to the liquidator, has acted in good faith and is therefore discharged of the debt (Article 24). Payments made before the publication are presumed, in the absence of proof to the contrary, to have been made in good faith, while later payments are presumed to have been made with knowledge about the opening of the proceedings.

Article 20(1) deals with situations where, despite the opening of main insolvency proceedings, a creditor has obtained a total or partial payment outside of those proceedings, for example, by a judgment enforcement on assets in another Member State. Such payment must be returned to the liquidator. A more complicated situation can arise where, due to the existence of parallel insolvency proceedings, a creditor has already obtained some dividends in other countries. In order to ensure equal treatment of creditors, Article 20(2) prescribes that such a creditor shall obtain a subsequent dividend only after all the other creditors of the same category have received a dividend equivalent to that which he had obtained abroad.

Article 25 deals with the recognition and enforcement of "other judgments" handed down in the Member State where insolvency proceedings have been opened, such as decisions concerning the course and closure of the proceedings, preservation measures, compositions and generally judgments deriving directly from and closely linked with the insolvency proceedings, even if handed down by another court. Such decisions are excluded from the scope of the Brussels I Regulation,[30] but Article 25 stipulates that they have to be recognized with no further formalities and that the Brussels rules regarding enforcement[31] in principle are to be applied to them.

According to Article 25(3), the Member States are not obliged to recognize or enforce a judgment that might result in a limitation of personal freedom or postal secrecy. There is also a traditional clause permitting a refusal on the grounds of public policy (Article 26).[32] However, it follows from Article 16(1) that the refusal must not be based on the fact that in the Member State where recognition is sought insolvency proceedings could not be brought against the debtor because of his capacity (natural person not engaged in business, public-law entity, *etc.*).

10.5   Secondary Proceedings

As has already been pointed out, the opening of main proceedings in the Member State where the debtor has the centre of his main interests does not preclude the opening of secondary proceedings in those other Member States where the debtor has an establishment. In fact, the opening of main proceedings makes the opening of such secondary proceedings easier, since it eliminates the need to examine whether the debtor is insolvent or not (Article 27). This means that secondary proceedings can be opened in a Member State, even if the substantive requirements (inability to pay which is not temporary, cessation of payments, *etc.*) stipulated by the law of that state are not fulfilled. Secondary proceedings are territorial and can be said to serve two seemingly mutually incompatible purposes: they protect the legitimate interests of some

---

[30] See section 3.2 *supra* and the ECJ judgment in the case of *Gourdain* v. *Nadler,* case 133/78, [1979] ECR 733.

[31] Article 25 refers to the 1968 Brussels Convention, but the Brussels I Regulation stipulates in Article 68(2) that any reference to the Convention is to be understood as a reference to the Brussels I Regulation.

[32] See *Eurofood*, case C-341/04, [2006] ECR I-0000.

creditors (usually the local ones) against the foreign main proceedings and, at the same time, assist and support the foreign main proceedings in various ways.

The principal reason why the Regulation accepts parallel insolvency proceedings in more than one Member State, and thus deviates from the ideals of unity and universality in their pure form, is that there are conceivable situations where such parallel proceedings are legitimately preferable from the point of view of certain groups of creditors, for example, when in the country of establishment there are many small creditors who would find it difficult to lodge their claims in the main proceedings opened in a distant Member State, or when the ranking of claims in the main proceedings differs substantially from the law of the country of the establishment.

Just like main proceedings, secondary proceedings in principle are governed by the law of the state where they are opened (Article 28), but they must be winding-up proceedings (Articles 3(3) and 27). The opening of secondary proceedings, pursuant to Article 29, may be requested by the liquidator in the main proceedings (for example, if he finds the assets in a particular Member State so complex that he prefers them to be handled in separate proceedings) or by any other person authorized to do so under local law (for example, an individual creditor who believes that his chances of obtaining a dividend from the local assets are better if these assets are distributed in local secondary proceedings than if they are distributed in the main proceedings in another Member State). The Regulation, however, does not require any specific legal interest on the part of the applicant; the provision envisaged in the preparatory discussions, whereby only those creditors who would benefit from a more favourable legal status (for example, a more favourable ranking) in the secondary proceedings could request the opening of such proceedings, has been deleted.[33] It appears that an individual small creditor in this way can extort the opening of secondary proceedings although the benefits this brings him are marginal and much lower than the disadvantages caused to the rest of the creditors (for example, the costs of having to appoint and pay a separate liquidator in the secondary proceedings). The only way of avoiding this seems to be to convince the creditor in question to withdraw his application, for example, by offering to buy his claim or to compensate him in some other manner.

The Regulation imposes, in particular in Articles 31 and 35, on liquidators in both main and secondary proceedings a far-reaching duty to cooperate in various ways, for example, by exchanging information and by transferring any surplus remaining in secondary proceedings to the liquidator in the main proceedings. The liquidator in secondary proceedings is obliged to give the liquidator in the main proceedings an opportunity to submit proposals on the liquidation or on the use of the assets in the secondary proceedings (Article 31(3)), but in order not to paralyze the work of the liquidator in the secondary proceedings, this obligation should reasonably be confined to important assets

---

[33] See the Virgos/Schmit Report, point 227.

and decisions only.[34] The liquidator in the main proceedings also is entitled to apply for a court order temporarily staying in whole or in part the process of liquidation in secondary proceedings (Article 33).

According to Article 32(3), the liquidator, whether appointed in main or secondary proceedings, is empowered to participate in other proceedings on the same basis as a creditor, in particular by attending creditors' meetings. However, he is not entitled to vote, unless he has obtained from individual creditors a power of attorney authorizing him to represent them and vote on their behalf.

If the law governing the secondary proceedings permits it, the proceedings may be terminated without a liquidation of the assets, for example, by a composition, in spite of the fact that secondary proceedings must be of a winding-up type (Article 34). This presupposes, however, the consent of the liquidator in the main proceedings if the interests of creditors in the main proceedings are affected. Furthermore, any stay of payment or discharge of debt granted in secondary proceedings may not have effect in respect of the debtor's assets in the other Member States "without the consent of all the creditors having an interest", but a comparison between Article 34(2) and Article 17(2) seems to indicate that the Regulation accepts such extraterritorial effects of territorial proceedings even without a unanimous consent of all the interested creditors, although only with regard to those creditors who have given their consent.

The fact that the Regulation does not impose any time limit on the right to apply for secondary proceedings can give rise to practical difficulties. The liquidator in the main proceedings, for example, may be involved in negotiations for the purpose of selling the debtor enterprise as a whole, but as long as important assets remain in another Member State where there is an establishment, any creditor can obstruct the negotiation at any moment by applying for the opening of local secondary proceedings there. The right of the liquidator in the main proceedings to apply, pursuant to Article 33, for a court order staying temporarily the process of liquidation in secondary proceedings does not suffice to provide a satisfactory solution in such a situation. Because of this risk, the liquidator in the main proceedings may be tempted to sell or move the assets hastily, which may be to the detriment of the bankruptcy estate.

10.6   Lodgment of Claims and Information to Creditors

Articles 39-42 deal with the provision of information for creditors and lodgment of their claims. Of particular interest is Article 39, which stipulates that even the tax authorities and social security authorities of other Member States have the right to lodge claims in the proceedings. This provision is important, because the traditional attitude in many countries is that foreign

---

[34] See the Virgos/Schmit Report, point 233.

public-law claims are not enforceable. The Member States naturally would be reluctant to hand over the local assets to the liquidator in a foreign bankruptcy where their legitimate tax claims and social security claims would be disregarded.

A creditor may lodge his claim in the main proceedings and in any secondary proceedings (Article 32(1)). One lodgment should normally be sufficient, because pursuant to Article 32(2) each liquidator is required to lodge in other proceedings claims which have already been lodged in his proceedings, provided that this serves the interests of the creditors in question and subject to their right to withdraw their claim. The practical value of such cross-lodgment of claims is debatable, as it may give rise to a complicated network of lodgments in the main proceedings and numerous secondary proceedings, where much effort will have to be spent on avoiding the risk of the same claim being given multiple dividends in parallel or even the same proceedings.

Another problem connected with the lodgment of claims is that those creditors who do not reside in the Member State where the proceedings are opened run the risk of not finding out about the opening, as the usual advertising in the Official Gazette of the country of opening has normally almost no real publicity effect in other countries. The idea of some kind of central advertising in an annex to the Official Journal of the European Communities (today Official Journal of the European Union) was discarded. Instead, Article 40 prescribes that known creditors habitually residing in other Member States shall be individually informed about the opening of insolvency proceedings and invited to lodge their claims.[35] This notice shall be provided in the official language of the country of the proceedings, but on a form under the heading "Invitation to lodge a claim. Time limits to be observed" in all of the official languages of the European Union, so that the recipients at least are made aware of what the notice is about (Article 42). Creditors from other Member States are allowed to lodge their claims in the language of their own country, provided that they do so under the heading "Lodgment of claim" in the language of the Member State of the proceedings, but this right to use their own language is of limited value as they may be required to provide a translation of the whole document into the language of the Member State where the proceedings take place. Unknown creditors and creditors with relatively small claims thus may face difficulties and relatively high expenses when lodging their claims.

---

[35] It should be noted that the opening of insolvency proceedings takes effect in the other Member States even if no notice has been given pursuant to Article 40, but the creditor affected may be entitled to compensation. See *Commission v. AMI*, case C-294/02, [2005] ECR I-2175, point 71.

CHAPTER II

Service of Documents, Taking of Evidence and Legal Aid

II.I   Service of Documents

The EC Regulation No 1348/2000 of 29 May 2000 on the Service in the Member States of Judicial and Extrajudicial Documents in Civil or Commercial Matters[1] is based substantially on an EC Convention from 1997, which has never entered into force[2]. The Regulation complements in certain respects the Hague Convention from 1965 on the Service Abroad of Judicial and Extrajudicial Documents in Civil and Commercial Matters. This Hague Convention in some parts has become outdated, as it focuses more on the service of the actual physical documents than on the conveying of the contents thereof, which today can be much more efficiently done by fax or electronic mail. In view of the first experiences with the application of the Regulation, the Commission has already proposed that it should be amended on a number of points.[3]

The Regulation applies – except in relation to Denmark[4] – in civil and commercial matters[5] where a judicial or extrajudicial document has to be transmitted from one Member State to another for service on a person with a known address (the Regulation does not apply where the address of the person to be served is unknown). Each Member State appoints both transmitting and receiving agencies, as well as a central body responsible for, *i.a.*, seeking solutions to difficulties arising during the transmission (Articles 2-3). The names and addresses of the receiving agencies, their geographical jurisdiction, the means of receipt of documents and the languages that may be used are communicated by each Member State to the Commission in order to be included in an annually updated manual (Article 17).[6]

---

[1] OJ 2000 L 160 p. 37.

[2] See OJ 1997 C 261 p. 1. The semi-official explanatory report on the Convention, published in OJ 1997 C 261 p. 26, can thus normally be very helpful even for the interpretation of the Regulation. See also, for example, Hess, *Rev.crit.d.i.p.* 2003 pp. 215-237; P. Kaye in von Hoffmann (ed.), *European Private International Law*, pp. 159-180; W. Kennett in Fentiman *et al.* (eds.), *L'espace*, pp. 199-232; Meyer, *IPRax* 1997 pp. 401-404; Stadler, *IPRax* 2001 pp. 514-521.

[3] See COM(2005)305 final.

[4] A special agreement has been concluded between the EC and Denmark, making the provisions of the Regulation applicable, with some amendments, in their mutual relations. See OJ 2005 L 300 p. 53 and section 1.2 *supra*. The agreement has not yet entered into force.

[5] There are no reasons to believe that the scope of civil and commercial matters under this Regulation differs from the prevailing interpretation of Article 1(1) of the Brussels I Regulation, see section 3.2 *supra*.

[6] See the Commission Decision No 2001/781 of 25 September 2001 adopting a manual of receiving agencies and a glossary of documents that may be served under Council Regulation (EC) No 1348/2000 on the Service in the Member States of Judicial and Extrajudicial Documents in Civil or Commercial Matters, OJ 2001 L 298 p. 1 (as amended), and the information communicated to Member States under Article 23 of the Regulation, OJ 2001 C 151 p. 4 (as amended).

Documents normally will be transmitted directly between the designated transmitting and receiving agencies in the two countries, using any appropriate means, provided that the content of the document remains true and legible (Article 4). This shows that it is not necessarily the actual physical document that has to be served and that the Regulation comprises also electronic transmission, provided that the procedural law of the countries involved considers it acceptable. The document has to be accompanied by a request on a standard form annexed to the Regulation. The receiving agency, as soon as possible and in any event within seven days, will send a receipt to the transmitting agency. The service itself takes place either in accordance with the law of the Member State addressed, or by a particular method requested by the transmitting agency unless the requested method is incompatible with the law of the addressed Member State. The service must be carried out as soon as possible; if it has not been possible to do so within a month, the receiving agency must inform the transmitting agency (Article 7). The date of service effected is determined on the basis of the law of the Member State addressed, but for the purposes of proceedings in the Member State of origin, it is fixed by the law of that state (Article 9). After the service has been effected, a certificate is sent to the transmitting agency (Article 10).

In connection with the service, the receiving agency has to inform the addressee that he may refuse to accept the document to be served if it is in a language other than either the official language of the Member State addressed or a language of the Member State of origin, which the addressee understands (Article 8). The ECJ has held that even if the addressee refuses to accept the document on such ground, the service is not invalid (a "non-service"), provided it is remedied by sending the necessary translation as soon as possible.[7] This is important, because it means that where a document must be served within a particular period of time in order to preserve the rights of the applicant, the date to be taken into account is the date of service of the initial document.

Among other permissible methods of service, the Regulation in Articles 12-15 mentions service through consular or diplomatic channels, direct service by post and direct service through competent officials of the Member State addressed. There is no hierarchy between the different methods provided for by the Regulation. In fact, it is even conceivable to use more than one method at the same time, in which case it is the first validly effected service that counts for determining the date of service for the purpose of procedural time-limits.[8]

Although the Regulation prevails in principle over other bilateral and multilateral agreements and arrangements concluded by the Member States, it does not preclude maintaining or even concluding new agreements or arrangements to expedite or simplify further the transmission, provided they are compatible with the Regulation (Article 20).

---

[7] See *Leffler* v. *Berlin Chemie*, case C-443/03, [2005] ECR I-9611.

[8] See *Plumex* v. *Young Sports*, case C-473/04, [2006] ECR I-1417.

Article 19 of the Regulation contains certain provisions on the relevance of service when the defendant, who has had to be served in another Member State, does not appear in the proceedings. A default judgment normally cannot be given, when the document instituting the proceedings must be served in another Member State, until it is established that the document was properly served or actually delivered in sufficient time to enable the defendant to prepare his defense. Similarly, the judge has the power to relieve the defendant from the effects of the expiration of the time for appeal from a default judgment, when the document instituting the proceedings or the judgment itself must be served in another Member State and the defendant, without any fault on his part, did not obtain knowledge of the document in sufficient time to present a defence or of the judgment in sufficient time to lodge an appeal, and he can show a *prima facie* defence on the merits.

11.2   Taking of Evidence

The EC Regulation No 1206/2001 of 28 May 2001 on Cooperation between the Courts of the Member States in the Taking of Evidence in Civil or Commercial Matters[9] applies, except in relation to Denmark, when the court of a Member State, in accordance with its law, requests the competent court of another Member State to take evidence or requests to be allowed to take evidence directly in another Member State.[10]

The last-mentioned, direct taking of evidence must be requested on a form annexed to the Regulation and may only take place if it can be performed on a voluntary basis without the need for coercive measures. The authorities of the requested Member State may refuse the request under certain circumstances, such as when the requested direct taking of evidence would be contrary to fundamental principles of its law (Article 17).

In most cases, however, the request asks for the taking of evidence by the competent court of the requested Member State. In contrast to the rules on the service of documents,[11] this Regulation does not provide for the designation of any transmitting or receiving agencies. The requests, on a special form annexed to the Regulation, normally are to be transmitted by the requesting court directly to the requested court (Article 2). Each Member State draws up *i.a.* a list of the courts competent to take evidence and also designates a central body responsible for such matters as supplying information and seeking solutions to

---

9   OJ 2001 L 174 p. 1. There are no reasons to believe that the scope of civil and commercial matters under this Regulation will differ from the prevailing interpretation of Article 1(1) of the Brussels I Regulation, see section 3.2 *supra*.

10   See, for example, Berger, *IPRax* 2001 pp. 522-527; Hess, *Rev.crit.d.i.p.* 2003 pp. 215-237; Müller, *Grenzüberschreitende Beweisaufnahme*.

11   See section 11.1 *supra*.

difficulties that may arise in respect of a request. On the basis of the lists and other information provided by the Member States, the Commission is to publish and regularly update a manual, which also is to be made available electronically (Article 19).

The request for the taking of evidence and other communications must be drawn up in the official language of the requested Member State or in another language, which that state has indicated it can accept (Article 5). The transmission is to take place by the swiftest possible means provided that the document accurately reflects the content and is legible (Article 6). The requested court shall acknowledge the receipt within seven days (Article 7) and execute the request within 90 days (Article 10). Delays have to be notified to the requesting court (Article 15). The execution of the request in principle will take place in accordance with the law of the requested Member State. If the requesting court calls for a special procedure, the requested court has to comply with such a requirement unless it is incompatible with the law of the requested Member State or would create major practical difficulties (Article 10). A request for the hearing of a person must not be executed when that person (for example, a priest, a doctor or an advocate) claims the right or duty to refuse to give evidence under the law of either the requesting or the requested Member State (Article 14). If it is provided for by the law of the requesting Member State, the parties or their representatives have the right to be present at the taking of evidence (Article 11), for example, in order to participate in the cross-examination of a witness. The representatives of the requesting court normally have the right to be present as well (Article 12). Where necessary, the requested court shall apply the coercive measures provided for by its own law (Article 13).

Similar to the Regulation on the service of documents, the Regulation on the taking of evidence prevails over other bilateral or multilateral agreements or arrangements concluded by the Member States, in particular, the 1954 Hague Convention on Civil Procedure and the 1970 Hague Convention on the Taking of Evidence Abroad in Civil and Commercial Matters. This does not preclude, however, the maintaining of existing or the concluding of new agreements and arrangements compatible with the Regulation and further facilitating the taking of evidence (Article 21).

11.3   Legal Aid

The procedures concerning cross-border disputes are often more complicated and often give rise to more expenses than purely domestic cases. This makes legal aid for persons who lack sufficient financial resources of their own particularly important in order to secure the effective access of such persons to justice in cross-border litigation. The purpose of Directive No 2003/8 of 27 January 2003 to Improve Access to Justice in Cross-border Disputes by Establishing Minimum Common Rules Relating to Legal Aid for Such

Disputes[12] is clearly indicated in its title. However, it must be noted that this is a directive, not a regulation. Consequently, it is not directly applicable but is addressed to the Member States (except Denmark), which are obliged to adapt their national rules on legal aid to comply with the Directive's requirements.

Cross-border disputes are defined in Article 2 of the Directive as those disputes where the party applying for legal aid is domiciled or habitually resident in a Member State other than the Member State where the court is sitting or where the decision is to be enforced. The domicile is to be determined in accordance with Article 59 of the Brussels I Regulation, which means that in order to ascertain whether the applicant is domiciled in another Member State, the law of that Member State will be applied.

Pursuant to Article 3 of the Directive, natural persons are entitled to receive appropriate legal aid, guaranteeing pre-litigation advice, legal assistance and representation in court, and exemption from costs and fees. Expenses incurred in having a judgment enforced are also covered (Article 9). Member States are, on the other hand, entitled to request that recipients pay a reasonable share themselves, as well as to demand a refund if the financial situation of the recipient has substantially improved or if legal aid has been granted on the basis of inaccurate information provided by the recipient. Member States must grant legal aid without discrimination not merely to Union citizens but even to third-country nationals residing lawfully in a Member State (Article 4). When assessing the economic situation of a person, Member States are permitted to define objective thresholds above which the applicants are deemed able to bear the costs themselves, but such thresholds must not prevent legal aid when the person concerned proves that he is unable to pay the costs as a result of differences in the cost of living between the Member State of habitual residence and the Member State of the forum (Article 5). Member States may also provide that legal aid can be refused for proceedings which appear to be manifestly unfounded (Article 6).

The application for legal aid may be submitted to the competent authority of either the Member State where the applicant is habitually resident (the transmitting authority) or the Member State of the proceedings (the receiving authority). Each Member State is required to designate such transmitting and receiving authorities and inform the Commission about them for the purpose of publication in the Official Journal of the European Union (Article 14). The Directive provides in Article 16 for a standard form for legal aid applications and for the transmission of such applications.[13]

---

[12] OJ 2003 L 26 p. 41.

[13] See Commission Decision No 2004/844 of 9 November 2004 establishing a Form for Legal Aid Applications under Council Directive 2003/8, OJ 2004 L 365 p. 27 *and* Commission Decision No 2005/630 of 26 August 2005 establishing a Form for the Transmission of Legal Aid Applications under Council Directive 2003/8, OJ 2005 L 225 p. 23.

The Directive does not prevent Member States from having rules on legal aid that are more generous than the minimum provisions in the Directive (Article 19). Provisions on legal aid also are found in some other Community instruments, such as Article 50 in both the Brussels I and the Brussels II Regulations, which stipulate that an applicant who, in the Member State of origin of the judgment, has benefited from complete or partial legal aid or exemption from costs or expenses is entitled, in the enforcement procedures under these Regulations, to benefit from the most favourable legal aid or the most extensive exemption from costs and expenses provided for by the law of the Member State where enforcement takes place.

According to Article 20, the Directive has precedence, as between Member States, over other bilateral and multilateral agreements, including the 1977 European Agreement on the Transmission of Application for Legal Aid and the 1980 Hague Convention on International Access to Justice.

Alphabetical Table of ECJ Decisions

Numerical Table of ECJ Decisions

313/85, *Iveco Fiat v. Van Hool*, [1986] ECR 3337 — 3.3.5

144/86, *Gubisch v. Palumbo*, [1987] ECR 4861 — 3.3.6

145/86, *Hoffmann v. Krieg*, [1988] ECR 645 — 3.4

9/87, *Arcado v. Haviland*, [1988] ECR 1539 — 3.3.2

158/87, *Scherrens v. Maenhout*, [1988] ECR 3791 — 3.3.4

189/87, *Kalfelis v. Bankhaus Schröder*, [1988] ECR 5565 — 3.3.2

32/88, *Six Constructions v. Humbert*, [1989] ECR 341 — 3.3.2

115/88, *Reichert v. Dresdner Bank*, [1990] ECR I-27 — 3.3.4

220/88, *Dumez v. Helaba*, [1990] ECR I-49 — 3.3.2

365/88, *Kongress Agentur Hagen v. Zeehaghe*, [1990] ECR I-1845 — 3.3.2

190/89, *Rich v. Impianti*, [1991] ECR I-3855 — 3.2

214/89, *Powell Duffryn v. Petereit*, [1992] ECR I-1745 — 3.3.2, 3.3.5

339/89, *Alsthom Atlantique SA v. Sulzer*, [1991] ECR I-107 — 2.2

351/89, *Overseas Union v. New Hampshire Ins.*, [1991] ECR I-3317 — 3.3.6

6 and 9/90, *Francovich v. Italy*, [1991] ECR I-5357 — 1.3

261/90, *Reichert v. Dresdner Bank*, [1992] ECR I-2149 — 3.3.2

280/90, *Hacker v. Euro-Relais*, [1992] ECR I-1111 — 3.3.4

26/91, *Handte v. Traitements*, [1992] ECR I-3967 — 3.3.2

89/91, *Shearson Lehman Hutton v. TVB*, [1993] ECR I-139 — 3.3.3

168/91, *Christos Konstantinidis*, [1993] ECR I-1191 — 2.2

172/91, *Sonntag v. Weidmann*, [1993] ECR I-1963 — 3.2, 3.4, 3.5

20/92, *Hubbard v. Hamburger*, [1993] ECR I-3777 — 2.1

92/92 and 326/92, *Collins v. Imtrat*, [1993] ECR I-5145 — 2.1

125/92, *Mulox v. Geels*, [1993] ECR I-4075 — 3.3.3

129/92, *Owens Bank v. Bracco*, [1994] ECR I-117 — 3.4

288/92, *Custom v. Stawa*, [1994] ECR I-2913 — 3.3.2

294/92, *Webb v. Webb*, [1994] ECR I-1717 — 3.3.4

398/92, *Mund & Fester v. Hatrex*, [1994] ECR I-467 — 2.1

406/92, *Tatry*, [1994] ECR I-5439 — 3.2, 3.3.6

414/92, *Solo Kleinmotoren v. Boch*, [1994] ECR I-2237 — 3.4

68/93, *Shevill v. Presse Alliance*, [1995] ECR I-415 — 3.3.2

292/93, *Lieber v. Göbel*, [1994] ECR I-2535 — 3.3.4

318/93, *Brenner v. Reynolds*, [1994] ECR I-4275 — 3.3.3

341/93, *Danværn v. Otterbeck*, [1995] ECR I-2053 — 3.3.2

364/93, *Marinari v. Lloyd's Bank*, [1995] ECR I-2719 — 3.3.2

439/93, *Lloyd's Register v. Campenon Bernard*, [1995] ECR I-961 — 3.3.2

55/94, *Gebhard v. Consiglio degli Avvocati*, [1995] ECR I-4165 — 2.2

214/94, *Boukhalfa v. Bundesrepublik Deutschland*, [1996] ECR I-2253 — 2.1

336/94, *Dafeki v. Landesversicherungsanstalt*, [1997] ECR I-6761 — 2.2

43/95, *Data Delecta AB v. MSL Dynamics Ltd.*, [1996] ECR I-4661 — 2.1

78/95, *Hendrikman v. Magenta*, [1996] ECR I-4943 — 3.4

106/95, *MSG v. Gravières Rhénanes*, [1997] ECR I-911 — 3.3.2, 3.3.5

220/95, *van den Boogaard v. Laumen*, [1997] ECR I-1147 — 3.2, 3.3.2

269/95, *Benincasa v. Dentalkit*, [1997] ECR I-3767 — 3.3.3, 3.3.5

Bibliography

Ancel, B., "The Brussels I Regulation: Comment", *Yearb.PIL* 2001 pp. 101-114.

Ancel, B. & Muir Watt, H., "L'intérêt supérieur de l'enfant dans le concert des jurisdictions: Le Règlement de Bruxelles II bis", *Rev.crit.d.i.p.* 2005 pp. 569-605.

Audit, M., "L'interprétation autonome du droit international privé communautaire", *Clunet* 2004 pp.789-816.

d'Avout, L., "La circulation automatique des titres exécutoires imposée par le règlement 805/2004 du 21 avril 2004", *Rev.crit.d.i.p.* 2006 pp.1-48.

Badiali, G., "Le droit international privé des Communautés européennes", *Rec.des cours* 1985, vol. 191, pp. 9-181.

Ballarino, T., "Les règles de conflit sur les sociétés commerciales à l'épreuve du droit communautaire d'établissement. Remarques sur deux arrêts de la Cour de justice des Communautés européennes", *Rev.crit.d.i.p.* 2003 pp. 373-402.

Ballarino, T. & Ubertazzi, B., "On *Avello* and Other Judgments: A New Point of Departure in the Conflict of Laws?", *Yearb.PIL* 2004 pp. 85-128.

von Bar, C. (ed.), *Europäisches Gemeinschaftsrecht und Internationales Privatrecht*, Köln *etc.* 1991.

Basedow, J., "Der kollisionsrechtliche Gehalt der Produktfreiheiten im europäischen Binnenmarkt: favor offerentis", *RabelsZ* 1995 pp. 1-55.

Basedow, J., "European Private International Law of Obligations and Internal Market Legislation – A Matter of Coordination", *Liber Memorialis Petar Šarčević*, München 2006, pp. 13-24.

Baur, M.-O., "Projects of the European Community in the Field of Private International Law", *Yearb.PIL* 2003 pp. 177-190.

Becker, C., "Insolvenz in der Europäischen Union. Zur Verordnung des Rates über Insolvenzverfahren", *ZEuP* 2002 pp. 287-315.

Behrens, P., "Das Internationale Gesellschaftsrecht nach dem Überseering-Urteil des EuGH und den Schlussanträgen zu Inspire Art", *IPRax* 2003 pp. 193-207.

Beraudo, J.-P., "Le Règlement (CE) du Conseil du 22 décembre 2000 concernant la compétence judiciaire, la reconnaissance et l'exécution des décisions en matière civile et commerciale", *Clunet* 2001 pp. 1033-1106.

Berger, C., "Die EG-Verordnung über die Zusammenarbeit der Gerichte auf dem Gebiet der Beweisaufnahme in Zivil- und Handelssachen (EuBVO)", *IPRax* 2001 pp. 522-527.

Besse, D., "Die justitielle Zusammenarbeit in Zivilsachen nach dem Vertrag von Amsterdam und das EuGVÜ", *ZEuP* 1999 pp. 107-122.

Boele-Woelki, K., "Brüssel II: Die Verordnung über die Zuständigkeit und die Anerkennung von Entscheidungen in Ehesachen", *ZfRV* 2001 pp. 121-130.

Boele-Woelki, K. & van Ooik, R.H., "The Communitarization of Private International Law", *Yearb.PIL* 2002 pp. 1-36.

Bogdan, M., "1980 års EG-konvention om tillämplig lag på kontraktsrättsliga förpliktelser – synpunkter beträffande den svenska inställningen", *TfR* 1982 pp. 1-49.

Bogdan, M., "The 'Common Market' for Judgments: the Extension of the EEC Jurisdiction and Enforcement Treaty to Nonmember Countries", 9 *Saint Louis University Public Law Review* 113-129 (1990).

Bogdan, M., *Sveriges och EU:s internationella insolvensrätt*, Stockholm 1997.

Bogdan, M., "The EU Bankruptcy Convention", 6 *Int.Insolv.Rev.* 114-126 (1997).

Bogdan, M., "Some Reflections regarding the New EU Directive on Injunctions for the Protection of Consumers' Interests", [1998] *Consumer L.J.* 69-375.

Bogdan, M., "Kan en Internethemsida utgöra ett driftställe vid bedömningen av svensk domsrätt och tillämplig lag?", *SvJT* 1998 pp. 825-836.

Bogdan, M., "Ordre public, internationellt tvingande rättsregler och kringgåendeläran i EG-domstolens praxis rörande internationell privaträtt", *SvJT* 2001 pp. 329-346.

Bogdan, M., "The E.C. Law of International Insolvency", *Revue des affaires européennes* 2001-2002 pp. 452-459.

Bogdan, M., "Om Bryssel/Luganoreglernas tillämpning i marknadsrättsliga mål", *JT* 2002-03 pp. 410-416.

Bogdan, M., "Rätt att välja bland nationella bolagsformer inom EU", *Ny Juridik* 2004, No. 1, pp. 7-20.

Bogdan, M., "Den italienska litispendenstorpeden", *Ny Juridik* 2004, no. 3, pp. 53-62.

Bonomi, A., "Conversion of the Rome Convention on Contracts into an EC Instrument: Some Remarks on the Green Paper of the EC Commission", *Yearb.PIL* 2003 pp. 53-97.

de Bra, P., *Verbraucherschutz durch Gerichtsstandsregelungen im deutschen und europäischen Zivilprozessrecht*, Frankfurt a.M. etc. 1992.

Braun, S., *Der Beklagtenschutz nach Art. 27 Nr 2 EuGVÜ*, Berlin 1992.

Briggs, A. & Rees, P., *Civil Jurisdiction and Judgments*, ed. 2, London etc. 1997.

Bureau, D., "La fin d'un îlot de résistance. Le Règlement du Conseil relatif aux procédures d'insolvabilité", *Rev.crit.d.i.p.* 2002 pp. 613-679.

Busch, M., "Schutzmassnahmen für Kinder und der Begriff der 'elterlichen Verantwortung' im internationalen und europäischen Recht – Anmerkungen zur Ausweitung der Brüssel II-Verordnung", *IPRax* 2003 pp. 218-222.

Byrne, P., *The European Union and Lugano Conventions on Jurisdiction and the Enforcement of Judgments*, Delgany 1994.

Calvo Caravaca, A.-L. (ed.), *Comentario al convenio de Bruselas relativo a la competencia judicial y a la ejecución de resoluciones judiciales en material civil y mercantil*, Madrid 1994.

Carpenter, M. et al., *The Lugano and San Sebastian Conventions*, London etc.1990.

Civil Jurisdiction and Judgments in Europe. Proceedings of the Colloquium on the Interpretation of the Brussels Convention by the Court of Justice considered in the Context of the European Judicial Area, Luxembourg 11 and 12 March 1991, London etc. 1992.

"Comments on the European Commission's Draft Proposal for a Council Regulation on the Law Applicable to Non-Contractual Obligations", submitted by the Hamburg Group for Private International Law, *RabelsZ* 2003 pp. 1-56.

"Comments on the European Commission's Green Paper on the Conversion of the Rome Convention of 1980 on the Law Applicable to Contractual Obligations into a Community Instrument and Its Modernization", submitted by the Max Planck Institute for Foreign Private and Private International Law, *RabelsZ* 2004 pp. 1-118.

Cuniberti, G., "*Forum Non Conveniens* and the Brussels Convention", 54 *I.C.L.Q.* 973-981 (2005).

Czernich, D. & Tiefenthaler, S., *Die Übereinkommen von Lugano und Brüssel. Europäisches Gerichtsstands- und Vollstreckungsrecht. Kurzkommentar*, Wien 1997.

Czernich, D., & Heiss, H., *Das Europäische Schuldvertragsübereinkommen. Kommentar*, Wien 1999.

Dashwood, A., Hacon, R.J. & White, R.C.A., *A Guide to the Civil Jurisdiction and Judgment Convention*, Deventer etc. 1987.

Donzallaz, Y., *La Convention de Lugano du 16 septembre 1988 concernant la compétence judiciaire et l'exécution des décisions en matière civile et commerciale*, vol. I-III, Berne 1996, 1997 and 1998.

Drasch, W., *Das Herkunftslandprinzip im Internationalen Privatrecht*, Baden-Baden 1997.

Drobnig, U., "Verstösst das Staatsangehörigkeitsprinzip gegen das Diskriminierungsverbot des EWG-Vertrages?", *RabelsZ* 1970 pp. 636-662.

Droz, G.A.L., *Compétence judiciaire et effets des jugements dans le Marché Commun*, Paris 1972.

Droz, G.A.L., *Pratique de la Convention de Bruxelles du 27 septembre 1968*. Paris 1973.

Droz, G.A.L., "Entrée en vigueur de la Convention de Bruxelles révisée sur la compétence judiciaire et l'exécution des jugements", *Rev.crit.d.i.p.* 1987 pp. 251-303.

Droz, G.A.L., "La Convention de Lugano parallèle à la Convention de Bruxelles concernant la compétence judiciaire et l'exécution des décisions en matière civile et commerciale", *Rev.crit.d.i.p.* 1989 pp. 1-51.

Droz, G.A.L. & Gaudemet-Tallon, H., "La transformation de la Convention de Bruxelles du 27 septembre 1968 en Règlement du Conseil concernant la compétence judiciaire, la reconnaissance et l'exécution des décisions en matière civile et commerciale", *Rev.crit.d.i.p.* 2001 pp. 601-652.

Duintjer Tebbens, H., "Judicial Interpretation of the 1988 Lugano Convention on Jurisdiction and Judgments in the Light of its Brussels Matrix: the Convergence Confirmed", *Yearb.PIL* 2001 pp. 1-25.

Duursma-Kepplinger, H.-C. & Duursma, D., "Der Anwendungsbereich der Insolvenzverordnung under Berücksichtigung der Bereichsausnahmen, von Konzernsachverhalten und der von den Mitgliedstaaten abgeschlossenen Konkursverträge", *IPRax* 2003 pp. 505-511.

Fallon, M., "Les conflits de lois et de juridictions dans un espace économique intégré. L'expérience de la Communauté européenne", *Rec.des cours* 1995, vol. 253, pp. 9-282.

Fallon, M. & Meeusen, J., "Private International Law in the European Union and the Exception of Mutual Recognition", *Yearb.PIL* 2002 pp. 37-66.

Fallon, M. & Meeusen J., "Le commerce électronique, la directive 2000/31/ CE et le droit international privé", *Rev.crit.d.i.p.* 2002 pp. 435-490.

Fentiman, R. et al. **(eds.)**, *L'espace judiciaire européen en matière civile et commerciale – The European Judicial Area in Civil and Commercial Matters*, Bruxelles 1999.

Fezer, K.-H. & Koos, S., "Das gemeinschaftsrechtliche Herkunftslandprinzip und die e-commerce-Richtlinie", *IPRax* 2000 pp. 349-354.

Fisknes, T., *Luganokonvensjonen og dens betydning i sjørettslige tvister,* Oslo 1991.

Fletcher, I.F., *Conflict of Laws and European Community Law*, Amsterdam etc. 1982.

Foyer, J., "Entrée en vigueur de la Convention de Rome du 19 juin 1980 sur la loi applicable aux obligations contractuelles", *Clunet* 1991 pp. 601-631.

Fuchs, A. et al. **(eds.)**, *Les conflits de lois et le système juridique communautaire*, Paris 2004.

Galanti, E., "The New EC Law on Bank Crisis", 11 *Int.Insolv.Rev.* 49-66 (2002).

Garrido, J.M., "Some Reflections on the EU Bankruptcy Convention and its Implications for Secured and Preferential Creditors", 7 *Int.Insolv.Rev.* 79-94 (1998).

Gaudemet-Tallon, H., "Le nouveau droit international privé européen des contrats", *Rev.trim.dr.eur.* 1981 pp. 215-285.

Gaudemet-Tallon, H., "Le Règlement no 1347/2000 du Conseil du 29 mai 2000: 'Compétence, reconnaissance et exécution des décisions en matière matrimoniale et en matière de responsabilité parentale des enfants communs'", *Clunet* 2001 pp. 381-445.

Gaudemet-Tallon, H., *Compétence et exécution des jugements en Europe*, ed. 3, Paris 2002.

Geimer, R, "Salut für die Verordnung (EG) Nr. 44/2001 (Brüssel I-VO)", *IPRax* 2002 pp. 69-74.

Geimer, R. & Schütze, R.A., *Europäisches Zivilverfahrensrecht*, ed. 2, München 2004.

Gillard, N. (ed.), *L'espace judiciaire européen. La Convention de Lugano du 16 septembre 1988*, Lausanne 1992.

Gothot, P. & Holleaux, D., *La Convention de Bruxelles du 27 septembre 1968*, Paris 1985.

Gruber, U.P., "Die neue EheVO und die deutschen Ausführungsgesetze", *IPRax* 2005 pp. 293-300.

Grundmann, S., "Binnenmarktkollisionsrecht – vom klassischen IPR zur Integrationsordnung", *RabelsZ* 2000 pp. 457-477.

Grundmann, S., "Das Internationale Privatrecht der E-Commerce-Richtlinie – was ist kategorial anders im Kollisionsrecht des Binnenmarkts und warum?", *RabelsZ* 2003 pp. 246-297.

Gsell, B., "Autonom bestimmter Gerichtsstand am Erfüllungsort nach der Brüssel I-Verordnung", *IPRax* 2002 pp. 484-491.

Hager, G. & Bentele, F., "Der Lieferort als Gerichtsstand – zur Auslegung des Art. 5 Nr. 1 lit. B EuGVO", *IPRax* 2004 pp. 73-77.

Halfmeier, A., "Vom Cassislikör zur E-Commerce-Richtlinie: Auf dem Weg zu einem europäischen Mediendeliktsrecht", *ZEuP* 2001 pp. 837-868.

Harris, J., "Stays of Proceedings and the Brussels Convention", 54 *I.C.L.Q.* 933-950 (2005).

Hartley, T.C., *Civil Jurisdiction and Judgments*, London 1984.

Hartley, T.C., "The European Union and the Systematic Dismantling of the Common Law of Conflict of Laws", 54 *I.C.L.Q.* 813-828 (2005).

Hatzidaki-Dahlström, L., *EU:s internationella privat- och processrätt. Den femte friheten*, ed. 2, Lund 2004.

Hertz, K., *Jurisdiction in Contract and Tort under the Brussels Convention*, Copenhagen 1998.

Hess, B., *Einstweiliger Rechtsschutz im europäischen Zivilrechtsverkehr (Art. 24 EuGVÜ)*, Berlin 1987.

Hess, B., "Die Integrationsfunktion des Europäischen Zivilverfahrensrechts", *IPRax* 2001 pp. 389-396.

Hess, B., "Nouvelles techniques de la coopération judiciaire transfrontalière en Europe", *Rev.crit.d.i.p.* 2003 pp. 215-237.

von Hoffmann, B. (ed.), *European Private International Law*, Nijmegen 1998.

von Hoffmann, B., "Richtlinien der Europäischen Gemeinschaft und Internationales Privatrecht", *ZfRV* 1995 pp. 45-54.

Hommelhoff, P. et al. (eds.), *Europäisches Binnenmarkt, IPR und Rechtsangleichung*, Heidelberg 1995.

Höpping, U., *Auswirkungen der Warenverkehrsfreiheit auf das IPR*, Frankfurt a.M. *etc.* 1997.

Huber, P. & Bach, I., "Die Rom II-VO. Kommissionsentwurf und aktuelle Entwicklungen, *IPRax* 2005 pp. 73-84.

Isenburg-Epple, S., *Die Berücksichtigung ausländischer Rechtshängigkeit nach dem Europäischen Gerichtsstands- und Vollstreckungsübereinkommen vom 27.9.1968*, Frankfurt a.M. *etc.* 1992.

Jänterä-Jareborg, M., "Marriage Dissolution in an Integrated Europe – The 1998 European Union Convention on Jurisdiction and the Recognition and Enforcement of Judgments in Matrimonial Matters (Brussels II Convention)", *Yearb.PIL* 1999 pp. 1-36.

Jänterä-Jareborg, M., "A European Family Law for Cross-border Situations – Some Reflections concerning the Brussels II Regulation and its Planned Amendments", *Yearb.PIL* 2002 pp. 67-82.

Jayme, E., *Ein Internationales Privatrecht für Europa*, Heidelberg 1991.

Jayme, E. (ed.), *Ein internationales Zivilverfahrensrecht für Gesamteuropa. EuGVÜ, LugÜ und die Rechtsentwicklungen in Mittel- und Osteuropa*, Heidelberg 1992.

Jayme, E. & Kohler C., "Zum Stand des internationalen Privat- und Verfahrensrechts der Europäischen Gemeinschaft", *IPRax* 1985 pp. 65-71.

Jayme, E. & Kohler C., "Das Internationale Privat- und Verfahrensrecht der Europäischen Gemeinschaft – Jüngste Entwicklungen", *IPRax* 1988 pp. 133-140.

Jayme, E. & Kohler C., "Das Internationale Privat- und Verfahrensrecht der EG – Stand 1989", *IPRax* 1989 pp. 337-346.

Jayme, E. & Kohler C., "Das Internationale Privat- und Verfahrensrecht der EG auf dem Wege zum Binnenmarkt", *IPRax* 1990 pp. 353-361.

Jayme, E. & Kohler C., "Das Internationale Privat- und Verfahrensrecht der EG 1991 – Harmonisierungsmodell oder Mehrspurigkeit des Kollisionsrechts", *IPRax* 1991 pp. 361-369.

Jayme, E. & Kohler C., "Das Internationale Privat- und Verfahrensrecht der EG nach Maaastricht", *IPRax* 1992 pp. 346-356.

Jayme, E. & Kohler C., "Das Internationale Privat- und Verfahrensrecht der EG 1993 – Spannungen zwischen Staatverträgen und Richtlinien", *IPRax* 1993 pp. 357-371.

Jayme, E. & Kohler C., "Europäisches Kollisionsrecht 1994: Quellenpluralismus und offene Kontraste", *IPRax* 1994 pp. 405-415.

Jayme, E. & Kohler C., "Europäisches Kollisionsrecht 1995 – Der Dialog der Quellen", *IPRax* 1995 pp. 343-354.

Jayme, E. & Kohler, C., "L'interaction des règles de conflit contenues dans le droit derivé de la Communauté européenne et des conventions de Bruxelles et de Rome", *Rev.crit.d.i.p.* 1995 pp. 1-40.

Jayme, E. & Kohler C., "Europäisches Kollisionsrecht 1996 – Anpassung und Transformation der nationalen Rechte", *IPRax* 1996 pp. 377-389.

Jayme, E. & Kohler C., "Europäisches Kollisionsrecht 1997 – Vergemeinschaftung durch 'Säulenwechsel'?", *IPRax* 1997 pp. 385-401.

Jayme, E. & Kohler C., "Europäisches Kollisionsrecht 1998: Kulturelle Unterschiede und Parallelaktionen", *IPRax* 1998 pp. 417-429.

Jayme, E. & Kohler C., "Europäisches Kollisionsrecht 1999: Die Abendstunde der Staatsverträge", *IPRax* 1999 pp. 401-413.

Jayme, E. & Kohler C., "Europäisches Kollisionsrecht 2000: Interlokales Privatrecht oder universelles Gemeinschaftsrecht?", *IPRax* 2000 pp. 454-465.

Jayme, E. & Kohler C., "Europäisches Kollisionsrecht 2001: Anerkennungsprinzip statt IPR?", *IPRax* 2001 pp. 501-514.

Jayme, E. & Kohler C., "Europäisches Kollisionsrecht 2002: Zur Wiederkehr des Internationalen Privatrechts", *IPRax* 2002 pp. 461-471.

Jayme, E. & Kohler C., "Europäisches Kollisionsrecht 2003: Der Verfassungskonvent und das Internationale Privat- und Verfahrensrecht", *IPRax* 2003 pp. 485-495.

Jayme, E. & Kohler C., "Europäisches Kollisionsrecht 2004: Territoriale Erweiterung und methodische Rückgriffe", *IPRax* 2004 pp. 481-493.

Jayme, E. & Kohler C., "Europäisches Kollisionsrecht 2005: Hegemonialgesten auf dem Weg zu einer Gesamtvereinheitlichung", *IPRax* 2005 pp. 481-493.

Jenard, P., *La Convention de Bruxelles du 27 septembre 1968 et ses prolonguements*, Bruxelles 1994.

Jobard-Bachellier, M.-N., "Les procédures de surendettement et de faillite internationales ouvertes dans la communauté européenne", *Rev.crit.d.i.p.* 2002 pp. 491-507.

Johnson, G.W., "The New European Union Convention on Insolvency Proceedings: A Critique of the Convention's Corporate Rescue Paradigm", 5 *Int.Insolv.Rev.* 80-107 (1996).

Juenger, F.K., "Parteiautonomie und objektive Anknüpfung im EG-Übereinkommen zum internationalen Vertragsrecht. Eine Kritik aus amerikanischer Sicht", *RabelsZ* 1982 pp. 57-83.

Juenger, F.K., "La Convention de Bruxelles du 27 septembre 1968 et la courtoisie internationale. Réflexions d'un Américain", *Rev.crit.d.i.p.* 1983 pp 37-51.

Junker, A., "Die einheitliche europäische Auslegung nach dem EG-Schuldvertragsübereinkommen", *RabelsZ* 1991 pp. 674-696.

Kassis, A., *Le nouveau droit européen des contrats internationaux*, Paris 1993.

Kaye, P., *Civil Jurisdiction and Enforcement of Foreign Judgments*, Abingdon 1987.

Kaye, P., *The New Private International Law of Contract of the European Community*, Aldershot 1993.

Kaye, P. (ed.), *European Case Law on the Judgments Convention*, Chichester etc. 1998.

Kaye, P., *Law of the European Judgments Convention*, vol. 1-5, Chichester 1999.

Kayser, N., "A Study of the European Convention on Insolvency Proceedings", 7 *Int.Insolv.Rev.* 95-140 (1998).

Kessedjian, C., "Le droit international privé et l'intégration juridique européenne", in *International Cooperation through Private International Law. Essays in Memory of Peter E. Nygh*, The Hague 2004, pp. 187-196.

Killias, L., *Die Gerichtsstandsvereinbarungen nach dem Lugano-Übereinkommen*, Zürich 1993.

Klauer, S., *Das europäische Kollisionsrecht der Verbraucherverträge zwischen Römer EVÜ und EG-Richtlinien*, Tübingen 2002.

Klinke, U., *Brüsseler Übereinkommen und Übereinkommen von Lugano über die gerichtliche Zuständigkeit und die Vollstreckung gerichtlicher Entscheidungen in Zivil- und Handelssachen*, vol I-II, ed. 2, Köln *etc.* 1993.

Kohler, C., "Interrogations sur les sources du droit international privé européen après le traité d'Amsterdam", *Rev.crit.d.i.p.* 1999 pp. 1-30.

Kohler, C., "Der Europäische Justizraum für Zivilsachen und das Gemeinschaftskollisionsrecht", *IPRax* 2003 pp. 401-412.

Kohler, C., "Der Einfluss der Globalisierung auf die Wahl der Anknüpfungsmomente im Internationalen Familienrecht", in *Internationales Familienrecht für das 21. Jahrhundert. Symposium zum 65. Geburtstag von Ulrich Spellenberg*, München 2005, pp. 9-27.

Kohler, C., "Das Prinzip der gegenseitigen Anerkennung in Zivilsachen im europäischen Justizraum", *Zeitschrift für Schweizerisches Recht* 2005 pp..263-299.

Kreutzer, K., "Zu Stand und Perspektivern des Europäischen Internationalen Privatrechts. Wie europäisch soll das Europäische Internationale Privatrecht sein?", *RabelsZ* 2006 pp.1-88.

Kropholler, J., *Europäisches Zivilprozessrecht*, ed. 7, Heidelberg 2002.

Lefranc, D., "La spécificité des règles de conflit de lois en droit communautaire derivé (aspects de droit privé)", *Rev.crit.d.i.p.* 2005 pp. 413-446.

Lagarde, P., "Le nouveau droit international privé des contrats après l'entrée en vigueur de la Convention de Rome du 19 juin 1980", *Rev.crit.d.i.p.* 1991 pp. 287-340.

Lagarde, P., "Développements futurs du droit international privé dans une Europe en voie d'unification: quelques conjectures", *RabelsZ* 2004 pp. 225-243.

Lagarde, P. & von Hoffmann, B. (eds.), *L'européisation du droit international privé – Die Europäisierung des internationalen Privatrechts – The Europeanisation of International Private Law*, Köln 1996.

Lando, O., "The EEC Convention on the Law Applicable to Contractual Obligations", 24 *C.M.L.R.* 159-214 (1987).

Lando, O., "Being first. On Uses and Abuses of the Lis Pendens under the Brussels Convention", in *Modern Issues in European Law. Nordic Perspectives. Essays in Honour of Lennart Pålsson*, Stockholm 1997, pp. 105-122.

Larsson, M., *Konsumentskydd över gränserna – särskilt inom EU. En studie i internationell privat- och processrätt*, Uppsala 2002.

Lasok, D. & Stone P.A., *Conflict of Laws in the European Community*, Abingdon 1987.

Layton, A. & Mercer, H. (eds.), *European Civil Practice*, ed. 2, vol. I, London 2004.

Lefranc, D., "La spécificité des règles de conflit de lois en droit communautaire dérivé (aspects de droit privé)", *Rev.crit.d.i.p.* 2005 pp. 413-446.

Leutner, G., *Die vollstreckbare Urkunde im europäischen Rechtsverkehr*, Berlin 1997.

Liukkunen, U., *The Role of Mandatory Rules in International Labour Law*, Helsinki 2004.

Mäder, S.A., *Die Anwendung des Lugano-Übereinkommens im gewerblichen Rechtsschutz*, Bern 1999.

Magnier, V., "La société européenne en question", *Rev.crit.d.i.p.* 2004 pp. 555-587.

Malatesta, A. (ed.), *The Unification of Choice of Law Rules on Torts and Other Non-Contractual Obligations in Europe. The "Rome II" Proposal*, Milano 2006.

Mankowski, P., "Wider ein Herkunftslandprinzip für Dienstleistungen im Binnenmarkt", *IPRax* 2004 pp. 385-395.

Mankowski, P., "Der Vorschlag für die Rom I-Verordnung", *IPRax* 2006 pp. 101-113.

Mari, L., *Il diritto processuale civile della Convenzione di Bruxelles. I. Il sistema della competenza*, Padova 1999.

Marmisse, A. & Wilderspin, M., "Le régime jurisprudentiel des mesures provisoires à la lumière des arrêts *Van Uden* et *Mietz*", *Rev.crit.d.i.p.* 1999 pp. 669-683.

Martiny, D., "Das Römische Vertragsrechtsübereinkommen vom 19. Juni 1980", *ZEuP* 1993 pp. 298-305.

Martiny, D., "Europäisches Internationales Vertragsrecht – Ausbau und Konsolidierung", *ZEuP* 1999 pp. 246-270.

Martiny, D., "Internationales Vertragsrecht im Schatten des Europäischen Gemeinschaftsrechts", *ZEuP* 2001 pp. 308-328.

Martiny, D., "Europäisches Internationales Vertragsrecht vor der Reform", *ZEuP* 2003 pp. 590-618.

Martiny, D., "Neue Impulse im Europäischen Internationalen Vertragsrecht", *ZEuP* 2006 pp. 60-95.

Matscher, F., "Der verfahrensrechtliche ordre public im Spannungsfeld von EMRK und Gemeinschaftsrecht – Bemerkungen zu den Urteilen des EuGH und des EGMR in der Sache Krombach", *IPRax* 2001 pp. 428-436.

Meeusen, J., Pertegás, M. & Straetmans, G. (eds.), *Enforcement of International Contracts in the European Union. Convergence and Divergence between Brussels I and Rome I*, Antwerp etc. 2004.

Mellqvist, M., *EU:s insolvensförordning m.m. En kommentar*, Stockholm 2002.

Mercier, P. & Dutoit, B., *L'Europe judiciaire: les Conventions de Bruxelles et de Lugano*, Bâle etc. 1991.

Merrett, L., "The Enforcement of Jurisdiction Agreements within the Brussels Regime", 55 *I.C.L.Q.* 315-336 (2006).

Meyer, J., "Europäisches Übereinkommen über die Zustellung gerichtlicher und aussergerichtlicher Schriftstücke in Zivil- und Handelssachen in den Mitgliedstaaten der Europäischen Union", *IPRax* 1997 pp. 401-404.

Moreau, A.-A., "Le détachement des travailleurs effectuant une prestation de services dans l'Union européenne", *Clunet* 1996 pp. 889-908.

Morse, C.G.J., "Consumer Contracts, Employment Contracts and the Rome Convention", 41 *I.C.L.Q.* 1-21 (1992).

Moss, G. et al. (eds.), *The EC Regulation on Insolvency Proceedings. A Commentary and Annotated Guide*, Oxford 2002.

Moura Ramos, M.R., "Public Policy in the Framework of the Brussels Convention. Remarks on Two Recent Decisions by the European Court of Justice", *Yearb.PIL* 2000 pp. 25-39.

Müller, A., *Grenzüberschreitende Beweisaufnahme im Europäischen Justizraum*, Tübingen 2004.

Newton, J., *The Uniform Interpretation of the Brussels and Lugano Conventions*, Oxford etc. 2002.

Nielsen, P.A., *International privat- og procesret*, København 1997.

Nourissat, C. & Treppoz, E., "Quelques observations sur l'avant-projet de proposition de règlement du Conseil sur la loi applicable aux obligations non contractuelles 'Rome II'", *Clunet* 2003 pp. 7-38.

Østergaard, K., "Selskabsstatuttet i EU. De internationale proces- og privatrettlige implikationer", *Nordisk Tidsskrift for Selskabsret* 2005 pp. 110-122.

Paefgen, W.G., "Kollisionsrechtlicher Verbraucherschutz im Internationalen Vertragsrecht und europäisches Gemeinschaftsrecht", *ZEuP* 2003 pp. 266-294.

Pålsson, L., "Nya lagvalsregler för försäkringsavtal", *SvJT* 1993 pp. 43-63.

Pålsson, L., *Romkonventionen – Tillämplig lag för avtalsförpliktelser*, Stockholm 1998.

Pålsson, L., *Brysselkonventionen, Luganokonventionen och Bryssel I-förordningen*, Stockholm 2002.

Partsch, P.-E., *Le droit international privé européen. De Rome à Nice*, Bruxelles 2003.

Péroz, H., "Le règlement CE no. 805/2004 du 21 avril 2004 portant création d'un titre exécutoire européen pour les créances incontestées", *Clunet* 2005 pp. 637-676.

Philip, A., *EU-IP. Europæisk international privat- og procesret*, ed. 2, København 1994.

Picone, P., *Diritto internazionale privato e diritto comunitario*, Padova 2004.

Pintens, W., "Marriage and Partnership in the Brussels IIa Regulation", *Liber Memorialis Petar Šarčević*, München 2006, pp. 335-344.

Pirrung, J., "Europäische justitielle Zusammenarbeit in Zivilsachen – insbesondere das neue Scheidungsübereinkommen", *ZEuP* 1999 pp. 834-848.

Plender, R. & Wilderspin, M., *The European Contracts Convention – the Rome Convention on the Choice of Law for Contracts*, ed. 2, London 2001.

Pocar, F., *La Convenzione di Bruxelles sulla giurisdizione e l'esecuzione delle sentenze*, ed. 3, Milano 1995.

Poillot-Peruzzetto, S., "Le créancier de la 'faillite européenne': commentaire de la Convention des Communautés européennes relative aux procédures d'insolvabilité", *Clunet* 1997 pp. 757-781.

Posch, W., "The 'Draft Regulation Rome II' in 2004: Its Past and Future Perspectives", *Yearb.PIL* 2004 pp. 129-153.

Puurunen, T., "Choice of Law in European Business-to-Consumer Electronic Commerce – A Trail out of a Political Impasse, *ZEuP* 2003 pp. 789-816.

Radicati di Brozolo, L.G., "L'influence sur les conflits de lois des principes de droit communautaire en matière de liberté de circulation", *Rev.crit.d.i.p.* 1993 pp. 401-424.

Rammeloo, S., *Das neue EG-Vetragskollisionsrecht*, Köln etc. 1992.

Rauscher, T., *Verpflichtung und Erfüllungsort in Art. 5 Nr. 1 EuGVÜ*, München 1984.

Rauscher, T. (ed.), *Europäisches Zivilprozessrecht. Kommentar*, München 2004.

Reichelt, G. (ed.), *Europäisches Kollisionsrecht. Die Konventionen von Brüssel, Lugano und Rom*, Wien 1993.

Reithmann, C. & Martiny, D. (eds.), *Internationales Vertragsrecht. Das internationale Privatrecht der Schuldverträge*, ed. 5, Köln 1996.

Rognlien, S., *Luganokonvensjonen. Internasjonal domsmyndighet i sivile saker*, Oslo 1993.

Roth, W.-H., "Der Einfluss des europäischen Gemeinschaftsrechts auf das internationale Privatrecht", *RabelsZ* 1991 pp. 623-673.

Roth, W.-H., "Angleichung des IPR durch sekundäres Gemeinschaftsrecht", *IPRax* 1994 pp. 165-174.

Roth, W.-H., "Internationales Gesellschaftsrecht nach Überseering", *IPRax* 2003 pp. 117-127.

Rozehnalová, N. & Týč, V., *Evropský justiční prostor v civilních otázkách*, Brno 2003.

Schack, H., "Die Gerichtsstands- und Vollstreckungsübereinkommen von Brüssel und Lugano. Eine Übersicht über aktuelle monographische Werke", *ZEuP* 1999 pp. 783-796.

Schack, H., "Das neue internationale Eheverfahrensrecht in Europa", *RabelsZ* 2001 pp. 615-633.

Schlosser, P.F., *EuGVÜ*, München 1996.

Schmidt-Parzefall, T., *Die Auslegung des Parallelübereinkommens von Lugano*, Tübingen 1995.

Scholz, I., *Das Problem der autonomen Auslegung des EuGVÜ*, Tübingen 1998.

Schulz, A., "Einstweilige Massnahmen nach dem Brüsseler Gerichtsstands- und Vollstreckungsübereinkommen in der Rechtsprechung des Gerichtshofs der Europäischen Gemeinschaften (EuGH)", *ZEuP* 2001 pp. 805-836.

Seatzu, F., *Insurance in Private International Law. A European Perspective*, Oxford *etc.* 2003.

Soltész, U., *Der Begriff der Zivilsache im Europäischen Zivilprozessrecht*, Frankfurt a.M. *etc.* 1998.

Spindler, G., "Herkunftslandprinzip und Kollisionsrecht – Binnenmarktintegration ohne Harmonisierung?", *RabelsZ* 2002 pp. 633-709.

Stadler, A., "Neues europäisches Zustellungsrecht", *IPRax* 2001 pp. 514-521.

Stadler, A., "Das Europäische Zivilprozessrecht – Wie viel Beschleunigung veträgt Europa? Kritisches zur Verordnung über den Europäischen Vollstreckungstitel und ihrer Grundidee", *IPRax* 2004 pp. 2-11.

Stein, A., "Der Europäische Vollstreckungstitel für unbestrittene Forderungen tritt in Kraft – Aufruf zu einer nüchternen Betrachtung", *IPRax* 2004 pp. 181-191.

Strömholm, S., *Upphovsrätt och internationell privaträtt*, Stockholm 2001.

Struycken, A.V.M., "Les conséquences de l'intégration européenne sur le développement du droit international privé", *Rec.des cours* 1992, vol. 232, pp. 257-383.

Struycken, A. (Teun) V.M., "Das Internationale Privatrecht der Europäischen Gemeinschaft im Verhältnis zu Drittstaaten und zur Haager Konferenz", *ZEuP* 2004 pp. 276-295.

Sujecki, B., "Europäisches Mahnverfahren", *ZEuP* 2006 pp. 124-148.

Traest, M., "Development of a European Private International Law and the Hague Conference", *Yearb.PIL* 2003 pp. 223-259.

Trunk, A., *Die Erweiterung des EuGVÜ-Systems am Vorabend des Europäischen Binnenmarktes*, München 1991.

Valloni, L.W., *Der Gerichtsstand des Erfüllungsortes nach Lugano- und Brüsseler-Übereinkommen*, Zürich 1998.

Vékás, L., "Der Weg zur Vergemeinschaftung des Internationalen Privat- und Verfahrensrechts – eine Skizze", *Liber Memorialis Petar Šarčević*, München 2006, pp. 171-187.

Villani, U., *La Convenzione di Roma sulla legge aplicabile ai contratti*, Bari 1997.

Wagner, R., "Vom Brüsseler Übereinkommen über die Brüssel I-Verordnung zum Europäischen Vollstreckungstitel, *IPRax* 2002 pp. 75-95.

Wagner, R., "EG-Kompetenz für das Internationale Privatrecht in Ehesachen?", *RabelsZ* 2004 pp. 119-153.

Wagner, R., "Die neue EG-Verordnung zum Europäischen Vollstreckungstitel", *IPRax* 2005 pp. 189-200.

Wagner, R., "Die zivil(-verfahrens-)rechtlichen Komponenten des Aktionsplans zum Haager Programm", *IPRax* 2005 pp. 494-496.

Wahl, N., *The Lugano Convention and Legal Integration*, Stockholm 1990.

Weiss, J., *Die Konkretisierung der Gerichtsstandregeln des EuGVÜ durch den EuGH*, Frankfurt a.M. etc. 1997.

Werlauff, E., *Common European Procedural Law*, Copenhagen 1999.

Weser, M., *Convention communautaire sur la compétence judiciaire et l'exécution des décisions*, Bruxelles etc. 1975.

Wilderspin, M. & Lewis, X., "Les relations entre le droit communautaire et les règles de conflits de lois des Etats membres", *Rev.crit.d.i.p.* 2002 pp. 1-37 and 289-313.

Wilderspin, M. & Rouchaud-Joët, A.-M., "La compétence externe de la Communauté européenne en droit international privé", *Rev.crit.d.i.p.* 2004 pp.1-48.

Von Wilmowsky, P., "EG-Vertrag und kollisionsrechtliche Rechtswahlfreiheit", *RabelsZ* 1998 pp. 1-37.

Zimmer, D., "Ein Internationales Gesellschaftsrecht für Europa", *RabelsZ* 2003 pp. 298-317.

Index